MW00629054

Praise for *American Gaslighting*

"American Gaslighting is an eye opening and enlightening investigation into how the 'liberal left' in America is actively using propaganda tactics to shame its fellow citizens and ruin the country. This book sets leftist gaslighting ablaze once and for all." (5 Stars)

– John Kelly
Detroit Free Press

"At this particular time, when thoughts about politics are polarized as left vs. right, blue vs. red, progressive vs. conservative (or however the media is electing to phrase), Shyti steps onto the platform with vigor and fervor, expressing his concerns by presenting a history of the growing impact of propaganda...Powerful and controversial, Shyti's book deserves a wide reading audience, no matter the political inclination." (5 Stars)

– Grady Harp
Top 100 Amazon Hall of Fame Reviewer

"While no nation's history is without blemish, Shyti uncovers the roots of the American Left's predatory nature over emotionalists through its longtime overt and subtle lies about the United States and its founders as seeped in through control of educational and cultural foundations... Perhaps this book will give its readers enough information to realize what has been done to them if they have not yet realized it. Highly Recommended." (5 Stars)

– Chris Cordani
Host, Book Spectrum

American Gaslighting

HOW AMERICA IS BEING SYSTEMATICALLY
TAUGHT TO HATE ITSELF

Daniel A. Shyti

Mind Union Media, LLC
Potomac Falls, Virginia

Mind Union Media, LLC
www.mindunion.com
Admin@mindunion.com

Ordering Information:
Quantity sales. Special discounts are available on quantity purchases by corporations, associations, and others. For details, contact the "Special Sales Department" at the address above.

American Gaslighting/ Daniel A. Shyti —1st ed.
ISBN 978-0-9897084-6-3

Contents

PREFACE XV

INTRODUCTION 1

THE FACTS ABOUT THE POLITICAL SPECTRUM............................2
THE LEFT IS ON A MISSION 4
THE FORCES PULLING AMERICA TOWARD MARXISM 7

HUMAN NATURE..10

BASIC HUMAN NEEDS...11
ARE WE EVER PERMANENTLY HAPPY? 15
EMOTIONALISM VS. RATIONALITY 16
OUR DESIRE FOR SAMENESS 16
OUR PATHETIC FUNGIBLE MINDS 19
HOW GASLIGHTING WORKS...22
HOW TO RESIST GASLIGHTING 40

A FAST WALK THROUGH HISTORY 41

TRIBES, EMPIRES, AND CONFLICT..41
SLAVERY: ORIGINS AND ITS ARRIVAL IN THE NEW WORLD....................46
BIRTH OF OUR NATION AND FOUNDING PRINCIPLES (1619 VS. 1776).....52
THE FOUNDING FATHERS—INDISPUTABLE PROOF OF THEIR HIGHER
VIRTUE 66
THE CHAIN OF EVENTS THAT FOREVER SHATTERED THE CHAINS OF
BONDAGE 69

MARXISM AND THE PROGRESSIVES....................................75

PROGRESSIVISM..76
FROM PROGRESSIVISM TO MODERN MARXISM 85
MARXISM WILL TAKE CARE OF YOU 92
CAPITALISM IS NOT THE PROBLEM 93

CRITICAL RACE THEORY—THE NEW RACIAL HATRED 98

ROBIN DiANGELO...102

IBRAM KENDI 109

MASTERFUL MARKETING STROKES OF THE LEFT................116

BLACK LIVES MATTER..118

SOCIAL MEDIA DRIVERS 124

SYSTEMIC RACISM—DOES IT EXIST?..................................126

THE HISTORY OF SYSTEMIC RACISM.............................128

THE SUPREME COURT'S IMPACT ON RACIAL EQUALITY 141

LAST GASP OF THE FORMER CONFEDERACY 144

THE CIVIL RIGHTS ERA OF THE 1960S. 146

THE GREAT SOCIETY 150

SO, WHERE IS ALL THE SYSTEMIC RACISM?........................157

MARXISM ON THE MARCH...160

AN AMERICAN TALE 160

THE OBAMA LEGACY 161

THE GREAT PROTECTORS OF DEMOCRACY 165

FOLLOW THE MONEY – THE LEFT GETS RICH......................169

THE AGE OF PROPAGANDA 174

DECEIT 174

SUBJUGATION...184

THE LEFT'S OBSESSION WITH DEATH 196

THE ABORTION DEATH CULT..197

ROOTS OF THE ABORTION INDUSTRY 199

THE ULTIMATE IN LEFTIST GASLIGHTING 205

OPERATION PUSH BACK...209

UNDERSTANDING THE POLITICAL LANDSCAPE......................209

THINKING CLEARLY...212

LEARN TO ARGUE EFFECTIVELY...217

SOCIAL MEDIA AND WOKE CULTURE...................................224

RECLAIM YOUR CHILD'S EDUCATION 234

BECOME POLITICALLY ACTIVE...236

SAVING OUR COUNTRY 238

EPILOGUE 241

DEFINITIONS AND USAGE 246

REFERENCES..249

INDEX..251

ABOUT THE AUTHOR 255

List of Figures

FIGURE 1-1: THE REAL POLITICAL SPECTRUM 2

FIGURE 2-1: MASLOW'S HIERARCHY OF NEEDS 12

FIGURE 2-2: FAIRFAX COUNTY PUBLIC SCHOOLS POLICY ON GENDER
    AFFIRMATION 35

FIGURE 2-3: FACEBOOK'S FIFTY-EIGHT GENDER OPTIONS 39

FIGURE 3-1: NUMBER OF SLAVES SENT TO THE NEW WORLD 50

FIGURE 3-2: EMANCIPATION MEMORIAL WASHINGTON DC........................55

FIGURE 3-3: RECORDS OF THE VIRGINIA COMPANY 58

FIGURE 3-4: LIBRARY OF CONGRESS TIMELINE ENTRY 58

FIGURE 4-1: NUMBER IN POVERTY AND POVERTY RATE: 1959 TO 2019 90

FIGURE 4-2: US POPULATION BY YEAR...94

FIGURE 5-1: CRT TRAINING SESSION..108

FIGURE 5-2: BLM WEBSITE IMAGE 118

FIGURE 6-1: NUMBER IN POVERTY AND POVERTY RATE: 1959 TO 2019 152

For my country that I love dearly

"The cause of America is in a great measure the cause of all mankind"

—Thomas Paine, *Common Sense*, 1776

Preface

Since you opened this book, there's a very good chance you love America. Maybe you're just curious; maybe you're deeply concerned about the direction in which our country is heading.

You may be a conservative, or you may be an independent, or you may even be a traditional Democrat voter. It really doesn't matter to me. I think we need to talk. To set the stage, I have a few questions for you. Do you have an open mind? Are you willing to listen to a perspective that maybe you do not share? Do you think we Americans are on the verge of losing our country?

As I began writing this book, I committed to keeping an open mind. I knew I would be delving into uncomfortable topics. I had to listen to people and read material that I did not agree with. Some of my opinions changed by the time the book was finished.

My answer to the last question above—I am extremely concerned that we are losing our country. If we do not ignite a rebirth of the American spirit, we'll soon reach the point of no return. I'll also share with you that I'm a conservative thinker. I have not arrived at my beliefs whimsically or because I've gorged myself on too much Fox News. I've analyzed history. I've assessed human behavior. I've drawn from my life experiences and those of my parents. My conclusion is that people thrive best when we can exercise the greatest degree of freedom. That freedom can only be enjoyed when government power is contained. This is the foundational tenet of conservatism—not the lies you hear on legacy media.

I wrote this book out of love for my country. The country that lifted my family out of poverty. I am deeply concerned that Americans are being systematically taught to hate their own country. That is why I chose to speak up and take a stand. There are increasing numbers of Americans that do not seem to value the constitutional framework that has held us together for nearly 250 years. They are being conditioned to "burn it down."

American Gaslighting will hopefully set you on a journey of understanding and speaking the truth. The goal is to enlighten as many people as possible no matter where they currently stand politically. Within these pages, you'll find an explanation of what freedom-loving Americans face, the tools used to divide us, a retracing of how we arrived at our current situation, an assessment of who is most culpable for our present state, and what to do to stop it.

We are living in the Age of Propaganda. Facts don't matter to the propagandists. They believe that any lie can be covered with enough traditional and social media messaging. This messaging relies on manipulating the mind through psychological techniques that are particularly effective against people who don't routinely exercise critical thinking skills. In American Gaslighting, I cover these psychological ploys. I provide a brief examination of human nature, a constant across the thousands of years of history. Understanding human nature is critical to understanding why leftist policies are doomed to failure and why they appeal to the weak-minded in the short run.

The text also covers a fast walk through history to accurately examine America's founding and political evolution. The conversation is critical because manipulation of history is a cornerstone of leftist propaganda. It paints America as systemically and irredeemably racist. The highest use of historical knowledge is to learn what not to do in the future. However, pulling history forward to the present and pretending that the ills of the past still exist is deceitful, to say the least. This is precisely how the left uses our history— cherry-picking what is useful in reopening old wounds to justify their extreme social upheaval.

I also cover the nature of woke ideology. According to its adherents, to be woke implies that one is awake and tuned into the belief that America is an irredeemably racist society worthy of self-loathing and contempt. Their solution is to tear it down and reconstruct America into a society based on equity. The self-appointed woke masters will decide what equity is. No need for you to worry about that detail. Woke ideology is ridiculous and deserves every ounce of scorn and ridicule that we can throw at it.

In the woke world, the stupid are wise, and the wise are stupid. To be woke is to believe that up is down, right is left, backward is forward, guilt is innocence, love is hate, insanity is sanity, math is racist, censorship is democracy, and men can actually have babies. In truth, to be woke is the closest you can get to being lobotomized without a surgeon actually cutting your skull open. Wokeness is brainwashing and anesthesia rolled into one.

The forces aligned against our American system are powerful, organized, and international. The people aiming to bring about our downfall are highly organized on a global scale. I'll explain who they are. Ultimately, their agenda is global socialism and complete control of the worldwide economy. Those ends cannot be achieved without placing America under their thumb. To a great extent, that has already happened, but their work is not complete. Their advancements are still reversible, but time is running out.

At various points, you'll encounter sprinklings of ridicule and sarcasm. These tools are effective and necessary in exposing the pathetic lack of logic on which woke ideology is founded. To the greatest extent possible, I've restrained my passions and not engaged in ad hominem attacks. The intense criticism of the left is directed at the political leadership and other entities active in advancing the leftist agenda, not rank-in-file voters, most of whom are simply being gaslighted by the propaganda.

It's also essential to establish a common understanding of key terms in a world where our words are frequently and arbitrarily redefined to suit the needs of the propagandists. To achieve consistency of meaning and usage within this text, I've included a definition and usage guide at the back of the book. You may want to read that before diving into the main text.

CHAPTER 1

Introduction

"It was the best of times, it was the worst of times, it was the age of wisdom, it was the age of foolishness, it was the epoch of belief, it was the epoch of incredulity, it was the season of light, it was the season of darkness, it was the spring of hope, it was the winter of despair."

—*Charles Dickens, A Tale of Two Cities, 1859*

Without question, Americans live in the freest, most prosperous, and welcoming nation that mankind has ever created. Despite this, America is being systematically taught to hate itself. The effort is coordinated, pervasive, and fundamentally corrosive to the core of our national identity. If you readily dismiss this as some nut-job conspiracy theory, you have been fooled and are well on your way to being a victim of gaslighting.

The term gaslighting originates from a 1938 stage play written by Patrick Hamilton. It was later made into a movie. The plot is about an abusive husband who torments his wife with a variety of psychological ploys meant to drive her insane. Gaslighting has become the term used to describe such abusers who manipulate and deceive, ultimately driving their victims to doubt the most basic elements of reality.

To resist the effects of political gaslighting one must first correctly identify who the gaslighters are.

The Facts About the Political Spectrum

As a first step, it's important that we establish some facts and dispel a crucial myth about the political spectrum.

When we speak of the political spectrum, we use terms such as the left and the right. The left represents authoritarian centralized government with almost no personal liberty at the extreme. The most repressive form of government on the left is communism.

Here's an easy quiz. If on the extreme left you have communism, what should we find on the extreme right? If at the extreme left, we find total control by government, logic dictates that the opposite would be no government at all. Otherwise known as anarchy. Realistically no society can exist under anarchy. Anarchy creates a power vacuum that simply leads us back to the left and authoritarian government when a strongman emerges to seize power. Refer to Figure 1-1 for a supporting illustration.

The right favors maximum personal liberty with minimal government control but must stop short of anarchy for society to function.

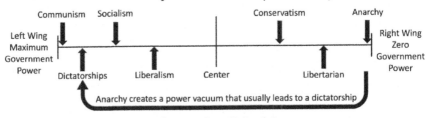

Figure 1-1: The Real Political Spectrum

Authoritarian governing structures are political systems where control is concentrated in the hands of a centralized body or a single person. Communism, based on the philosophy of Karl Marx, and various forms of dictatorships represent authoritarian systems with total central control. Examples of these include the former Soviet Union, present-day China, North Korea, Cuba, and Venezuela.

Monarchies fall under dictatorships and can range from moderate government to extreme authoritarian systems. The degree of authoritarian rule flies with the whims of the monarch.

Socialism is another type of authoritarian government that can vary in the degree of centralized control. Typically, under an extreme socialist system, the government controls nearly all aspects of the economy but does not directly own the means of production. This contrasts with communism where the government owns all means of production and private property does not exist.

With this discussion, I dispel a common myth advanced by the left that fascist governments are right wing. Consider this the first lie exposed in American Gaslighting. The left likes to label fascism as right wing, but the truth is fascism is an extreme form of socialism, which is most certainly a left-wing ideology. In fact, Nazi was short for a member of the National Socialist German Worker's Party. Does that sound right wing to you?

Fascism is really just socialism with a more nationalistic spin. These were the characteristics of Nazi Germany under Hitler and Italy under Mussolini. The left uses the nationalism characteristic of fascism to gaslight people into believing that fascism is right wing. Because conservatives tend to have a strong sense of nationalism, they are labeled fascist by the left. This pervasive lie about conservatism pervades nearly every form of media.

Throughout this book, I use the terms "the left" to describe individuals and organizations who favor heavy government control to the detriment of personal liberty. I sometimes apply the label Marxist to leftists as a literal tag when the shoe fits and as a pejorative term when I want to highlight the left's extremism.

Marxism is the more extreme form of leftist ideology that we currently see in America. It is the totalitarian philosophy that wants to concentrate all political and economic power in the hands of the state. The American left has now clearly drifted dangerously close to Marxism.

The American political spectrum's left wing used to be predominantly liberal. An old-fashioned American liberal still loved his country. Marxists, the more extreme left, hate America. I never thought I would pine for good old-fashioned liberalism. Unfortunately, liberalism is the preferred conduit of the left's ultimate goal of Marxism because the liberal mind is particularly susceptible to big government solutions for nearly everything. Bigger government only leads to less liberty, which in turn leads to totalitarian systems like Marxism. Liberalism is effectively dead. Killed by the rising extreme leftists – the Marxists.

The Left is on a Mission

The organized leftist gaslighters are on a mission to tear down every institution, historical reference, and social and economic structure that underpins American society. The targets of destruction are our founding ideals, belief in a creator God, the nuclear family, our Constitution, and all aspects of capitalism.

Their tools to affect this destruction are racism, sexual identity, speech control, and politicized science. The primary threat to anyone resisting these tools is cancellation—the public shunning on social media, loss of employment, censorship, and character destruction. The secondary, and more severe threat is physical destruction through attacks by leftist mobs or corrupt government agencies that have been weaponized against the American public.

The leftist strategy is to first create a type of societal insanity whereby the populace begins to doubt the value of every traditional social structure including one's own gender identity. Secondly, they instigate social unrest to pit society against itself. They accomplish this by inflaming the passions of the ignorant.

Karl Marx, Marxism's co-creator, used social class to divide the populace into two groups, the oppressors and the oppressed. The capitalist and bourgeoisie were the oppressors, while the workers were oppressed. Social division along economic lines was a tough sell in America, where upward mobility has always been possible through skill, hard work, and education. The American brand of Marxists selected race and identity politics as their preferred tools to divide and conquer. The oppressors are all white people. The oppressed are all so-called people of color (POCs). Once at war with itself, the populace becomes easier to control and still easier to gaslight. We are well on our way.

To say America has a checkered past regarding racism is a gross understatement. Over the centuries, our country has made many egregious mistakes regarding race and most specifically the treatment of Black Americans. However, the purity of virtues enshrined in the Declaration of Independence and our Constitution served as the foundation for national self-correction. Those who had suffered injustice could find solace, redress, and ultimate justice simply by pointing to those national virtues. We fought the Civil War, the most ghastly and bloody war in our history, to correct the evil of slavery. We passed numerous civil rights acts to outlaw discrimination. We were well on our way to becoming a race-neutral society at the start of the 21st century. The landscape changed significantly in 2008. Society started coming unglued as extreme leftist philosophies reemerged with a vengeance. Leftists are unrelenting.

Since its creation, Marxism has had a foothold in America. So-called intellectuals began to view the American Constitution as stale. The emergence of the commonly named robber barons of the late 19th and early 20th centuries made some intellectuals want to rethink capitalism. The modern-day open attacks on America's ideals can also be traced back to President Woodrow Wilson, one of the foremost proponents of progressive thought—a precursor to the present-day left. Using their twisted ideology, Marxist attacks on the American way of life are not new.

Leftist gaslighters seek to empty your mind of historical fact while heaping shame and guilt upon innocent people. The primary tools used to accomplish this brainwashing are the 1619 Project and Critical Race Theory (CRT). The 1619 Project is a propaganda initiative by the New York Times that seeks to change the recognized founding of America to 1619 as opposed to 1776. The year 1619 is significant because it marks the first landing of presumed enslaved Africans on the American mainland. CRT is a once-obscure academic ideology modeled after Marxism by dividing everyone into two classes—the oppressors and the oppressed.

Once your mind is scrubbed clean like a freshly washed blackboard, they are free to write in whatever they wish to suit their goals. You will be the unwitting recipient of their worldview that America is detestable, you are not an American first and foremost, but rather a citizen of the world, and lastly, if your skin is the wrong shade, you are an oppressor. The ultimate goal is absolute power by making America conform to the emerging global socialism being pushed by globalist elites.

Doubt is the cornerstone of gaslighting. Gaslighting is most effective when it is based on the half-truth. Leftists uses the half-truth to instill doubt. Using the half-truth, the leftist introduces a problem partially rooted in fact and then offers remedies to cure the patient's ills. However, history has proven time and again that the left's remedies do not work, and their so-called cures will actually "kill the patient" ideologically, morally, and ultimately physically. The remedies that the left offers for society's ills are merely meant to systemically advance their cause and consolidate control. The battle for the soul of America is on. America is at the tipping point.

The Forces Pulling America Toward Marxism

Powerful forces are threatening our Constitutional Republic by pulling our country drastically to the left. Various groups share common goals that often lead to organized cooperation and collusion in transforming America. In other cases, alignment of their interests is temporary and coincidental.

First, we have overtly Marxist groups that advocate the complete replacement of capitalism and the free market with a centrally managed economy in the name of equity. These advocates clearly wish to completely teardown the American system and replace it with their concept of utopia. These groups include individuals who advance the tenets of CRT and also declared Marxists.

The overtly Marxist are aided by elected officials who either directly share the same views or are quick to pander to their demands for political gain. Such is the case with members of Congress who have declared themselves Democratic Socialists. Others, who claim to just be liberal Democrats, often cave into leftist demands to gain votes and campaign contributions. For simple political expediency, so-called Liberal Democrats may not have defined themselves as socialists, but their deeds and voting records indicate their full alignment with the dominating left.

Leftist ideologies are about control by powerful, monied elites. Marxism appeals to the have- nots because they see it as way to gain more control over material wealth. Wealthy leftist elites use the have-nots as pawns by playing to their desires and jealousies, but the elites are really only interested in gaining more power for themselves. The elites are willing to undermine our Constitution as they manipulate the poor for their own benefit. The weakening of our Constitution draws the country toward leftist totalitarian control.

This results in either oligarchy or a bloodbath that ultimately ends in Marxist style domination if their violent tactics succeed.

The pull toward Marxism overwhelmingly comes from the Democrat side of the aisle, but believe me there are plenty of Republicans that sell out as well. So, if you think that all you have to do is vote Republican, think again. Both the Republican and Democrat parties are highly influenced by globalism where American sovereignty is being eroded in favor of foreign interests. These interests assert their power through initiatives such as climate change, gun control, and pandemic control, which is a recent addition to their toolkit. The leading organization interested in establishing global socialism is the World Economic Forum (WEF).

Adversary states such as China and Russia are instigators and beneficiaries of our internal strife that has resulted from America's decay toward Marxism. The leaders of these states understand that our global dominance and competitiveness is a direct outgrowth of our freedoms. I believe their leaders understand this key factor better than many Americans. From Russia and China's perspective, anything that internally divides us accrues to their benefit. Naturally, they help stoke hatred and division through social media influence in service of their cause.

In an October 2020 speech in Philadelphia, Former President Barrack Obama said, "What is new is a growing movement for justice, equality, and progress on so many issues. This is really a tipping point. And that momentum only continues if we win this election. In times as polarized as these, your vote doesn't just matter; it matters more than ever before."

Through an orchestrated blend of legitimate and illegitimate tactics, the left won the 2020 election. With the leftists now in control, the destruction of our institutions will accelerate to a point from which there may be no return unless freedom-loving people act. Obama knows we are at the crescendo of leftist domination—the tipping point. Ironically, Obama's words hold true for freedom-loving Americans as well as leftist ideologues. "In times as polarized as these, your vote doesn't just matter; it matters more than ever before."

This book provides a balanced historical reference, exposes leftist tactics, raises awareness that you are being gaslighted by liars, and reinforces the imperative to apply logic as your tool for combating gaslighting. The text also explains how the aforementioned forces are simultaneously converging to weaken American society either coincidentally or in collusion with internal proponents of leftist ideologies. Finally, the book outlines an action plan to win the fight for America's soul.

Never in my wildest dreams would I have imagined that we would be combating Marxism in 21st century America. My generation is the cold war generation. Once the Soviet Union fell, Marxism was dead, relegated to the "ash heap of history"—so we thought. Little did we know of the cancer growing inside our own borders, steadily eating away at our national identity. And now, we find ourselves burdened with a defining generational challenge. No generation escapes a great tribulation. The 21st-century neo-Marxist movement is our great tribulation. Surely, even greater and more severe suffering will follow if America collapses into Marxism. It must be defeated, or America is lost forever.

CHAPTER 2

Human Nature

"Human action can be modified to some extent, but human nature cannot be changed."

—*Lincoln, Speech at Cooper Union, 1860*

The Founding Fathers of the United States were astute students of human nature. They were some of the most learned men of their time. Our Founders were products of the Age of Enlightenment also known as the Age of Reason. The 17th and 18th centuries were a time when knowledge and exchange of ideas flourished. During the Age of Enlightenment, the concepts of liberty, religious tolerance, scientific reasoning, and opposition to absolute monarchy proliferated throughout European society and also spread across the Atlantic to the New World.

The Age of Enlightenment was enabled by the printing press invented by Johannes Gutenberg (c1450.) This crucial invention facilitated written mass communication and the publishing of books and scientific papers. The transformative impact of this first knowledge age is directly comparable to the effects of the internet on 20th century society.

America's Founders treasured access to books and studied the history of the world. They studied all prior forms of government. They learned well that concentration of power in the hands of one person or even a select few was the wellspring of tyranny. They could easily foresee that concentration of power would lead to abuse due to man's corruptible nature. Not long after winning our independence from Britain and signing the Treaty of Paris in 1783, our Founders began specifically framing a constitutional structure designed to protect mankind from itself.

Today's corrupt news media gives no credit to the Founders for the depth of their insight. Leftist attacks use every imaginable reason to discredit them despite the gifts of freedom their foundational actions gave to subsequent generations. As I read history and learn about what our Founders knew, I'm deeply impressed at their profound insights and how similar the drivers of human activity are across the millennia.

Humans had changed little in the millennia preceding 1787 when our Constitution was adopted, and we have changed even less since. As I wrote in my book, *Ten Timeless Rules for Life – Things Every Young Person Should Know for a Perfect Launch*, all people since the dawn of humanity have 99.5% of their DNA in common. That means that we are very close to identical in physiological makeup. That 0.5% difference accounts for all biological variations such as gender, height, hair and eye color, strength, speed, intellect, and yes—skin color. The Population Reference Bureau guesstimates that 108 billion people have been born since mankind's appearance on earth some 50,000 years ago. Guess what? We are all 99.5% identical. We also all have a common set of needs.

Basic Human Needs

The drivers of human decision-making in 1787 and before are the same as what drives us today. While our Founding Fathers could not benefit from volumes of psychological and social research, they nonetheless had a comprehensive understanding of these human needs. Let's consider Figure2-1, the well-known Maslow's Hierarchy of Needs. This model is an encapsulation of what most humans want in varying degrees.

We start with the bare essentials of food, water, shelter, etc. Without these, we die. With the essentials satisfied, we then pursue safety. When we know we are safe, we turn to psychological and social needs of love and belonging and esteem. From there, we can finally aspire to become the most we can be through creative pursuits. However, everyone does not reach the self-actualization phase. Assuming self-actualization is the desired state for all, in present-day America, failure to achieve self-actualization is predominantly determined by the choices one makes. Oppression is not the obstacle. However, it's clear that many stop short of self-actualization and settle for contentment short of reaching their personal potential. Drive, ambition, and optimism are the chief determinants of reaching one's full potential.

Figure 2-1: Maslow's Hierarchy of Needs

You can see how our Bill of Rights reflects the enablement of our human needs. The inherent wisdom in the structure of our Constitutional Republic creates stability for us to fulfill the two bottom needs—physiological and safety. Our God-given rights enshrined in our founding documents further enable all Americans to focus on the *pursuit of happiness* reflected in the upper three needs of Maslow's model. Very little listed in the hierarchy of needs is a direct right. It is the protective framework of the Bill of Rights in our Constitution founded on the concept of our God-given rights to *life, liberty, and the pursuit of happiness* that makes it possible for us to meet our own needs through individual endeavor.

We take the bottom tier of the hierarchy for granted in modern American society. Some even claim that the government must meet their physiological needs, and it is their right to receive such largess. Government involvement in our lives at this level is simply another entry point for control and tyranny.

Our Constitutional framework enables each individual to easily take care of themselves if they so choose. Through our economic and social structures, it's safe to say that the number of people who die from starvation in the US is virtually zero. You can undoubtedly find malnourished people due to poverty, but death by starvation effectively does not exist unless due to psychological factors such as anorexia. Even if you find one case of starvation, it does not invalidate the argument that people in America do not die of starvation.

This is in stark contrast to the so-called "developing world," where famine is still commonplace. No one will recline in leisure and write a symphony or create a scientific breakthrough when their stomach aches from hunger. There is no opportunity for advancement when tier one of the hierarchy is unaddressed. The overwhelming majority of people in the US are fortunate to be able to spend much of their time pursuing the satisfaction of needs in the top four layers of the hierarchy. Our system provides inherent, built-in opportunities for everyone in America.

Some might say, "Hold on, shelter is a basic physiological need. Haven't you noticed the homelessness crisis?" Yes, we have homelessness issues heavily skewed toward California and the west coast and other major urban centers. But the majority of homelessness is connected to mental illness, alcoholism, and drug abuse. Physical disability is another significant contributing factor. Very few healthy, non-addicted people stay permanently homeless. These are the situationally homeless who typically find a solution once they receive some sort of assistance to stabilize their housing situation.

In 2019, the US population was 328,239,523 according to the US Census Bureau.[1] According to a 2019 study by the Department of Housing and Urban Development, the homeless population totaled 567,715.[2] That's just 0.17% of the total population. A 2021 meta-analysis published by the Public Library of Science (PLOS)[3] and posted to the NIH website estimated that as many as 76.2% of the homeless are mentally ill, drug or alcohol addicted, or some combination of the three. Homelessness is clearly driven by addiction and mental illness not simple economic misfortune.

Our standard of living and ability to meet basic needs far exceeds many other parts of the world. The majority of Americans have no appreciation for our standard of living. In America and much of western society, survival through your ability to meet basic physiological and safety needs is practically guaranteed. This fact alone creates an opportunity for a better life that many around the globe simply do not have.

---

[1] U.S. Census Bureau website, release number CB19-981, December 30, 2019

[2] The U.S. Department of Housing and Urban Development, The 2019 Annual Homeless Assessment Report (AHAR) to Congress

[3] "The prevalence of mental disorders among homeless people in high-income countries: An updated systematic review and meta-regression analysis," August 23, 2021, PLOS Medicine, by Stefan Gutwinski, et al.

Are We Ever Permanently Happy?

Even when we succeed in finding happiness, it is fleeting. We are simply never permanently happy. We may achieve a goal or experience an event in our lives that brings us tremendous joy, but how long does that feeling last? Maybe a couple of days? Sometimes more. Then what? We return to our humdrum everyday lives and keep looking for something else to make us happy. It seems that we can never find a permanent state of happiness.

Do you think that Thomas Jefferson knew this when he wrote, "We hold these truths to be self-evident, that all men are created equal, that they are endowed by their Creator with certain inalienable rights, that among these are life, liberty and the *pursuit* of happiness."

Happiness, here on earth at least, is a never-ending pursuit. And that's a good thing in many ways. This yearning drives us forward. It spurs us to want to climb Maslow's "ladder." Not just for material things, but to establish meaningful relationships with others, achieve worthy goals, form a spiritual connection with our Creator, and for the self-actualizers—search and discover our hidden talents and creativity.

We can easily fall victim to excesses that ultimately lead to evil and a life devoid of virtue if our pursuit of happiness is not tied to worthy goals that benefit others and ourselves. Everyone wants to be happy even dictators and power-hungry politicians. Power is what gives these types of people their momentary happiness. Throughout history, their version of "pursuit of happiness" has proven time and again to not be good for the rest of us. Here again, is why the Founders created a constitution to protect us from ourselves. Our Constitution was designed to reign-in the power hungry.

Emotionalism vs. Rationality

Can you think rationally when you're angry and emotionally out of control? It's certainly much harder. That's why we use the term "crime of passion." In the extreme, someone may become so angry that they physically attack someone else even when they previously had not exhibited violent tendencies. Their anger overwhelms all rational thinking. That is the state to which the Marxists are driving our society. Half of all Americans have been whipped up into such a frenzy that they won't even listen to opposing points of view. Remember Obama's "get in their face" exhortation?

> "I need you to go out and talk to your friends and talk to your neighbors. I want you to talk to them whether they are independent or whether they are Republican. I want you to argue with them and get in their face."[4]

Much has been written on whether humans are rational or emotional creatures. Lately psychology texts and popular discourse have tilted toward viewing humans as far less rational than we think we are. The less rationally we behave, the more we begin to resemble animals. Rationality is one significant trait that separates us from animals. We actually achieve each stage in Maslow's hierarchy through a complex combination of rationality and emotionalism. We must force ourselves to think rationally. It takes effort.

Our Desire for Sameness

Our emotional responses are heavily influenced by hardwired physiological factors. Humans have a hardwired desire for sameness.

---

[4] Barack Obama, Campaign speech, Elko, Nevada, 2008

Anthropologists have long studied human tribal history. We began long ago in small geographically separated hunter-gatherer groups, that bonded around their everyday struggle for survival. Over thousands of years our common needs, physical proximity, and shared social structures imprinted a desire for sameness and identity in the human mind. We carry this desire with us still.

When forging new relationships, we seek sameness. We ask ourselves, "What do we have in common?" In sales training, representatives are explicitly taught to build bonds with customers, seek common interests, and even mirror the behavior and body language of the prospect as a way to achieve sameness. Sameness tends to build trust on a biological level.

Let's say you're an average white dude who has been invited to a party by a white friend. You arrive at the location and the door swings open. You notice that everyone in the room is black except you, your date, and your friend. You get a sudden attack of butterflies. In the race baiter's world, this reaction is due to your inner repressed racism.

The truth is that your emotion is a common human reaction to unexpected absence of sameness. This reaction alone does not indicate that you're racist. It is simply a feeling of uneasiness, neither right nor wrong. These feelings are impulses. It is how you choose to act that matters. Taken as an isolated reaction, your uneasiness simply indicates that you were expecting some level of sameness based on appearance and the expectation was not met.

As you enter the room, the host greets you warmly. You strike up a friendly conversation. She introduces you to her husband and a few friends and shows you where the food and drinks are. You relax as you realize that all people are basically the same. Having had a positive experience, the next time a similar situation arises, your feeling of uneasiness will likely not happen.

I had a similar experience when I traveled to Taiwan on business. It often seemed that I was the only white guy in a sea of Chinese. As I made friends with local engineers, and we traveled around Taipei, I realized that no one seemed to care that I didn't look like them though I'm sure I stood out in a crowd. I connected on a human level with almost everyone I met, and I later found myself at great ease wherever I went.

Humans are visual creatures. We interpret the world primarily through our eyes. Moving beyond appearance and connecting on deeper levels is how we form bonds with others. In other words, find common ground no matter what people look like.

Our desire for sameness, while natural, must be tempered to fit modern society. While in ancient times, tribes identified with superficial aspects such as skin color, today we must transcend such boundaries. Very few countries today are truly homogenous societies. Our mobility has shrunk the globe. America has been the foremost social experiment in merging people of diverse national heritage, races, and creeds into a functioning society. Yet sameness still has a purpose in creating unity.

Until recent times, we have been able to rally around a common flag of sameness—the American identity. This identity is what is enshrined in our founding documents. To be American is to believe in God-given rights, equal justice before the law, and the rule of law itself. To be American means the rights of the individual reign supreme, and the people give government its power and not the other way around.

Our national motto "E Pluribus, Unum" means from many, one. Originally, it expressed the coming together of thirteen colonies into one nation. Over the years it has also come to signify from many people, one nation. Leftists seeks to reverse this concept to create "E Unum, Pluribus," or out of the one, many. They seek to fracture the American populace into as many fragments as possible. The more they divide, the more easily society can be demolished and rebuilt into the perpetually elusive "Marxist Utopia."

Despite what the leftists would have you believe; America has thus far succeeded remarkably well at creating a functioning society from a very diverse population. However, all of what's good about America is on the brink of destruction due to ignorance of our history, the false narrative of systemic racism, and pervasive gaslighting.

Our Pathetic Fungible Minds

Let's reexamine the question, "Are we rational or emotional creatures?" The answer is we are both. However, it takes far more effort to engage our rational minds, and it is instinctively easier to react emotionally. It takes energy to logically examine any proposition, circumstance, or course of action. Our rational minds require frequent visits to the mental gymnasium. That takes effort and discipline.

Our schools used to be that gymnasium, the place where the rational mind was nurtured and fortified. Where critical thinking was exercised. Where argumentation based on facts and evidence was taught. In an overwhelming number of schools and university campuses, that is no longer true. Critical thinking is not encouraged and neither is debate on controversial subjects. Try arguing that you do not believe in man-caused global warming. Try telling a science professor that carbon-dioxide does not produce the so-called greenhouse effect. Try telling a liberal social sciences professor that America does not systemically oppress anyone. You will be labeled a climate denier and a racist respectively. Submission to leftist orthodoxy is all that matters. People that engage their rational mind are difficult to control because they question too much. Therefore, our schools are now tasked with dumbing down our children's minds and indoctrinating them with self-loathing ideology.

This is not to say that our emotional mind has no purpose and must be suppressed. Quite the contrary. A balance of both the rational and emotional are essential to decision-making. The emotional mind is what spurs action. We can scrutinize any situation with a rational and rigorous examination of facts, but a decision to act is only rendered once things "feel right."

The leftist gaslighter precisely knows how to manipulate your fungible mind. They exert focused effort into stoking anger and fear. When kept in a constant state of anger and fear, people tend to stop thinking rationally. This is the root of mob mentality. When people are triggered into an overwhelming state of fear that threatens their safety, they will readily surrender freedoms in exchange for survival. Prime examples of the fear tactic are man-caused global warming and the hysteria surrounding the COVID-19 pandemic.

Some couples are so afraid of the supposed impending doomsday of climate change that they have committed to not having children. During the pandemic, vast segments of Americans readily surrendered their most fundamental freedoms. You must resist being swept up into emotional currents designed to press you into action without stopping to think.

One common psychological tactic to start people moving down the road to accepting leftist orthodoxy is priming. Priming involves creating a predisposition designed to lead someone to the answer you want. Daniel Kahneman, in his outstanding book, *Thinking, Fast and Slow*, explained how priming works.

> People were asked to complete the ambiguous fragments W_ _ H and S _ _ P. Those recently asked to think of an act of which they are ashamed are more likely to complete those fragments as WASH and SOAP and less likely to complete them as WISH and SOUP.

Now, think about this in terms of the so-called social justice movement where we are constantly reminded that slavery once existed in America. Think of the numerous systemically oppressive actions committed against black people in our history. Know that these actions were almost exclusively committed by white people. Now I want you to rate your whiteness on a scale of privilege and oppression. If you're white, you've just been primed to judge yourself harshly. You are actually more likely to blame yourself for the ills of the past.

Sadly, many weak-minded people are being subjected to Critical Race Theory training, also known as diversity, equity, and inclusion training, or culturally responsive training. This type of "training" is a form of indoctrination through priming. It has become the preferred tool for spreading leftist ideology by dividing people into either oppressor or oppressed.

People exposed to this diabolical indoctrination become psychologically diminished by feelings of guilt that their race is composed of evil oppressors. They "willingly" take the sins of the past onto their own shoulders even though they had nothing to do with the actions of past generations. The supposedly "oppressed" are also psychologically diminished by feelings of powerlessness, cynicism, and victimhood. Critical Race Theory is priming the minds of our youth to hate their country, and our public schools at all levels are driving the hate bus.

Kahneman drives home his point on priming this way, "Feeling that one's soul is stained appears to trigger a desire to cleanse one's body, an impulse that has been dubbed the Lady Macbeth effect."

A desire to cleanse one's soul. Imagine that. This is the core of American gaslighting. If we can get enough people to want to cleanse their souls, we can then present the detergent. Woke ideology is the cleanser designed to wipe away our evil, white, patriarchal, systemically racist foundations to make way for a completely reimagined society like the fictitious Marxist utopia. And the only way for your soul to be cleansed is to join their movement and become a social justice warrior. Let's get real here. This garbage happens in communist China every day, but this nightmare is actually happening here in America, right under your nose.

How Gaslighting Works

Gaslighting is a psychological manipulation strategy designed to make the targeted victim question their own reality. Its modus operandi is persistent programming through a barrage of messages that create mental instability by constantly plucking emotional strings in the victim's mind.

Gaslighting destroys what an individual believes and knows to be true and replaces it with what the gaslighter wants you to believe. Gaslighting perfectly aligns with the leftist Saul Alinsky strategies outlined in his subversion manual, "Rules for Radicals." According to Alinsky, "All change means disorganization of the old and organization of the new." The left uses Alinsky's playbook as their sacred scripture. They are now in process of trying to disorganize the American mind so they can reorganize your thinking into their worldview.

Stephanie Sarkis, Ph.D., has published extensively on gaslighting techniques. Her book, *Gaslighting: Recognize Manipulative and Emotionally Abusive People—and Break Free* details the tactics of gaslighters. She is a highly credentialed and licensed counselor. Using her work as a guide, let us examine how the political left employs the diabolical tools of gaslighting to tear down the reality of America.

Gaslighters Tell Blatant Lies

This gaslighting tactic could fill the whole book on its own. The left lies incessantly, and our corrupt corporate media never calls them on it. In fact, the media are so corrupt that it's hard to distinguish if they are pulling or pushing the leftist agenda. Not only is the traditional corporate media such as the New York Times, Washington Post, ABC, CBS, NBC, CNN, and MSNBC totally in bed with the left, but now we also have social media censorship to contend with. Voices of reason are routinely silenced online while big tech freely offers its platforms to the Taliban, Hamas, the Ayatollahs, and China.

Representative Maxine Waters (D) is free to incite violence. She is not canceled, yet people speaking out against the left are routinely silenced. In a detailed study of big tech, the Media Research Center detailed the extensive bias and censorship practiced by big tech.[5] When they are occasionally caught red-handed, they sometimes claim that the suppression of conservative voices was by mistake. How convenient that no leftist was censored by mistake. The censorship of conservative voices continues unabated whenever the message does not align with woke leftist talking points.

The internet was founded with great promise as a tool of liberation capable of giving voice and opportunity to ordinary people. Together with traditional media, it has morphed into the most powerful propaganda tool ever invented—spreading lies when it suits the left and suppressing dissent with alarming frequency. Let's take a look at some common leftist lies.

The left is saving our democracy. Let us not pretend even for a second that leftist organizations and movements we face today are

---

[5] "CENSORED! How Online Media Companies Are Suppressing Conservative Speech," by Ashley Rae Goldenberg and Dan Gainor, Media Research Center 2018

not rooted in Socialism, Marxism, and Fascism. They are all about centralizing control. Centralized control is the antithesis of democracy. The left is obsessed with destroying democracy not saving it.

Fascism is a right-wing ideology. It is a typical ploy of leftists to brand communism as left wing and fascism as right wing. That is a leftist lie. Fundamentally, there is very little difference between the two systems. In communism, the state owns all means of production. Under fascism, government and industry elites form an unholy alliance that works in concert very similar to what the global billionaire elites are planning today. Either way, both communism and fascism concentrate power in the hands of the few and create tyranny for the general population.

It is common for the left to call the right fascist. During World War II, the fascist allies, Hitler and Mussolini, fought the Russian communists. To build their own brand, they pushed the bold claim that fascism is the number one enemy of communism as if the two ideologies were diametrically opposed systems of government. This myth is perpetuated today by those who claim fascism and communism are at opposite ends of the political spectrum. In one sense, when a modern leftist is quick to call you a fascist, they are, in essence, admitting they are communists. The truth always has a way of floating to the surface.

The American left is gripped by Marxism. Therefore, labeling right-wing leaders Hitler remains their default ploy. The left cannot stand being exposed so they attempt to suppress anyone who disagrees with them with shouts of, "Hitler!" Our uneducated activist youth readily succumb to the hyperbole despite learning so little of history that they probably know nothing about the real Hitler. The hyperbole serves to condition them that anyone who disagrees with them is Hitler. When the next Hitler really emerges, they won't know what they're looking at.

The Supreme Court is broken. On April 15, 2021, the extreme leftist Democrat Senator Edward Markey from Massachusetts announced a bill designed to pack the Supreme Court of the United States. His claim: President Donald Trump and then Senate Majority Leader Mitch McConnell broke the court because they pushed through three appointments. Trump's appointments were made by a legitimate, lawfully elected president through entirely legal means. His conservative appointees sometimes disappoint the right because their job is to interpret the Constitution not to legislate from the bench the way leftists do. The reverse is not true. The appointments from the left rarely disappoint their masters. Just examine the judicial record of Ruth Bader-Ginsberg who believed the Constitution was a "living document" that could be reinterpreted with the times. The leftist desire is clear—completely circumvent the democratic process and the Constitution.

In a press conference, the leftist ideologue Markey proclaimed: "Our democracy is in jeopardy today because the Supreme Court standing is sorely damaged. The way we repair it is straightforward. We can undo the damage that the Republicans have done by restoring balance. And we do it by adding four seats to the Court to create a 13-member Supreme Court." Restoring balance? That is truly laughable. Expanding the Supreme court from nine to thirteen, giving the leftists a seven to six advantage is balance? That's not balance. That's a shameless attempt to legitimize totalitarian power.

Notice the doublespeak to use Orwell's term. Our democracy is in jeopardy so the way to fix it is to destroy the constitutional process upon which our democratic republic is founded. Leftist domination is redefined as restoring balance. This court packing maneuver is fresh as of the writing of this book. If the leftists succeed, there will be no more justice in America. The left will violate the Constitution with impunity; lawsuits will fly, and activist justices will vote against anything they don't like, bending, twisting, and ignoring the Constitution as they see fit. Thereby rendering it useless.

Marxism will create a utopia free from want. Marxism has never worked and will never work. That won't stop the Marxist gaslighter from telling you it will solve everything that's wrong with capitalism. The problem, they say, is that Marxism has never really been done correctly. Since we are now so much smarter here in America, and we have so much more technology at our disposal, we can now do Marxism right and a utopia will flourish. In truth, Marxism destroys every fundamental human right and thereby crushes all incentive to contribute to society. The state becomes the grantor or withholder of all rights based on the corrupt whims of a few powerful people. As Winston Churchill once said of Marxism, "It's inherent virtue is the equal sharing of misery." Just ask anyone fleeing Venezuela.

America is systemically and irredeemably racist. Perpetually charging America as racist is the tool by which the Marxists intend to divide and conquer in an attempt to pit all the so-called people of color against white folks. It is simply a substitute for the class struggle rhetoric used in the Communist Manifesto. If America is irredeemably racist and such an unjust society, why are migrants literally dying to enter the country by any means they can? Can the Marxists point to a single law today that is designed to keep minorities down? I can point to dozens of laws and initiatives designed for the exact opposite such as affirmative action, preferential treatment of minorities for college entry, preferential treatment of minority owned businesses when contracting at the federal, state, and local levels, college tuition assistance programs for minorities, housing assistance, and welfare benefits. The list is long indeed. Despite all these attempts to give minorities a jump start, the blatant lie of racism repeated enough times becomes truth to uninformed, guilt-ridden voters who have been successfully gaslighted by the cunning Marxist.

We must strive for equity. You have more, and I have less. Therefore, you should give me some of yours to make things fair. That's the Marxist definition of equity. It ignores individual effort and achievement. Our system strives to create *equality* under the law and equal opportunity—not equal outcomes. Both of those principles are often subverted by the left as well.

We live in a meritocracy where people achieve what they can based on their individual effort and talent. The meritocracy is, of course, viewed as racist and must be destroyed. It is idiotic to subscribe to this thinking.

One of the critical weaknesses of communism is the removal of individual incentives. That is why totalitarian countries ultimately implode. Their economies fail when the state moves in and nationalizes industries. At that point, it doesn't matter how hard you work. Your reward is the same no matter what. Leftist ideology is really not about solving problems for the ordinary person. Benevolence is a smokescreen. If you're a true believer in leftist ideology, you would have to also be ignorant of human nature. Self-interest is a fundamental driver of our behavior, and there is no shame in this. It's part of our biologically innate survival mechanism.

The Founding Fathers have no credibility. The left routinely highlights that several of America's founding fathers were slaveholders. Among these were George Washington, Thomas Jefferson, and James Madison. Because of their slaveholding ways, these men have no credibility. Therefore, everything they did must be discounted, ignored, or torn down.

Consider this thought exercise. On a clear, crisp spring day, the sky is blue. That is a fact. If Mother Theresa told you this fact, or Adolf Hitler tells you the same, does it make the statement any less accurate depending on who tells you? No matter who says it, the fact remains true—the sky is blue on a clear, crisp spring day. However, you may want to verify everything that comes from a despot's mouth. My point is that truth is truth regardless of its source.

So, we must also ask ourselves, "Is it worth living by the principle that all men are created equal?" Jefferson wrote these words in the Declaration of Independence. Are they less valid because he was a slaveholder? America's principles are sound. We have not always been perfect in living by them, but the principles remain sound as bedrock, nonetheless.

James Madison was also a slaveholder. He was also chiefly responsible for the ten amendments to the Constitution known as the Bill of Rights. Among these are freedom of religion, freedom of speech, freedom of the press, protection against illegal search and seizure, and more. The Bill of Rights is part of what gives America its foundation of greatness and virtue. Shall we throw them all away because Madison was a slaveholder? Would you like to live in an America where the Bill of Rights is revoked? The leftists say, "Yes. Burn it down!"

Gaslighters Deny They Ever Said or Did Something, Even Though You Have Proof

Critical Race Theory is not happening. This rose can be pinned on the carpetbagger, Terry McAuliffe, who made this statement while campaigning for Governor in Virginia. Fortunately, and with great delight, he was defeated and sent back to the dark recesses of the leftist swamp. It has rapidly become a leftist talking point to dispel concerns over CRT. This evil indoctrination scheme has caused many independents and soft Democrats to rethink their support. The leftists know that it could potentially be their Achilles' heel. So, their strategy is to deny that CRT is being taught in schools across our country. CRT is used in schools across a broad portion of curriculums as a lens through which any subject can be viewed as racist if one wants to twist facts to the extreme.

They often rename CRT and try to repackage it, but they press on with teaching its core principles relentlessly. Renaming CRT as Culturally Responsive Training is not particularly imaginative since it is still abbreviated to CRT. Hey, no one said leftists are imaginative, but they are diabolically clever. The dual use of the acronym CRT is just another attempt at obfuscation.

There is no crisis at our southern border. Within days of Joe Biden's election, the rush to the border began. Illegal immigrants started pouring in by the thousands hoping to gain entry with the added promise of massive public assistance provided by the leftists in power. The Biden administration has provided lodging and transportation on request, with many of these desperate people arriving infected with COVID while legal citizens continued to suffer restrictions to our freedoms. In testimony before Congress, Department of Homeland Security Secretary Mayorkas insisted "the border is closed" as thousands of illegal immigrants keep pouring across—a blatant lie and more Orwellian doublespeak.

Gaslighters Use What Is Near and Dear to You as Ammunition

Disrespect of the American flag. Old Glory is a sacred symbol to most patriotic Americans. It stands for our identity and the many sacrifices that generations have made to defend the country. It represents all that we patriots hold dear, so naturally the leftist gaslighter sees it as a target. They burn the flag and refuse to stand for her during the national anthem.

In September 2017, the NFL sent the Jacksonville Jaguars and Baltimore Ravens to play a game at Wembley Stadium in London. During the playing of the American National Anthem, the devoted gaslighted wokester athletes promptly took a knee in protest. They are often quick to say that it's not disrespect. They just want to use the moment to highlight their grievances. Sorry, I don't accept that. Not one player kneeled during God Save the Queen. I guess they do understand that standing during such moments is a matter of respect, courtesy, and just simple good manners. Unfortunately, they cannot show the same deference to the symbol of their own country.

Destruction of monuments. The destruction of statues and monuments is an orchestrated attack point of the left. Anyone who tells me that they suddenly awakened one morning and felt offended by a statue of Robert E. Lee is just not credible. It is simply the starting point for tearing down all statues the left deems offensive. And believe me, they can always find a reason. If not stopped, they will tear down every statue from Mr. Rogers to Jesus and replace them with Ché Guevara and Marx.

I've studied the Civil War extensively, and frankly, I'm not fond of Confederate heroes. In fact, I'm inclined to view them as traitors to our country. Despite this view, the statues honoring these men have a place in our history as ugly as it was back then. While such statues were indeed erected by Confederate sympathizers to honor their own, many statues were erected when the country was still healing from the ravages of war. Today, I don't personally see much purpose in honoring these Confederates. Still, I view the statues as an essential part of our history and a reminder of the catastrophic consequences that extreme internal divisions can cause. Whether these controversial statues still have a place in the public square is a matter for debate and legislative action—not mob rule.

I asked someone who participated in the protests in Richmond, Virginia if he could tell me anything about Robert E. Lee besides that he fought for the Confederacy and therefore to preserve slavery. I heard nothing but crickets, but he was vehement in his belief that the statue must be torn down. Ignorance is infectious.

Every America-loving patriot knew the real strategy when the demolition of statues began. Once the Confederate statues came down, so must all the others. When does it end? Statues of Abraham Lincoln, the Great Emancipator who gave his life in opposition to slavery, were torn down. The race hustler, Al Sharpton started calling for the Jefferson Monument to be defunded. I'm not sure what they would do with Martin Luther King's statue. His views on race and national healing do not align with the modern-day leftist social warriors.

Gaslighters Wear You Down Over Time

The left is relentless. They frequently employ professional protestors who are funded by radical sources and the back-alley channeling of tax dollars into activist organizations. Through their corruption, they have managed to attach a vacuum hose to our national treasury and suck your tax dollars into grants and pet projects that funnel money to radical groups. A prime example is the letting of contracts to Critical Race Theory consultants. The Federal Government has spent millions on teaching CRT garbage. State and local governments have channeled millions more.

People who oppose the left are busy and typically content with our American way of life. They have responsibilities like working, taking care of their children, and generally living their lives as responsible law-abiding Americans. The left is always on offense and uses paid, perpetual malcontents that they frequently bus-in for riots and protests. Leftists are the ones seeking to tear down American society at every level. Staying on offense gives them the strategic initiative. It's exhausting to even defend against the simplest attack.

Gaslighters Know Confusion Weakens People

This leftist gaslighting strategy is designed to assault our social moorings across a spectrum of attack points. The more the left can sow confusion across society, the more likely they are to weaken the ties that bind our nation.

Destruction of faith. The left constantly uses science to sow disbelief in God. When scientists make a discovery, the left promotes it as evidence that God doesn't exist, "You see there's no mystery here. Everything can be explained through science." This tactic is designed to separate the country form God. I'm not intending to debate the myriad of theological contradictions and exclusions across various religious faiths, sects, and denominations. I'll leave that to the theologians, but I'll happily debate the existence of God with anyone. The Founders believed firmly in a Creator as well. Although the Catholic Church had lost much of its political power across the world as it emerged from the Age of Reason, our Founders maintained a firm faith in the Almighty while some distanced themselves from organized religions. They are often called Deists by historians.

While the Constitution restrains the government from establishing an official state religion, our founding documents are deeply rooted in the existence of a Creator God. This is fundamental to our nation because it is from God that we obtain our basic human rights. No man can take away our unalienable rights because we are "endowed with them by our Creator." This is not only a matter of faith, but it is an important political issue that has grave implications. If the left extinguishes God in our social structures, the state becomes your god. The state becomes the grantor and withholder of rights. Since our Founders knew this, they integrated the concept that our rights come from God into our national fabric. As we become unmoored from God, we become a society adrift and ripe for "reimagination" as the leftists like to say.

Destruction of parental authority. The state continues to advance its grip on your child while driving a wedge between you and your precious progeny. Their favorite instrument is public schools. Several school districts and jurisdictions are pushing laws that allow children to make potentially life changing decisions without the consent of their parents.

In keeping with the Alinsky inspired mantra, "Never let a good crisis go to waste," the COVID pandemic was used to assert public school power and diminish parental authority. Several school jurisdictions have said they will offer COVID vaccinations to children without parental consent. The District of Columbia passed a law that allows officials to vaccinate children in public schools without first notifying their parents. A municipal regulation known as the "Minor Consent to Vaccinations Act of 2020" allows a child aged 11 and up to consent to vaccination.[6] This law also keeps the child's immunization record private and presents a blank immunization record to parents thereby even depriving parents of complete knowledge of their child's health history. It is a draconian leftist measure that subverts parental authority. One has to ask, is this America or China?

The legal system has consistently upheld eighteen as the age required for legal consent. Subversion of the age of consent creates vast implications across the legal spectrum. If a child is presumed to comprehend the risks of vaccination, will they also in the future be presumed to have consented to sex with an adult stranger? Alteration of established norms must be resisted and accepted only after careful consideration from all sides. You must understand that lawyers love to play the "if this...then that" game. That's how legal precedent is established and constantly twisted to win future litigation.

Parental concerns regarding secret vaccination are valid based on parental rights and from a medical perspective. According to the

---

[6] Council of the District of Columbia, D.C. Law 23-193

Center for Disease Control's (CDC) own data, there have been troubling reports of children developing life-threatening heart inflammation after receiving these emergency use vaccines, despite children being at almost zero risk of dying from COVID. So why vaccinate a healthy child who is not at risk? Who will take care of the child if he or she becomes one of the unlucky few that develops heart problems? Will the DC Government foot the bill for their medical needs? Can these children's hearts even be restored to health? What happened to doing only what is medically necessary for a patient? Leftists care only about advancing their control. Forcing you to bow to their power is all that matters.

Sexual confusion and all manner of gender bending. Encroachment upon parental rights doesn't stop with the COVID "emergency" actions that schools implemented. In 2021 the Virginia Assembly enacted VA Code 22.1-23.3 into law enabling school districts to advance the transgender movement through their policies. Schools in Virginia are now aggressively promoting the pansexuality agenda and providing "gender affirming" support for children who claim to be of a gender that does not align with their biological sex.

If a boy declares that he is a girl, the school must support him and provide access to all facilities that match whatever he claims. Fairfax County Public School (FCPS) policy 2603 was developed and adopted to carry out the new law. Under the policy, *there is no parental consent required*, and they don't even have to inform you. You put Johnny on the school bus in the morning. Then around lunchtime, he decides that he's feeling more like a Dorothy. Would you not want to know that your child is going through a crisis?

Refer to Figure 2-2 below obtained from training that all Fairfax County teachers must complete. Left-leaning school boards across the country have either preceded Virginia's regulations or will soon follow suit.

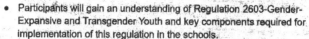

≡ Supporting Gender Expansive and Transgender Youth

Learning Objectives

- Participants will gain an understanding of Regulation 2603-Gender-Expansive and Transgender Youth and key components required for implementation of this regulation in the schools.
- Participants will recognize that identities are fluid and our identities intersect, influencing one another to create unique experiences.
- Participants will identify and understand the use of identified pronouns and chosen name.
- Participants will understand the steps to take when a transgender or gender-expansive student reports that they have been bullied or harassed.

Click NEXT to continue

Supporting Gender Expansive and Transgender Youth

Screenshot

‹ PREV   NEXT ›

≡ Supporting Gender Expansive and Transgender Youth

Legal Name and Chosen Name

Option 1	Option 2	Option 3
Name Change in Class	**Name Change in Virtual Platforms**	**Name Change on All Records**
• Teachers use a student's chosen name	• Teachers use the chosen name in class	• Name change will be reflected in SIS, SEA-STARS and all other records
• Teachers ensure that substitute class lists use chosen name	• Teachers ensure that class lists use chosen name	• Student's Legal Name will be stored in the Protected Information View
• Student may use a chosen name in some classes and not others	• Student may use a chosen name in some classes and not others	• Students will receive diplomas and transcripts with both the legal and chosen name
• Parental permission is not required	• Parental permission is not required	• Parental permission is not required
	• Virtual platforms such as BBCU and G Suite reflect chosen name	• Legal name change documentation is not required

Supporting Gender-Expansive and Transgender Youth

Screenshot

Figure 2-2: Fairfax County Public Schools Policy on Gender Affirmation

Sexual confusion is a powerful ploy to undermine traditional social foundations, sow more profound division, and keep the populace in a state of high anxiety. The constant reinforcement that one may not really be a boy or a girl despite what your body looks like can lead to tremendous insecurity in our children. They become confused about the most fundamental aspect of their existence. Our children are being barraged with messages that it's okay if they don't feel that they identify with their biological sex. No need to talk to your parents about it. Certainly, no need to see an honest therapist. It's all good.

In addition, leftists are pushing minor consent laws to allow children with gender dysphoria to proceed with permanent life altering "gender reassignment" procedures. This includes puberty suppression through hormone therapy and even physical mutilation like radical mastectomies and penectomy. In an October 2016 town hall meeting, then candidate Joe Biden embraced the idea of 8-year-olds being able to decide that they are transgender. In typical, barely coherent Biden style, he said, "The idea that an eight-year-old child, a ten-year-old child, decides, you know, 'I want to be transgender. That's what I think I'd like to be. It'd make my life a lot easier'—there should be zero discrimination."

The politicians speak as if they are experts and are quick to pander to special interests despite the overwhelming evidence that biological sex is fixed down to the cellular level at conception. Further, harmful "therapies" and life-altering procedures are being pushed onto children while ignoring the statistics that 80-95% of children with gender dysphoria eventually accept their biological sex according to the American College of Pediatricians. Instead, the insane left pushes children into transgenderism. The following is an abstract from the American College of Pediatricians' position on gender dysphoria.

Gender dysphoria (GD) of childhood describes a psychological condition in which children experience a marked incongruence between their experienced gender and the gender associated with their biological sex. When this occurs in the pre-pubertal child, GD resolves in the vast majority of patients by late adolescence. Currently there is a vigorous, albeit suppressed, debate among physicians, therapists, and academics regarding what is fast becoming the new treatment standard for GD in children. This new paradigm is rooted in the assumption that GD is innate and involves pubertal suppression with gonadotropin releasing hormone (GnRH) agonists followed by the use of cross-sex hormones—a combination that results in the sterility of minors. A review of the current literature suggests that this protocol is founded upon an unscientific gender ideology, lacks an evidence base, and violates the long-standing ethical principle of "First do no harm."[7]

As you saw in the FCPS policy, the accepted leftist orthodoxy is that "identity is fluid." They blindly and willingly accept this position without any scientific backing. So, let's dive headlong into enabling children to act on their psychological issues instead of providing compassionate counseling to help them resolve their inner conflicts. Let's all break out into our happy dance as we needlessly destroy the lives of vulnerable kids all sacrificed at the altar of identity politics, and of course let's not forget the almighty dollar. The insanity of giving children life altering hormones and even physical body modifications is akin to providing diet pills to an anorexic and claiming that you've helped them accept their true inner self.

Social media certainly plays its part in ensuring that gender confusion reigns supreme. You can ask to be called whatever you want if you're an adult. You can produce whatever non-traditional identity you desire. But for children, the social media environment again

---

[7] "Gender Dysphoria in Children," American College of Pediatricians – November 2018

creates reinforcement for their inner conflicts. Figure 2-3 shows Facebook's 58 gender choices when opening a new account. Facebook claims that it is merely responding to the demands of its user base. This may be true because gender confusion reigns supreme.

Agender	Androgyne	Androgynous
Bigender	Cis	Cisgender
Cis Female	Cis Male	Cis Man
Cis Woman	Cisgender Female	Cisgender Male
Cisgender Man	Cisgender Woman	Female to Male
FTM	Gender Fluid	Gender Nonconforming
Gender Questioning	Gender Variant	Genderqueer
Intersex	Male to Female	MTF
Neither	Neutrois	Non-binary
Other	Pangender	Trans
Trans*	Trans Female	Trans* Female
Trans Male	Trans* Male	Trans Man
Trans* Man	Trans Person	Trans Person
Trans Woman	Trans* Woman	Transfeminine
Transgender	Transgender Female	Transgender Male
Transgender Man	Transgender Person	Transgender Woman
Transmasculine	Transsexual	Transsexual Female
Transsexual Male	Transsexual Man	Transsexual Person
Transsexual Woman	Two-Spirit	

Figure 2-3: Facebook's Fifty-eight Gender Options[8]

Gaslighters Project

The left directly accuses the right of the very things of which the left is blatantly guilty. The left repeatedly accuses the right of trying to destroy democracy. According to the left, conservatives are fascists. Conservatives are the ones who promote totalitarian policies. This is the most extreme and ridiculous form of gaslighting, but it works because of pervasive media messaging. It leverages the what-you-see-is-all-there-is (WYSIATI) mental phenomena that Kahneman explores in depth in his aforementioned book.

Most people fail to search for hidden evidence. They simply do not make the effort to dig deeper into an issue, to seek statistical substantiation, to weigh both sides of an argument. They simply accept what they see because leftist ideology is all they see every day on nearly every corrupt media outlet. What they see the most frequently and consistently becomes their reality.

WYSIATI is a mechanism our minds use to rapidly observe and make sense of the world around us. While in everyday life, the mechanism helps us cope, it is a destructive and lazy thinking pattern in politics. You must never assume that any political proposition stands on WYSIATI. The leftist readily avails himself of this psychological trick to project. They position their dastardly ploys as the tactics of their adversaries when in reality, the opposite is true.

A rudimentary examination of philosophies will rapidly reveal leftist projection by asking some simple questions. Which philosophy diminishes the rights of the individual? Which philosophy promotes the rights of the individual? Which system would allow you

---

[8] Source: ABC News online, "Here's a List of 58 Gender Options for Facebook Users," Russell Goldman, February 13, 2014

to live by the rights of "life, liberty and the pursuit of happiness" with the fewest restrictions?

Gaslighters Tell You Everyone Else Is a Liar

The left lies, lies, and lies some more, and then tells you that everyone else is a liar. The modern leftist claims everything you've been taught about American values and history is a lie. After all, you've been taught by white people. Therefore, everything you know is automatically not true. The American system was created by white people; therefore, it must be burned down.

How to Resist Gaslighting

Human behavior tends to be simple and consistent, but the human mind is complex and easily manipulated if you are a low energy thinker. Rational thought is the only antidote to gaslighting. Whenever you hear a proposition that doesn't ring true, you can resist gaslighting by simply asking "Does that make sense?" Remain firm in your beliefs until irrefutable evidence is presented. Ask probing questions relentlessly until you receive satisfactory answers. A propagandist stands on a quicksand bed of lies. Persistent probing quickly sinks the liar.

Learning to think statistically instead of succumbing to emotional anecdotes is also critical in dispelling leftist lies. For example, are black people really being hunted in the streets every day? This will be explored further in later chapters. For now, I encourage you to accept that a simple examination of statistics reveals that the idea is blatant lie. Yet so many people believe it. Gaslighters are indeed diabolical.

CHAPTER 3

A Fast Walk Through History

"Sometimes our neighbors want the things we have, or have the things we want, so we both fight until they take ours or gives us theirs."

—*Jonathan Swift, Gulliver's Travels, 1726*

Tribes, Empires, and Conflict

Mankind has been in some state of war almost since the appearance of the first tribes on planet Earth. As populations multiplied, tribes eventually grew into empires and kingdoms, some vast and some small. Throughout human history, competing empires inevitably came into conflict with each other. That is not to say that primitive tribes didn't fight as well, but as empires expanded, skirmishes transformed into significant and ever greater wars. The common objective has consistently been acquisition of land and resources. The catalysts for conflict can usually be traced to an imbalance of military strength, greed, and mutual distrust.

Ultimately, the British Empire became the most successful in all human history, controlling 25% of the world's landmass at its peak in 1920. This remarkable level of conquest was achieved even after having long since lost its American colonies that spawned the

United States. British empire-building far eclipsed even the vaunted Roman Empire, which controlled only 3.7% of the world at its peak in 117 AD. Who knows what the Romans might have accomplished if they had comparable superior resources and technology?

Every rational peace-loving person wishes that human conflict and the clash of empires might become an avoidable outcome. But it seems that perpetual global competition repeatedly deteriorates into warfare. The stability of any group is determined primarily by its military and economic strength. Adherence to virtue alone is no shield against conquest unless it is also accompanied by military superiority. Therefore, nations are forever embroiled in a chess game of strategic military one-upmanship, alliance, and counter-alliance. Weakness and strategic error invite geopolitical and social instability leading to ultimate doom for weaker nations.

One need only perform a cursory review of world history to see that the Asians, Europeans, Arabs, Africans, and just about every civilization, race, and ethnicity have at some point in history benefitted and suffered from the conflict of empires. Nor is it even remotely accurate to think that these groups only attacked each other through racially organized cartels "oppressing" one another. They have fought internally as much, if not more.

In fact, it is a gross oversimplification to believe that the four continental supergroups mentioned above have consistently operated in unison to achieve common geopolitical goals. These supergroups are extraordinarily diverse and competitive within their borders.

For example, Libyans, Ethiopians, and Ghanaians are all technically Africans yet exceptionally ethnically and culturally diverse. In fact, Africa is so diverse that we count 54 countries, 800 ethnic groups, and 1000 languages according to the Department of Defense. Leftist rhetoric mashes Europeans together as white. In reality, Europeans are as culturally diverse as the populations of Africa.

Across the centuries, numerous rivalries pitted European countries against each other. Precursors of the Spanish, Portuguese, French, and British empires all fought to compete for superiority on the European continent.

Fast forward some more to the watershed voyage of Columbus in 1492, European rivalries not only continued in Europe but were now expanded to colonial interests abroad. The nations of the North and South American continents are the outgrowths of these four former empires. The British and French ultimately gained dominance in North America, while the Spanish and Portuguese dominated South America.

The colonization of what is now America and subsequent conquest of Indian lands is an extension of the perpetual conflict of empires and civilizations that can be traced back to time immemorial. This is not a justification or an absolution. It is merely an observation of fact. When civilizations begin to expand beyond some pre-established territorial equilibrium, conflict erupts and continues until one side emerges victorious.

There is no doubt that European colonizers invaded lands that were sparsely occupied by other civilizations. At Columbus' arrival, approximately 4-6 million Indians lived in the entire landmass that today comprises the Continental United States. Approximately 53 million occupied all of North and South America.[9] There is no moral basis for the European invasion. But neither is there any moral justification for most other invasions carried out by any other empire dating back millennia. No race, ethnicity, country, or continent can claim "clean hands" in the perpetual violent struggle for survival, superiority, and dominance. The expansion of civilizations and

---

[9] Denevan, William M. (September 1992). "The Pristine Myth: The Landscape of the Americas in 1492". Annals of the Association of American Geographers.

lustful acquisition of lands and resources of others is a sad universal human behavior.

Geologists estimate that the first arrivals of Indians in North America occurred somewhere around 13,000 BC. These settlers multiplied and spread across the continent, and possibly nomadic tribes split off into Mexico and South America. The Aztecs, Mayans, and Incas settled throughout Mexico and Central and South America.

In contrast, the first appearance of modern humans in Europe can be traced to somewhere between 55,000-35,000 BC. Clearly European civilization had a head start in development of at least 23,000 years over the tribes of North America. European society's technological and military progress compared to North American civilization was inordinately out of balance by the time they came in contact.

The lifestyle of Europeans evolved around static cities and villages. Although some Indian tribes did establish stationary villages, Indians remained largely nomadic, particularly in the great plains of what is currently the Central United States. Contrasting social structures engendered vastly different concepts of government and property ownership. The nomadic lifestyle most likely hindered technology development as well. By the time the Europeans arrived on North American shores, the imbalance and contrast between the two civilizations were stark indeed. Arriving Europeans viewed the local inhabitants as primitive and even savages.

Leftist rhetoric would have you believe that before the arrival of the "evil Europeans," the red man lived in a peaceful Garden of Eden environment unspoiled by greed, disease, and war. This is a myth. Indigenous tribes routinely fought one another. Tribes encroached on valuable hunting land occupied by other tribes and conflict resulted.

Eastern North American tribes were also known to conduct "mourning wars" intended to replace lost members of their own tribe. Mourning wars helped compensate for the depopulation of a tribe. Warriors from one tribe would attack a neighboring group and capture individuals to replace their lost members. Captives found unsuitable for integration in the tribe were often tortured and killed.

The Aztecs used warfare as a tool for empire expansion, comparable to the ancient Romans. They conquered neighboring groups, extracted tribute, and enslaved captives. Those not enslaved were used for human sacrifice. The Incas of South America did the same. The behavior pattern of these groups again underscores the common human traits of lust for superiority and conquest. In this sense, they were no different from the Europeans who crossed the Atlantic

Leftists argue that white European colonizers stole the land from the so-called Native Americans. Therefore, everything in America today is the outgrowth of an original evil act and should not exist. One must ask a few pointed questions regarding the leftist stolen land argument.

Conflict and the need for military strength seem to be universal conditions across the globe that span thousands of years. So, why does the left single out America as a particularly evil outgrowth of empire expansion when every civilization that pre-dates our founding has behaved the same way? The United States' existence is owed to a cascade of geopolitical actions, wars, and conquests that are morally no better or worse than any other civilization since the dawn of time.

As for the argument that America's existence is based on an original wrong, what could possibly be the remedy for acts initiated over four centuries ago? Where does one draw the line in trying to reverse the series of historical conquests that ultimately led to where humanity finds itself today? Shall the world offer redress for every single conquest ever committed by every civilization? Shall we just obliterate our Constitution, dissolve the United States, and hand everything over to the Marxists for redistribution? In turn, I'm sure they would "do the right thing" and give everything back to the Indians starting with Manhattan. In fact, I'm sure they would start with the Upper West Side—a hardcore leftist and very wealthy neighborhood.

By reflecting on these questions, the leftist strategy becomes clear. The left is only interested in generating national self-loathing to destroy America and install their new brand of slavery.

Slavery: Origins and Its Arrival in the New World

In these few pages, it is difficult to convey the abhorrent, inhumane, and utterly detestable practice of slavery. To gain a deeper understanding of what it was like, I immersed myself in the writings of Fredrick Douglass, the fervent abolitionist who was once enslaved. Despite the privations and dehumanizing treatment he endured, Douglass taught himself to read, became a respected orator, and even befriended Abraham Lincoln. He managed to rise from slave to gentleman and was received at the White House by Lincoln on multiple occasions. There are many lessons to be learned from Douglass' story. What it teaches us about our national evolution is a subject for reflection. For now, let's step back and examine slavery from a historical perspective and its arrival on American shores.

By the end of the African slave trade, nearly 10 million slaves would be shipped across the Atlantic. Philip Curtin, a former Professor Emeritus of Johns Hopkins University, was a leading historian on the African Slave trade. In 1969, he published "The African Slave Trade: A Census" which estimated that between 9 and 10 million slaves had been sent across the Atlantic. His estimate was remarkably close. In 1990, researchers decided to create a single authoritative multi-source database to estimate the volume of the slave trade. The project began in earnest in 1993 and that database now resides online, hosted at Rice University, and can be found at https://www.slavevoyages.org. It is the source for most of the related data cited herein.

The database grew from in-depth analysis of ship manifests documenting slave voyages across the Atlantic. The manifests often showed the count of slaves onboard and their destination. No dataset is ever 100% accurate. However, considering the undertaking, only minor holes exist in this data mostly in early voyages where ships' records were less accurate or were lost to the ravages of time. According to the database, 10,016,771 slaves were transported from Africa by various European empires with 9,838,642 being sent across the Atlantic.[10] Of that number, 364,000 disembarked at ports that are now part of the United States. The last arrivals to the US occurred in 1860 mainly in Georgia and Florida. As a percentage of the transatlantic slave trade, only 3.6% of slaves arrived in North America. However, by the 1860 US census, the number of enslaved black people in America had ballooned to 3,950,000.[11] This is most likely attributed to reproduction and possibly movement of enslaved people from the Caribbean islands to mainland North America.

Just like the clash of empires had existed for millennia, so too had slavery before the start of the European-African slave trade. Slavery had flourished for centuries in Europe, Africa, Asia, and the Middle East. It was typical for a conquering empire to take captives and convert them to slaves. This practice also existed among warring black African tribes and was commonplace at the dawn of the colonial period. Wars between African tribes became the primary supply source for the slave trade with the Europeans. The expanse and depth of this enterprise can be most fully understood by reading, *The Slave Trade: The Story of the Atlantic Slave Trade: 1440-1870 by Hugh Thomas*.

---

[10] Data derived from the Slave Voyages Database, www.slavevoyages.org
[11] US Census, 1860, www.census.gov

Another rich and detailed reference is *Where the Negroes Are Masters by Randy J. Sparks.*

In the mid-fifteenth century, the Fante were the dominant tribe in the region that became known as the Gold Coast. Their main rivals in the interior were the Asante. The Fante became wealthy and powerful by establishing themselves as the middlemen of European trade centered on the town of Annamaboe, the most important trading post on the Gold Coast. They held this position from the 1400s to the late 1700s. The Fante established a broad base of trade with the Europeans of which the principal part was the supply of slaves.

As the Fante flourished on the coast during the 1680s, the Asante grew more powerful through their conquests in the African interior and subsequent delivery of their prisoners to the coast for sale as slaves. The Gold Coast supply of slaves to the Europeans was almost entirely in the hands of Africans. Both the Fante and Asante profited from this arrangement until the Asante eventually conquered the Fante and sold most of their people into slavery. This might be viewed as poetic justice since the Fante had been selling Africans into slavery for well over two centuries before. The subsequent outlawing of the Transatlantic slave trade by the United States and Britain by 1808 brought an end to the "Wall Street" of slavery that was Annamaboe.

The first recorded European transfer of slaves from the African coast occurred in 1444 with the direct capture and transport of 235 slaves to Portugal. African slaving was a novelty to the Portuguese at the time with their principal focus of exploration still being the discovery of gold. The Portuguese were the dominant European force on the Gold Coast starting in 1455 and lasting through 1642 when they were displaced by the Dutch. Slave trading on a small scale occurred sporadically early on. Still, the organized European-African slave trade began in earnest around 1481 with the permanent establishment of the Portuguese trading post at Elmina on the Gold

Coast. The Portuguese opened markets along western trade routes leading to the Mediterranean that avoided direct competition with Muslim traders who were using trans-Saharan routes to ship goods and slaves back to Muslim empires in the Middle East.

By 1642, the Portuguese abandoned their position on the Gold Coast when their trading post at Elmina fell to the Dutch. By 1679, the Dutch were displaced by the English who remained the dominant force at Annamaboe through the close of the 18th century.

The slave trade steadily escalated when the Portuguese and other European traders that followed realized that "black gold" was just as lucrative as the glimmering yellow metal. The opening of plantations in the New World, particularly in the Caribbean and South America, created an explosive demand for labor in the early 1500s. The Europeans and their African partners quickly deduced that a nearly insatiable market had been born.

The earliest date in the slave voyage database indicating a transatlantic shipment of slaves is 1520 when a merchant ship of unknown flag sailed from Portuguese Guinea and arrived in San Juan with a delivery of 259 African slaves. Figure 3-1 shows the scale of slave shipments over the years. Shipments peaked in 1829 when 101,105 slaves were sent west from Africa. Somewhere between 10-20% would die in transit. At times, entire ships were lost at sea.

The first shipment of slaves to America arrived in 1655 at New York with 391 slaves disembarking. The peak shipment of slaves occurred in 1807, with 20,028 disembarking in that year at various ports on the mainland. After 1807, the importation of slaves dropped to nearly zero as the Act Prohibiting the Importation of Slaves was voted into law on March 2, 1807 and took effect on January 1, 1808. Thomas Jefferson had called upon Congress to pass the act in his 1806 State of the Union Address. The Act made it illegal for all ships to import slaves whether foreign or domestic.

The internal American slave trade was not affected and slavery would continue for another half-century. Numerous acts and maneuvers to curtail and contain slavery would be attempted. So too would laws be passed, and compromises reached to protect it. Through the ensuing decades, abolitionist sentiments steadily grew, and Southern slavery proponents felt their economy increasingly threatened until finally the issue reached a boiling point and America exploded into a bloody civil war.

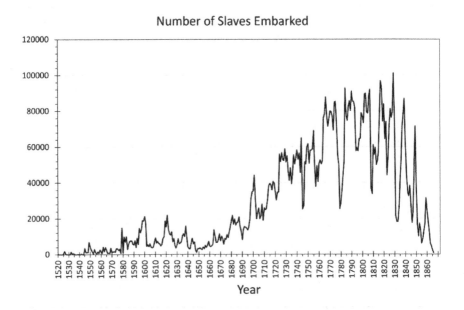

Figure 3-1: Number of Slaves Sent to the New World[12]

I've endeavored to provide a quick summary of the critical points shaping the origins of slavery and a view of its magnitude and pervasive practice. The key takeaway from this admittedly cursory summary is that slavery was a human problem driven by greed and lust

---

[12] Data derived from the Slave Voyages Database, www.slavevoyages.org

for power. It was not just a white problem or an American problem. Arabs were entrenched practitioners of African slavery long before the Europeans began exploiting it on a grand scale. Black African tribes were equally complicit in its development and perpetuation along with their European counterparts.

Of course, rationalizations and blame-shifting abound to ensure that all blame falls squarely and solely on the white man—the preferred propaganda of the modern American left. Blame shifting can be traced as far back as 1749 to the memoirs of the Danish West Indian and Guinea Company containing discussions with Fante counterparts.

> It is you, you whites ... who have brought all the evil among us. Indeed, would we have sold one another if you, as purchasers, had you not come to us?

Certainly, the contact with Europeans and the discovery of the New World led to a confluence of events that fueled demand for labor, subsequently filled by the greed and lust of the European emperors, popes, and African people. No one involved has clean hands in this contemptible practice of converting people into property.

Despite the western world having rejected and extinguished the practice, slavery still thrives today in Africa, the Middle East, and most systematically in China. Regardless of cause or complicity, the fact that slavery flourished in the Western World for over 400 years is certainly no justification for the Marxist argument to "burn down" our American Constitution and destroy our institutions as restitution for this abhorrent and pervasive practice. The essence and importance of our Constitution is an entirely separate discussion.

Birth of Our Nation and Founding Principles
(1619 vs. 1776)

Many Americans who follow politics are by now aware of the 1619 Project. It is a significant propaganda initiative concocted and marketed by the New York Times. It is controversial by choice, first to sell newspapers and second to advance the Marxist agenda. From the start, Nikole Hannah-Jones has been the front person for the project though it has many contributors. She is featured prominently in the initial work published in the New York Times Magazine on August 18, 2019.

Historians have already blasted major holes in the 1619 Project, and I don't plan to repeat their skillful rebuttals here. My goal is to highlight some specific falsehoods of the project and to properly frame it as Marxist propaganda and demonstrate how it improperly presents America's history.

As I read the 1619 Project, I found it filled with some valid points and true stories of the suffering of black people during the slave era and Post-Civil War America. It provides a greater appreciation for black people's injustices, struggles, and contributions. These are the good parts. The intent is not to show that the 1619 Project is entirely false. Much of it is true. The key issue is its twisted conclusions based on some willful lies and omissions.

I also found that the 1619 Project deliberately cherry-picks history to serve its specific propaganda purposes. Through its silence on the role of white people in ending slavery, it pretends that white people played no part in advancing abolition and civil rights. Blacks were indeed the victims of vast injustice, but not all whites were responsible, and many whites stood up to end slavery. The Civil War is mentioned 26 times. Never is the war discussed in terms of the lives sacrificed to preserve the union and end slavery. Just as it would be racist to lump all black Americans into one category for whatever purpose, it is equally racist to lump all whites together as oppressors. Nikole Hannah-Jones does precisely this. In speaking of the rise of Jim Crowe laws, she says:

> … black Americans, simply by existing, served as a problematic reminder of this nation's failings. **<u>White America</u>** dealt with this inconvenience by constructing a savagely enforced system of racial apartheid that excluded black people almost entirely from mainstream American life—a system so grotesque that Nazi Germany would later take inspiration from it for its own racist policies. (Emphasis added)

White America did not act in unison to oppress black people. A special kind of white Americans did this. Certainly not all. The discussion of who the real oppressors were is a morsel to be savored in later chapters. But the rhetoric of Black America vs White America is precisely the agenda that the 1619 Project seeks to legitimize.

Unfair and Misleading Treatment of Lincoln

Lincoln is the greatest president America has ever had. Still, the left casts Lincoln as a racist instead of the more deserving title of The Great Emancipator. Lincoln was revered and thought of in the most affectionate terms by generations of black people that preceded the authors of the 1619 Project. Like most people of his day, Lincoln had prejudices and misconceptions about black people. But a racist is much more defined by what he does than what he thinks. Thoughts are reshaped through reason and introspection. Actions cut deeply, have a more lasting effect, and are difficult to take back. Lincoln may have thought the wrong things at times, but his efforts were ever faithful to truth and justice. He skillfully and patiently navigated the most treacherous period in American history to save our country and end slavery.

I have delved deeply into the life and character of Abraham Lincoln. I'm sure he would chastise anyone for saying this because he was humble, among many other positive character attributes. I'll say it anyway. Lincoln deserves the reverence we would give to a saint. For the truth about Lincoln, we can turn to the words of Frederick Douglass, who gave a balanced, accurate, and heartfelt summation of what Lincoln meant to all Americans. On April 14, 1876, in Washington DC, at the dedication of the Emancipation Memorial (Figure 3-2), eleven years after Lincoln's death, Douglass said:

> When, therefore, it shall be asked what we have to do with the memory of Abraham Lincoln, or what Abraham Lincoln had to do with us, the answer is ready, full, and complete. Though he loved Caesar less than Rome, though the Union was more to him than our freedom or our future, under his wise and beneficent rule we saw ourselves gradually lifted from the depths of slavery to the heights of liberty and manhood; under his wise and beneficent rule, and by measures approved and vigorously pressed by him, we saw that the handwriting of ages, in the form of prejudice and proscription, was rapidly fading away from the face of our whole country…

Douglass closed his speech thus:

> We have done a good work for our race today. In doing honor to the memory of our friend and liberator, we have been doing highest honors to ourselves and those who come after us; we have been fastening ourselves to a name and fame imperishable and immortal; we have also been defending ourselves from a blighting scandal. When now it shall be said that the colored man is soulless, that he has no appreciation of benefits or benefactors; when the foul reproach of ingratitude is hurled at us, and it is attempted to scourge us beyond the range of human brotherhood, we may calmly point to the monument we have this day erected to the memory of Abraham Lincoln.

Frederick Douglass was a former slave who suffered greatly under the lash of cruel overseers. The first few pages of his autobiography, "Narrative of the Life of Frederick Douglass, an American Slave" will move any empathetic reader to tears. If any contemporary public figure of Lincoln's time had a grudge against Lincoln, it would be Douglass. Despite his suffering, he resolved his opinion of Lincoln with balance and understanding that Lincoln was a good and decent man whose thoughts evolved and whose life, though tragically cut short, culminated in freedom for all Americans. Whose words should we trust more, Frederick Douglass or the propagandists of the 1619 Project? Lest I be accused of cherry-picking, the full text of Douglass' oration is readily available online.[13]

Figure 3-2: Emancipation Memorial
Washington DC

---

[13] Oration in Memory of Abraham Lincoln WASHINGTON, D.C., APRIL 14, 1876, by Frederick Douglass

In June 2020, Marxist Black Lives Matter (BLM) protestors began targeting The Great Emancipator memorial as racist because in their words it depicts a black man in a subjugated position. They threatened to destroy the statue. Eleanor Holmes Norton seized the opportunity to pander to the left. She vowed to introduce legislation to remove the monument that Fredrick Douglass spoke about with such pride.

In Boston, the city council voted to remove a replica of the statue in downtown Boston. The removal was completed on December 29, 2020. In their ignorance of history, they succeeded in removing an iconic statue that honors Lincoln and depicts slaves as human beings rising out of slavery. Indeed, the Boston City Council and Eleanor Holmes Norton ought to spend a little time reading history and less time pandering to Marxist demands. The true goal behind the Marxist BLM protests is the cancellation of Lincoln, not sensitivity for their phony fragile feelings.

When viewing the statue from the perspective of an inner-city black youth on school field trip, I can understand how someone might interpret the statue negatively because it portrays black people in a diminished status. This interpretation arises from lack of context and knowledge of history. Tearing down the statue is not the solution. Instead, we can use the statue to teach the story behind it, honor Lincoln for his resolve, and honor Frederick Douglass for his courage and suffering. All of these opportunities will be lost if we fecklessly acquiesce to leftist temper tantrums.

We often look at the past through our cloudy 21st century lens and apply today's opinions to distant events. Frederick Douglass was not offended by the statue, and he was enslaved. Yet, a present day American who was never enslaved should feel offended?

Wrongly Proclaims the Birth of America as 1619

The illustrious propaganda piece opens with this bold declaration on the front cover:

> In August of 1619, a ship appeared on this horizon, near Point Comfort, a coastal port in the British colony of Virginia. It carried more than 20 enslaved Africans, who were sold to the colonists. **America was not yet America**, but this was the moment it began. No aspect of the country that would be formed here has been untouched by the 250 years of slavery that followed. On the 400th anniversary of this fateful moment, it is finally time to tell our story truthfully. (Emphasis added)

It is true that some number close to 20 Africans disembarked near Jamestown in 1619. Jamestown was a business venture from its start. It was operated by the Virginia Company, chartered by King James I. Its purpose was to establish a profitable colony that would ship raw materials to England. In 1624, after several violent encounters between settlers and the indigenous Powhatans, Virginia was made a royal colony by King James I. This meant that England took direct control over affairs, and the Virginia Company was disbanded.

Figure 3-3 shows the text of the records from the Virginia Company regarding the transaction involving the 20 Africans. Historians disagree on whether the Africans were treated as slaves or indentured servants. In the 1600's it was common for poor people with low skills to effectively sell themselves in service to a master in exchange for passage to the New World. The period of servitude would typically last seven years.

About the latter end of August, a Dutch man of Warr of the burden of a 160 tuñes arriued at Point-Comfort, the Comando⁺ name Capt Jope, his Pilott for the West Indies one Mʳ Marmaduke an Englishman. They mett wᵗʰ the Trēr in the West Indyes, and determyned to hold consort shipp hetherward, but in their passage lost one the other. He brought not any thing but 20. and odd Negroes, wᶜʰ the Governoʳ and Cape Marchant bought for victualle (whereof he was in greate need as he p̃tended) at the best and easyest ratε they could. He hadd a lardge and ample Coñ̃yssion from his Excellency to range and to take purchase in the West Indyes.

Figure 3-3: Records of the Virginia Company

The Library of Congress website shows a timeline of the Virginia colony and specifically claims the Africans became indentured servants. This is certainly possible since no slave laws were yet enacted in the colonies during this early period. The entry from August 1619, shown in Figure 3-4, is taken from a collection of Thomas Jefferson's Historical Notes on Virginia.

The first African slaves are brought to Virginia by Captain Jope in a Dutch ship. Governor Yeardley and a merchant, Abraham Piersey, exchange twenty of them for supplies. These Africans become indentured servants like the white indentured servants who traded passage for servitude. John Rolfe to Edwin Sandys, Jan 1619/20, "About the latter end of August..."

Figure 3-4: Library of Congress Timeline Entry
From the Papers of Thomas Jefferson

The English role in the slave trade is well established, and Hannah-Jones clearly acknowledges that "America was not America yet." The arrival of settlers and European control over colonies is indeed the starting point for colonization. Still the ideals that framed the Declaration of Independence and the Constitution were certainly not born at Jamestown out of the Virginia Company. Our American ideals are far more connected to the Mayflower Compact signed in

1620 by the pilgrims landing at Plymouth who had escaped religious persecution. The text follows:

> IN THE NAME OF GOD, AMEN. We, whose names are underwritten, the Loyal Subjects of our dread Sovereign Lord King James, by the Grace of God, of Great Britain, France, and Ireland, King, Defender of the Faith, &c. Having undertaken for the Glory of God, and Advancement of the Christian Faith, and the Honour of our King and Country, a Voyage to plant the first Colony in the northern Parts of Virginia; Do by these Presents, solemnly and mutually, in the Presence of God and one another, covenant and combine ourselves together into a civil Body Politick, for our better Ordering and Preservation, and Furtherance of the Ends aforesaid: And by Virtue hereof do enact, constitute, and frame, such just and equal Laws, Ordinances, Acts, Constitutions, and Officers, from time to time, as shall be thought most meet and convenient for the general Good of the Colony; unto which we promise all due Submission and Obedience.

This truly is the spark of the American spirit as we know it and most closely resembles our republican roots. The pilgrims enslaved no one. In contrast, when the English profiteers calculated that indentured servitude wasn't enough to drive their enterprises, they began replacing the practice with slavery. Why settle for a mere seven years of servitude when one could buy a slave for a lifetime?

Hannah-Jones declares, "America Wasn't a Democracy, Until Black Americans Made It One." Well, alert the media. America wasn't a democracy then, isn't a democracy now, and by the grace of God never will be. We are a republic. Democracy would devolve to ever-shifting mob rule where a simple majority could perpetually oppress any minority for any reason based on a simple majority vote. Democratic rule is a most fickle proposition.

The United States of America is a republic where we elect representatives and where law-abiding citizens subject themselves to a standard set of laws just as the pilgrims did at Plymouth. Unfettered democracy is another path to Marxism. That's why leftists love to extol and clothe themselves in democracy while working like beavers to solidify their grip on power.

The formation of the United States of America officially began in 1776 with the signing of the Declaration of Independence. In 1787, our Constitution and Bill of Rights completed the foundations. It is in these documents where our national identity as a sovereign nation is codified.

Prior to 1776, colonial governing bodies were growing ever more frustrated with King George III. His rule was capricious and inconsistent, and his word was worthless. Many problems in the thirteen established British colonies were ignored. His decrees and promises would change to suit the needs of the Crown. Despotic rule results when power is in the hands of one man. He is accountable to no one. Just like a monarchy, Marxism is despotism.

America Was Not Founded on a Lie

Thomas Jefferson is credited with composing the essence of the Declaration of Independence. Though like most authors, he suffered the editor's pen strokes, no one disputes that he wrote the Declaration's preamble:

> We hold these truths to be self-evident, that all men are created equal, that they are endowed by their Creator with certain unalienable Rights, that among these are Life, Liberty and the pursuit of Happiness.

Jefferson wrote the words that would shape our national destiny. Yet, at the same time, he owned over 600 slaves that worked his Monticello estate.

The 1619 Project treats these foundational ideals as follows: "Our founding ideals of liberty and equality were false when they were written. Black Americans fought to make them true." And, "The United States is a nation founded on both an ideal and a lie." This is, at best, very loose language and, at worst, a deliberate lie in itself.

Nothing that is a lie can ever be made true. A lie is a lie, and the truth is truth. Our founding ideals are true and just, and they form the framework for the best government mankind has been able to devise. No honest historian would claim that America has always lived up to these ideals. However, the ideals enshrined in our national identity are the North Star we can point to when course correction is needed, as Martin Luther King was able to do during the civil rights era.

The authors of the 1619 Project must think that Jefferson was either a cunning hypocrite or some sort of witless scribe. If he was a cunning hypocrite, he would not have forever linked his name to writing words that would prove him so. Based on what we know of his remarkable intelligence, we can safely say he was not a witless scribe either. He precisely knew what he was writing. He understood that the ideals of the Declaration of Independence would one day have to be squared with the reality of slavery.

Again, if one wants to cherry-pick quotes and historical facts, one could paint Jefferson as simply another white racist oppressor. This would be a vast oversimplification of his life and a complete disregard for the collateral goodness he helped create. Jefferson did often speak and act against slavery. To cast him as a crusader against slavery would also not be accurate. He was obviously a conflicted person. My assessment is that his failure to free all of his slaves can be summed up in just one word—debt. Jefferson spent a good portion of his life with a heavy debt load hanging over his head. When he died, he was still deeply in debt. No apologies on his behalf suffice, nor should we fabricate excuses about Virginia laws preventing a slaveholder from freeing his slaves. Jefferson's actions regarding his slaves were acts of self-preservation consistent with general human nature. It is really just that simple.

Rest assured, Jefferson knew the future implications of his words. He knew slavery was deeply wrong. He looked for ways to contain it and ultimately phase it out. He also knew that slavery had the potential to destroy the nation through civil war. He was correct in his prediction. So, today, we are moving toward the same outcome. Leftists know the deep scar that slavery inflicted on the nation and have chosen to tear open the stitches again, to create a fissure by which they can permanently fracture the nation. The 1619 Project is but one tool by which they chisel away at our stability.

The Revolutionary War Was Not Fought to Preserve Slavery

The assertion that the thirteen colonies fought the Revolutionary War to preserve slavery is false and another willful Marxist lie. In her opening essay, Hannah-Jones states:

> Conveniently left out of our founding mythology is the fact that one of the primary reasons the colonists decided to declare their independence from Britain was because they wanted to protect the institution of slavery.

The Declaration of Independence lists 27 grievances that were boldly laid before King George III of Great Britain. Without delving into all 27, the following provides a brief summary of the primary issues that led to declaring independence.

Mercantilism was the predominant economic policy across Europe during the colonial period. Of particular relevance to the American Colonies was Britain's strict policy enforcement. As a small island nation, Britain had far fewer natural resources than its colonies. Mercantilism's core principle was to minimize the importation of finished products to Britain while maximizing exports of finished products, thereby creating a favorable trade balance. This gave Britain the upper hand in the world economy. The colonists were restricted in shipping finished products to Britain. For example, they could supply cotton but could not sell finished clothing abroad. In turn, Britain would be the producer of finished goods that it would sell back to the Colonies and other markets.

Restriction of trade was another grievance that negatively impacted the colonial economy. This was closely tied to mercantilism. Colonists were only allowed to sell certain products to British merchants. This included tobacco, sugar, iron, furs, and indigo, a plant used for dye. Trade restrictions created a British monopoly for the purchase of colonial raw materials. They could set the price as they wished and severely limit colonial economic growth prospects.

Taxation without representation was another major grievance. The colonists did not have representation in the British Parliament. While the king still had the final word on all matters of state, British citizens had representation and could submit supplications to their government. Colonials had assemblies to pass local laws, but those assemblies reported to their respective colonial governor, who was bound to obey the king's decrees. At any time, the king could invalidate any law passed by a colonial assembly through his decrees to the governor. Parliament passed a series of acts raising raise taxes on the colonists. These angered the colonists, who claimed that Parliament had no right to tax the colonists.

Abolishing legislatures was Britain's most extreme political suppression of colonial self-rule. When assemblies began to drift too far toward independent governance, royal governors issued a decree to disband the offending assembly. For example, in 1768, the Massachusetts governor disbanded the colonial assembly after a row over the circulation of a letter written by Samuel Adams. The letter was critical of taxes called the Townsend Duties and attempted to enlist the assistance of all the other colonial assemblies. When the Massachusetts assembly refused to withdraw support for the letter, the governor, Francis Bernard, disbanded the assembly. The New York assembly suffered a similar fate for its protests over the Quartering Act. The Virginia and North Carolina assemblies were also dissolved when they objected to British taxation.

Refusal of assent was a deliberate neglect tactic exercised by the king. When disputes arose, and supplications were made to the king, he would simply ignore the colonists. As long as trade flowed and Britain prospered, all other concerns were secondary. When assemblies managed to pass laws and forward them through the Governor to the king, he would simply withhold his assent and ignore the problems.

These, among other issues, finally triggered the Continental Congress to convene and authorize the drafting of the Declaration of Independence.

The very next line of Hannah-Jones' essay contains another falsehood regarding slavery as the reason America fought the Revolutionary War,

> By 1776, Britain had grown deeply conflicted over its role in the barbaric institution that had reshaped the Western Hemisphere. In London, there were growing calls to abolish the slave trade.

I'm sure that in 1776 there were British voices raised in opposition to slavery. In America, there were calls against slavery as well. The fact that the Founders considered including a clause in the Declaration of Independence denouncing slavery indicates that there were indeed respected voices opposing it. The 1619 Project even mentions the clause denouncing slavery that was stricken from the final draft. While the Marxist essay uses this as evidence to place the blame of slavery at the feet of the colonists, it is totally misleading to infer that Britain was "getting religion" on the issue and had become morally opposed. The British would have done nothing to upend their lucrative trade triangle underpinned by slavery. The British placed the slave trade on steroids in North America, while the Portuguese did the same for South America.

Once the British were defeated in the Revolutionary War, the American South was still heavily dependent on slave labor. It was then easy for the British to ban the slave trade in 1807 through the Slave Trade Act. By then the United States of America was already moving to stop the importation of slaves as early as 1800. The Act Prohibiting the Importation of Slaves took effect in 1808. If Britain had not banned the slave trade, their slave merchants would no longer have had a market in America anyway. Besides, I'm sure that their reasoning also included retribution by undercutting their former colonies' access to free labor.

Also, consider another angle to this story. What if the American Colonies had convened their individual assemblies and unanimously agreed to abolish slavery? Would the crown have interpreted that as a threat to British trade and profits? Would the king have allowed it since British slavers profited handsomely and the colonies used the labor to ship goods back to Britain?

I reiterate that many hands were dirty in perpetuating the abominable practice of slavery. Winning the Revolutionary War set the stage for ultimate universal freedom. The beginning of the end of slavery was marked by the birth of the United States of America starting with Jefferson's pen and culminating with the blast of colonial muskets through which we won the right to form a nation.

The Founding Fathers—Indisputable Proof of Their Higher Virtue

As many as 41 of the 56 signers of the Declaration of Independence owned slaves. Because of this fact, the left would have you cancel the Founding Fathers. They want you to hate our Founders so much that you will be willing to tear down their monuments, burn the Declaration of Independence, and shred the Constitution. The central purpose of the 1619 Project is to convince you that America is evil. The filter it uses to examine history is captured in the phrase, "Anti-black racism runs in the very DNA of this country." Ask yourself this question, "Can you change your DNA?" Their filter implies that since racism is part of our DNA and DNA cannot be changed, we must burn down all our institutions and start with something new. Only "useful idiots" think that Marxism is a new and better way.

The truth about America is the exact opposite of what the left would have you believe. Racism is not in our DNA. The inalienable rights of life, liberty, and the pursuit of happiness are the DNA of our nation. That is why we have consistently self-corrected whenever the rights of any group are trampled upon. Our higher ideals serve as the true north of the American spirit. When we lose our way on an issue, we look to those ideals, and they guide us to what the right answer should be. This is why Martin Luther King was victorious because he could point to those higher ideals and say, "Wait a minute. What about us?"

There is no excuse for the Founders' enslavement of fellow human beings. No one held a gun to their heads and forced them to own slaves. Many of them were born with the system in place and inherited plantations. Jefferson inherited his slaves. Washington as well. One trap in examining history is that we tend to judge historical figures through a lazy and convenient filter based on modern moral thinking and laws. We consistently peer at the past through our 21st-century goggles. This filter makes many feel morally superior and quick to judge the Founders harshly. The ugly truth is that taken as a whole, humanity is no more moral and righteous today than in 1776. If you think our Founders were hypocrites, do you also believe that hypocrisy in human rights is a thing of the past?

Since leftists are so willing to point out the hypocrisy of the Founders, we should call out all the woke corporations that make massive profits from China's systemic slave labor system. In fact, it's entirely appropriate that we make LeBron James the poster child for modern hypocrisy on the issue of slavery. The entire National Basketball Association (NBA) is complicit in the suffering of the Uyghur population forced into slave labor by the Chinese Communist Party (CCP). Every NBA player and coach is forbidden to speak out against human rights abuses in China, while they are encouraged to put BLM slogans on their jerseys that support our domestic Marxist liars. Why? Because China will threaten the NBA with banning televised games if the NBA does anything that makes the CCP look bad.

In contrast, social justice virtue signaling is in fashion domestically and gives spoiled millionaire athletes a sense of moral superiority. They can speak freely about American social issues without fear of retribution. They have that freedom because of the Bill of Rights our Founders embedded in America's DNA.

So, if anyone thinks he is morally superior to the Founders, be aware that there are many areas in today's society where the Founders would think that modern Americans have actually devolved and replaced their brains with Swiss cheese. In 1776, slavery was a global human problem. Sadly, it was a way of life. America was but one place touched by this scourge.

Therefore, consider the grander virtue of our Founders despite their human failings. Each of the signers of the Declaration of

Independence is a hero. Upon placing their names on that glorious document, they committed treason from the British Crown's perspective. They fully expected that their declaration would be met with military force. In fact, by 1775, the king had already declared the colonies to be in open rebellion. Regardless, with their ragtag militias, the puny colonies chose to confront the most powerful military force on the planet. If they had failed, all of the signers would have been executed. This prompted Benjamin Franklin to say, "We must hang together, or we shall surely hang separately." Despite putting their lives and all they owned at risk, these brave men signed anyway. This is courage that most cannot comprehend. Under the leadership of the magnificent and most honorable George Washington and the skillful diplomacy of Benjamin Franklin, America actually wins. Our victory is but one link in the chain of events that led to freedom.

Having won independence, what did our Founders do next? They could have selected a king and established a monarchy that mirrored the one they had just defeated. Some colonists close to Washington approached him with the prospect of becoming king. He met the idea with a stern rebuke and forbade them from ever mentioning it again. Washington believed in the grander ideals for which he fought. He wasn't a corrupt sellout like so many of our present-day leaders. Having gained independence and concentrated their power, the Founders did something magnificent. They simply gave that power away. They gave it to you and me. They gave it to "We the People." That indicates a higher commitment to virtue. This proves our Founders were essentially virtuous men while many were still erring severely in one aspect of their character. This is a much more balanced and unifying perspective than the disparaging characterizations advanced by the 1619 Project.

The Chain of Events that Forever Shattered the Chains of Bondage

When I was still in corporate life as a vice president at a Fortune 100 company, I realized that many business problems were due to people being promoted into their first leadership position without formal leadership training. These poor victims of neglect would commit egregious errors in handling people that would often prove disruptive to a company's culture and performance.

The leadership problems I observed are pervasive, not only in corporations, but also in government and politics. Based on what I saw and experienced, I decided to write my first book, *4 Power Leadership: Your Pathway to Leadership Success,* to help newly minted leaders avoid the most common pitfalls.

To promote my book, I would accept speaking engagements wherever I could. I was once invited to speak at a Rotary Club meeting in Fairfax, Virginia. Part of my speech addressed the role of mentorship in developing leaders. In cases where adequate mentorship is not readily available to a junior leader, I recommended the study of virtuous historical figures. In particular, I cited Washington, Jefferson, and Lincoln. Three of the historical figures I admire most.

When I concluded my talk, a black gentleman approached me at the front of the room. He politely suggested that I reconsider whom I cited as virtuous leaders. I immediately zeroed in on his point, but nonetheless, I pretended to not understand and asked, "How do you mean?" He said, "Well, Washington and Jefferson were slave owners. Some people might be offended."

I paused for a few seconds and gathered my thoughts before responding, "There are four people in American history who I believe are most responsible for creating the opportunity for you and me to stand here as equals and gentlemen and have a conversation. Would you care to step through who they are?" He said, "Sure." I said, "Let me start with the most recent and work backwards. The first two I'm sure you will not find controversial."

Martin Luther King. He led the civil rights movement. He was instrumental in forcing the end of Jim Crow laws and segregation and setting the stage for the civil rights amendment. He gave us the unforgettable and inspirational "I Have a Dream" speech. His personal quest for equality came to an abrupt and shocking end when an assassin's bullet struck him in the right side of his neck. He gave his life for his noble cause. Without Dr. King, black people would not be where they are today. He gave us the immortal words about judging people by the content of their character and not the color of their skin. So far, no objection from my new friend.

Abraham Lincoln. He led the North to victory through his leadership and steadfast resolve. He issued the Emancipation Proclamation freeing all slaves throughout the South. He also championed the passage of the 13th Amendment to the Constitution, abolishing slavery. Lincoln, too, gave his life in pursuit of a grand cause. Shortly after the South's surrender, a vile assassin shot him in the back of his head, ending the life of our greatest president. If America did not have Lincoln's Leadership to lead us through the disastrous period of the civil war, slavery might possibly have continued in America for 50 more years. Again, my new friend had no objection. I warned him that my next choice would be controversial to him.

Thomas Jefferson. As the principal writer of the Declaration of Independence, Thomas Jefferson gave us the foundational words that have guided the nation's morals for over two centuries.

> We hold these truths to be self-evident, that all men are created equal, that they are endowed by their Creator with certain unalienable rights, that among these are Life, Liberty and the Pursuit of happiness.

Have we always, as a nation, lived up to these ideals? No. History clearly shows that the nation strayed from these noble aspirations on many occasions. Jefferson's ownership of slaves has caused many to tag him as a hypocrite in modern times. Critics have also said that he wasn't considering blacks as men. Neither of these statements is true. As already mentioned, Jefferson knew precisely what he was writing. He knew that the American colonies' yearning for freedom could not be reconciled with the acceptance of slavery. Without Jefferson writing "all men are created equal," Lincoln and King would not have had much of a platform on which to justify their actions. Jefferson's writing was a critical plank in the ultimate demise of slavery and the civil rights movement's success. My friend considered my point as I moved on.

George Washington. Any serious study of George Washington readily reveals the profound courage and integrity he possessed. Read the biography of George Washington written by Washington Irving. The descriptions of privations that Washington and the Continental Army endured securing our nation's freedom are genuinely heart-rending. You are encouraged to read about Valley Forge and the other campaigns where Washington skillfully maneuvered his army, engaging when he could and eluding when the situation did not favor him. His patience and wisdom were the keys to his ultimate triumph at Yorktown.

Yes, he, too, owned slaves. He inherited his brother's plantation, and the heinous institution was ingrained in Virginia society for decades before. But yes, slave transactions did continue during his ownership. Nonetheless, the colonies do not gain independence from Great Britain without Washington's leadership. Without independence, there is no America. All the Founders would likely have been executed for treason. Lincoln never becomes president. The history of the world would be altered in ways we cannot imagine. All Americans, black people certainly included, owe Washington a considerable debt of gratitude and profound respect for his courage and integrity.

By the end of my explanation, I can't say I had definitely won over the gentleman who approached me, but I can say that he gained a perspective he had not considered before. He either didn't want to argue or didn't have an adequate rebuttal to my view. He thanked me, we shook hands, and he walked away. These conversations are precisely what we should strive for in sharing our differing perspectives.

There are several points I want to drive home through this story. First, the actions and roles of these four men were absolutely pivotal in creating modern-day America. If the left is so devoted to the religion of evolution, they must readily admit that societies can only evolve as our societal norms evolve. We evolve not only in physical traits but in our thoughts, beliefs, and values. American society has indeed grown in its perspectives on race. Our societal evolution was made possible because of the excellence of our national moral framework.

While slavery is still rampant in many parts of our 21st-century world, over half the globe now believes that slavery is abhorrent. That was not the case in Washington's day. The concept that "all men are created equal" was an outgrowth of the Enlightenment, a philosophical and political movement of which Jefferson was a devout subscriber. Even today, Jefferson's words continue to influence American society because they form the moral bedrock for true social justice in our nation. Despite the historical importance of Jefferson's words, the left is desperate to cancel Jefferson and everything he said. The "created" part gives them trouble because if our rights come from God, no totalitarian government can be tolerated in America. The "equal" part is not good enough for the lefties. They want to replace it with "equity," where the government is somehow trusted to guarantee equal outcomes for everyone. Revisiting the slavery issue is just the excuse to cancel Jefferson and our history.

The linkage of the four historical figures just discussed is an example of how we all stand on the shoulders of giants who lived before us. Washington and Jefferson were contemporaries who each had a pivotal role in forming America as a nation. Lincoln stood on their shoulders for justification in opposing slavery, issuing the Emancipation Proclamation, and ultimately defeating the rebel army. He is justly called The Great Emancipator.

Dr. King stood on the shoulders of Washington, Jefferson, and Lincoln. By 1955 when King rose to prominence, America had become a world power. We were the leader in championing freedom worldwide by defeating the Nazis and opposing Marxist regimes across the globe. King had a platform for his noble movement because of Jefferson's words and the courage of Washington and Lincoln. While many others contributed to abolishing slavery and the advancement of civil rights, these four men remain the most critical links in the evolution toward racial equality. They indeed form the chain that broke the chains of bondage.

The United States did not start the slave trade. It was well established by various colonial powers well before the founding of the United States in 1776. At the onset of the revolutionary war, measures to curtail and abolish slavery were already emerging.

However, America was not the first major western power to abolish slavery. Britain and France had the advantage of more favorable internal politics and were able to act sooner. Napoleon abolished slavery in France in 1815. France later permanently outlawed slavery in its colonies in 1848. Britain banned the practice entirely through the Slavery Abolition Law, which gained royal assent in 1833.

The Marxists say that America did not lead in the abolitionist movement. This criticism is based on an oversimplified and slanted recounting of history. America's first 85 years passed under the constant weight of negotiation and compromise with southern slave states. It took time for America to form its political system, pay off heavy debt incurred during the revolution, and finally turn to the reformation of a vast segment of its economy that depended on slavery. America has always had the right ideals embedded in our founding documents. However, it took a frustrating amount of time and a bloody war to restructure our society and finally resolve the slavery issue.

The 1619 Project does deliver a vivid portrayal of the past sufferings and injustices endured by black Americans. It is also deliberately biased as a piece of self-acknowledged political activism. The recounting of America's founding is pure fabrication. The 1619 Project willfully ignores the contributions of our Founders and white Americans, in general, that specifically led to the ultimate abolishment of slavery.

Every American ought to kneel before our Heavenly Father and give thanks each day that they live in America. Every American ought to be thankful that they won the cosmic lottery—even the descendants of enslaved people. Through their suffering, today, those descendants can live in the world's freest, most racially inclusive country. The question is, do we have the national will to keep it? Will we be able to beat back the corrupt leftist ideologues?

CHAPTER 4

Marxism and the Progressives

"It is a capital mistake to theorize before one has data. Insensibly one begins to twist facts to suit theories, instead of theories to suit facts."

—*Sir Arthur Conan Doyle,* A Scandal in Bohemia, *1891*

Marxist infiltration of our society grew from the progressive movement, which this chapter examines. The 1619 Project is a crucial propaganda piece for Marxists who want you to conclude that America is fundamentally flawed, irredeemably evil, and our system of government must be rebuilt from scratch. Once enough Americans are gaslighted into believing this, the Marxists will replace our system of government with their tyrannical machine.

Marxists want you to believe that their ideas are progressive. Progressive is such a nice-sounding word. After all, who doesn't want progress? In truth, Marxist philosophy is not progressive at all. It is regressive. It will lead to the total subjugation of all Americans. That is their aim. The left is about domination, not freedom, and not some righteous quest to avenge the errors of the past. Progressivism is their superhighway to domination.

In this chapter, I'll cover the roots of progressivism and how Marxists have embraced the philosophy as a half-step to implementing what they truly want. So-called progressives are merely their temporary allies.

Progressivism

Progressivism emerged in the latter part of the 19th century and gained popularity during the first two decades of the 20th. The ideology was initially embraced by factions of both the Republican and Democratic parties though it is now fully owned by Democrats. Progressivism sought to address the growing concentration of wealth in the hands of elite business tycoons during a period of explosive economic growth. Progressivism was formed through an unwritten alliance between politicians, academics, journalists, and activists seeking to create a more robust and centralized national government. Their stated purpose was to respond better to the perceived social and economic problems created by rapid industrialization.

The early progressives began shaping the political landscape by deemphasizing individual rights, particularly when the assertion of rights was used to defend big business interests. They also initiated a trend to diminish the power of legislatures at the national and local levels and to concentrate more power in the hands of unelected bureaucrats. This empowered a vast cadre of so-called government specialists and experts who wield immense powers abdicated to them by our elected officials through broad, loosely defined legislation. Thus, the administrative state was born and has ballooned into the gargantuan bureaucracy we live with today.

While its origin may have been a sincere and legitimate attempt to address emerging societal issues, the core principle of the progressive movement was to question the concept of self-government created by our Founders. American individualism was to be replaced by collectivism, and who would organize collectivism but the federal government. This thought process poured fuel on the debate over the Constitution as a fixed literal framework versus the progressive view of treating it as a "living" document that could be reinterpreted as needed to reflect changing times. This was viewed as "progress" by initiating a post-constitutional era that considers our Constitution and founding documents essentially obsolete. The post-constitutional concept is central to progressivism and underpins the extremist neo-Marxist thinking we are threatened by today.

Our Founders designed our system of government based on their knowledge of human nature. They conceived a timeless framework that was intended to endure forever. As I've established, human nature has not changed when comparing our motivations across historical periods. The Founders were prescient in this regard because they understood that human nature has the wellsprings of tyranny within it. The progressives, in contrast, believe that our founding documents are not timeless but merely served to solve the issues of the day. Therefore, they are obsolete and should be reinterpreted to suit current society. This is the quintessential gambit adopted by the modern leftist gaslighter.

An inch quickly becomes a yard with any political shift that erodes our rights. Once a political party or coalition advocates for more centralized power based on a need to solve a specific problem, the power gained is rapidly abused to justify even more centralized control. This is how the early progressives started left and kept moving left inch by inch. Today we have full-blown Marxists as an outgrowth of the most recent wave of progressivism. Leftists always seem to want to "out left" each other to demonstrate hardcore commitment to their extremist base. Ideologically, progressives and Marxists both desire a stronger central government, with the Marxists advocating total state control.

Theodore Roosevelt's Progressive Legacy

Theodore Roosevelt receives the lapel pin as the Father of Progressivism even though he was a Republican. Roosevelt ascended to the presidency in 1901 upon the assassination of William McKinley. He was re-elected in 1904 and served until 1909.

During Roosevelt's ascendence, the country was undergoing explosive economic growth. While benefiting from rapid progress, the nation also suffered from immense and rapid transformation. Large corporations and trusts had emerged that increasingly concentrated economic power in the hands of approximately 30 business tycoons who were often derisively labeled robber barons. Corruption throughout government was rampant. The national mood looked for change.

The net benefit of the so-called robber barons is a subject open for debate. Many engaged in ruthless anti-competitive, monopolistic, and sometimes unethical practices. However, on the whole, their efforts reorganized the American economy into a powerful manufacturing juggernaut that focused on efficiency and concentration of capital for the success of massive industrialization. This transformation ultimately led to establishing America as the undisputed world leader. Had we not accomplished this stunning transformation, "the Eiffel Tower would today be a strudel stand," as Johnny Carson once quipped. It was American might that twice helped rescue Europe from the clutches of evil despots.

It was also American ingenuity that enabled the construction of the Panama Canal, where the French had earlier failed and lost 22,000 men, primarily to disease. To his credit, TR was responsible for securing American rights to the canal project through deftly executed foreign policy maneuvers.

The gigantic strides America made during this period of industrialization were not without problems. This is where the progressives found their foothold. The environment was deteriorating rapidly, natural resources were being consumed at alarming rates without thought given to conservation, and labor practices unfairly favored the industrialists. Something indeed had to be done. The federal government was viewed as the only counterbalancing source of power that could reign in abuses. Under Theodore Roosevelt, the government underwent an equally dramatic metamorphosis and was transformed into today's perpetually growing administrative state.

Roosevelt expanded the federal government's power. He revived the Sherman Antitrust Act passed in 1890 to aggressively pursue monopoly trusts, and he founded the Bureau of Corporations. Though initially the agency was weak and held very little real power, it was the precursor to the Federal Trade Commission. He signed numerous business regulations into law, such as the Elkins Act of 1903, the Hepburn Act of 1906, and the Federal Employers' Liability Act for Labor of 1908 expanding the powers of the Interstate Commerce Commission. He established consumer protection, such as the Federal Meat Inspection Act of 1906 and the Pure Food and Drug Act of 1906, which created the precursor to the Food and Drug Administration (FDA).

During his second term, beginning in 1905, Roosevelt morphed into an activist president and began exercising executive powers not enumerated for the president in the Constitution. This approach directly contradicted the Founders' view that powers not expressly enumerated in the Constitution are reserved for the states or the people. TR's aggressive approach became a new standard for subsequent presidents. He defined himself as a "steward of the people," using this refrain as justification for actions that could not be directly tied to a specific constitutional authority granted to the president. TR's view was that if something wasn't expressly forbidden, he was empowered to act. This perilous migration of power undermined our republican tradition of small government. It allowed Roosevelt and subsequent presidents to draw power straight from the people and bypass the legislative process. Actions could be thinly veiled as constitutional under the guise of "general welfare." Executive orders continue to increase in frequency today as the president's power is rarely reigned in.

In 1908, TR did not seek re-election and ceded the presidency to political ally William H. Taft. Roosevelt would later become disillusioned with his old friend for not fully embracing his progressive agenda. TR then re-entered politics to seek a third term. Roosevelt formed the National Progressive Party after losing the Republican nomination to Taft. The split vote gave the election to Woodrow Wilson.

Woodrow Wilson's Progressive Legacy

While Theodore Roosevelt was the first progressive president, Woodrow Wilson also left an indelible progressive mark on American politics. To appreciate Wilson's perspective, consider his view of our founding documents. First, let's review the preamble of our Declaration of Independence:

> When in the Course of human events, it becomes necessary for one People to dissolve the Political Bands which have connected them with another, and to assume among the Powers of the earth, the separate and equal Station to which the Laws of Nature and of Nature's God entitle them, a decent Respect to the Opinions of Mankind requires that they should declare the causes which impel them to the Separation.

> We hold these Truths to be self-evident, that all Men are created equal, that they are endowed by their Creator with certain unalienable Rights, that among these are Life, Liberty, and the pursuit of happiness—That to secure these Rights, Governments are instituted among Men, deriving their just Powers from the Consent of the Governed,
>
> ...

Wilson's opinion of the preamble:

> If you want to understand the real Declaration of Independence, do not repeat the preface.[14]

While the preamble establishes the timelessness of human nature and creation by invoking the Almighty, natural rights, and the immutable laws of nature, Wilson denigrates all of these principles by his terse dismissal. His comment reduces our Declaration of Independence to a simple list of economic grievances. Wilson is further quoted:

> The Declaration of Independence did not mention the questions of our day. It is of no consequence to us unless we can translate its general terms into examples of the present day and substitute them in some vital way for the examples it itself gives, so concrete, so intimately involved in the circumstances of the day in which it was conceived and written. It is an eminently practical document, meant for the use of practical men; not a thesis for philosophers, but a whip for tyrants; not a theory of government, but a program of action. Unless we can translate it into the questions of our own day, we are not worthy of it, we are not the sons of the sires who acted in response to its challenge.
>
> What form does the contest between tyranny and freedom take to-day? What is the special form of tyranny we now fight? How does it endanger the rights of the people, and what do we mean to do in order to make our contest against it effectual? What are to be the items of our new declaration of independence?[15]

Wilson wanted to enact the reforms he sought to counter the powerful trusts and corporations of the day. The separation of

---

[14] Woodrow Wilson address, 1911, at the Jefferson Club of Los Angeles
[15] "What is Progress?", Woodrow Wilson, "The New Freedom", 1913

powers embedded in our Constitution was an obstacle to him. These separations were rooted in the Declaration as the principal structure for preventing tyranny. Wilson tried to recast the tyranny of despotism of our Founder's time with the new tyranny of special interests dominated by businessmen that Wilson often railed against. He, therefore, sought to restructure the government into an administrative organization of experts that would be insulated from the machinations of politics. This was a seismic shift from the Founders' philosophical pillar of "consent by the governed." As nasty and reprehensible as politics can be, legislative debate by elected representatives remains the best way for the people's will to be translated into law. Wilson's writings in the lead-up to his election reflect the ideas of a man frustrated with Washington's gridlock.

Ironically, Wilson uses the language of the Declaration of Independence to justify his view that the American government should be redesigned to fit the times.

> The men of that generation did not hesitate to say that every people has a right to choose its own forms of government—not once, but as often as it pleases—and to accommodate those forms of government to its existing interests and circumstances.[16]

Our Founders were products of the Age of Reason when scientific knowledge increased tremendously due to men like Sir Isaac Newton. His discoveries of various laws of physics and the development of advanced mathematics gave scientists of the day a new understanding of the earth and our solar system. Many of Newton's laws were viewed as immutable laws of nature. These discoveries probably shaped the culture at the time of America's founding.

---

[16] Woodrow Wilson address, 1913, at the rededication of Congress Hall, Philadelphia

Wilson claims that our Founders were merely swept along with the current of contemporary thinking and extended the immutable laws of nature to the political realm. This then infused the Founders' thinking that laws of human nature are also immutable. Wilson cites the development of the Theory of Evolution as knowledge that the Founders did not have. Darwinian Theory became the dominant perspective among the intelligentsia of Wilson's era. On this basis, Wilson advanced the false analogy that the Constitution must be viewed as a living thing. Just as evolution was the theory of his day, Wilson believed that the Constitution must evolve as living things evolve. This is made clear in the following quote:

> The makers of our Federal Constitution read Montesquieu with true scientific enthusiasm. They were scientists in their way, the best way of their age, those fathers of the nation. Jefferson wrote of "the laws of Nature,"—and then by way of afterthought, — "and of Nature's God." And they constructed a government as they would have constructed an orrery, —to display the laws of nature. Politics in their thought was a variety of mechanics. The Constitution was founded on the law of gravitation. The government was to exist and move by virtue of the efficacy of "checks and balances."[17]

> The trouble with the theory is that government is not a machine, but a living thing. It falls, not under the theory of the universe, but under the theory of organic life. It is accountable to Darwin, not to Newton.[18]

This is the foundation of modern progressive thinking that gives them license to trample the Constitution as they please, appoint activist judges that reinterpret the Constitution to suit their agenda, and move regulation into the shadows of the administrative state.

---

[17] "The New Freedom," Speeches of Woodrow Wilson 1913

[18] "What is Progress?", Woodrow Wilson, "The New Freedom", 1913

During his two terms in office, Wilson left several indelible marks on the American Government that reshaped the country, such as creating the Federal Income Tax, establishing the Federal Reserve, and creating the Federal Trade Commission to enforce antitrust actions. Among other achievements, he pushed for the passage of women's suffrage. Congress passed the 19th Amendment in June of 1919, and it was later ratified by the states in 1920. He also led the country through World War I and negotiated the Peace Treaty of Versailles.

Wilson was an academic at heart who thought big. At the conclusion of WWI, he sought to establish a new world order. Wilson pushed hard for the ratification of the Treaty of Versailles through an aggressive speaking tour across America. Since Congress bears responsibility for ratifying treaties, his idea was to use the American People to pressure legislators. Congress ultimately voted down the treaty of Versailles because it would have forced the United States to enter the League of Nations.

Wilson's grand progressive legacy endures with his beliefs enshrined in his book *The New Freedom*. It continues to be a tool for the post-constitutional crowd who view the Constitution as a living document that can be reinterpreted with the changing times. It is plain to see that using a "floating framework" as progressives desire, one could justify virtually anything based on the crisis du jour. Such as we saw with restrictions imposed during the COVID pandemic. Totally malleable laws are in effect, no law at all. The meaning of a constitutional clause today will be reinterpreted to mean something completely different tomorrow.

The transformation of the presidency from a constitutionally constrained executive to a magnet for the concentration of power and the rise of the administrative state that is unaccountable to the people are legacies belonging to Teddy Roosevelt and Woodrow Wilson administrations. The concentration of power is viewed as a good thing for progressives because they can "get things done" by minimizing the need for legislative action by a glacial Congress. To those who value the rule of law and believe the Constitution to be a static framework, the modern presidency and administrative state represent a slippery slope to tyranny.

A prime example is the power to implement binding international treaties. The authority for the United States to enter into unpopular treaties continues to be subsumed by activist presidents. President Obama pushed us into the Paris Climate Accord, which is in effect a treaty. But by calling it an accord, Obama sidestepped Congress. President Trump pulled the country out of it, only to have President Biden re-enter it. Biden is also angling for ways to force the United States into the UN Small Arms Treaty, effectively global gun control. Again, our Constitution stands in his way because Congress must first ratify it, and also, the treaty would be in direct conflict with our Second Amendment. His desire to enter this subversive agreement would also place internal US law under the auspices of the United Nations, the most corrupt international body in the world.

From Progressivism to Modern Marxism

A simple hopscotch game can portray the shift from progressivism to Marxism. The movement is not one dramatic leap per se, but a series of small hops executed through a continual game of "if this, then that." The powerful elite always thirst for more power. Their desire for absolute control is never quenched. They accumulate more power in small hops by continually pushing the envelope of their interpretation of Constitutional powers. Once one hop is accepted, it is used as a precedent for the next hop. Each hop is justified by faulty logic based on precedence—if this, then that.

When progressives expand government power, many right-wing politicians who claim to stand for our republican legal structure rarely, if ever, reverse progressive power grabs once they are in control. The reasons are money and that they too crave power. So, onward we hop like ignorant bunnies accepting all the carrots our "benevolent" enslavers lay before us in each square of their diabolical hopscotch game. One day we will look back from the final square with a longing eye toward the square from where we started. We'll then ask, how did the freest nation in the world make the leap to Marxism? The answer—one hop at a time.

As I said in Chapter 1, Marxism is a totalitarian philosophy that concentrates all political and economic power in the hands of the state. Its original central tenets are based on perpetual struggle between the owners of capital (the bourgeoisie) against the working class (proletarians). The Marxist philosophy is shamelessly defined in the Communist Manifesto written by Karl Marx and Frederick Engels and initially published in 1848. The ten principles below are pulled directly out of the manifesto:[19]

1. Abolition of property in land and application of all rents of land to public purposes.

2. A heavy progressive or graduated income tax.

3. Abolition of all rights of inheritance.

4. Confiscation of the property of all emigrants and rebels.

5. Centralization of credit in the hands of the State, by means of a national bank with State capital and an exclusive monopoly.

6. Centralization of the means of communication and transport in the hands of the State.

---

[19] "Communist Manifesto," Karl Marx and Frederick Engels, republished November 2006 by Socialist Labor Part of America

7. Extension of factories and instruments of production owned by the State: the bringing into cultivation of waste lands, and the improvement of the soil generally in accordance with a common plan.

8. Equal obligation of all to labor. Establishment of industrial armies, especially for agriculture.

9. Combination of agriculture with manufacturing industries: gradual abolition of all the distinction between town and country, by a more equable distribution of the population over the country.

10. Free education for all children in public schools. Abolition of children's factory labor in its present form.

Consider the degree to which these principles stand in contrast to our Constitution and, in particular, our Bill of Rights. Would you really want to live in an America where these are the new societal rules? The Communist Manifesto advocates central control of everything in the hands of the state, including your children. This is the recipe for tyranny. A tyranny that far exceeds the authoritarian rule of King George III that our Founders fought to defeat.

The critical difference between the new Marxism and classic Marxism of the late 19th and early 20th centuries is the definition of oppressors and oppressed. In the current reappearance of this cancer, the oppressors are all white people, and the oppressed are all people of color. This is a still further leap from viewing just black people as the oppressed class. The Marxists want to include everyone with skin of some shade darker than white in their oppressed class because even if 100% of black people were duped by their propaganda, they would only comprise 13% of the population. Therefore, the Marxists want you to believe that somehow all darker-skinned people are automatically and systemically oppressed.

This racist Marxist propaganda ploy crumbles when you consider the Asian "problem" to their argument. The Census Bureau conglomerates all people from the Far East (Chinese, Japanese, Koreans, Vietnamese, etc.) and East Indians into the Asian category. When we examine the Asians as a group, they outperform even whites on the socioeconomic ladder.[20] Therefore, the Marxist argument that our system is rigged against people of color falls apart.

Marxism is a philosophy that appeals to two kinds of people independent of race—megalomaniacs and losers. Megalomaniacs seeking the complete domination of others use this twisted philosophy to amass power. Losers embrace its principles due to jealousy of those more successful and desperation induced by their own often self-inflicted difficult circumstances. Marxism is a system for losers. Now, before leftists blow a gasket and accuse me of calling all poor people losers, consider this perspective.

My parents were poor. My father was a serf in his native country of Albania. A serf is just one small step above a slave. My parents immigrated to America shortly after WWII and lifted themselves up through hard work. My father adored the American system and the American Dream. In America, he was free to start a business, take care of his family, and generate as much success as he wished. He supported my mother and enabled her to stay home and care for us children. It wasn't a perfect life, we didn't have many frills, but our home life was stable and created opportunities for my brother and me. This story is not unique to my family. Millions of immigrants have enjoyed realizing the American Dream, where a person can start from nothing and build a life of comfort and wealth.

Losers are the ones who, generation after generation, blame others for their circumstances and rarely do anything to help

---

[20] Source US Census Bureau, "Income and Poverty in the United States: 2019," September 2020

themselves. Losers have a poor or non-existent work ethic. Most often, they do the bare minimum. Losers are pessimists and believe that they do not have the power to change their own condition. To anesthetize themselves and dull their personal pain, they often turn to drugs, alcohol, and promiscuous sex, which leads to unwanted pregnancy that further deepens their burdens or leads to abortion. They are more likely to get arrested and build a criminal record. They become society's pariahs and blame "the system" for their troubles. Losers generally feel they are owed handouts. Marxism plays directly to the mentality of these people because it gives them a psychological out by allowing them to blame the system instead of examining their own choices.

If I had to guess, I would say the fastest-growing segment of losers is composed of pampered suburban white kids who never struggled to improve themselves. With our public schools embracing the 1619 Project and its poisonous propaganda twin, Critical Race Theory, America will simply create more losers. Our public schools teach white kids that they are oppressors while teaching black kids that the system is rigged and that they can't get ahead because of it. In both cases, the school system is creating losers by ingraining pessimism instead of embracing and extolling the optimism of the American Dream. The Marxists want to deliberately create generations of failures to drive us further away from our founding ideals.

In contrast, the poor immigrants who come here with the will to better themselves succeed rapidly in our free-market society. In America, millions of hard-working, industrious people have climbed the economic ladder by their force of will. Immigrants come to our country with barely a few dollars in their pockets just as my father did. Within one generation, they rise to the middle class and above. This is the story of my parents. In contrast, Marxism is deliberately designed to suppress everyone and ensure "the equal sharing of misery," as Winston Churchill said. Marxism's true purpose is the seizure of power.

Capitalism is the system that lifts people out of poverty not Marxism. Government economists often look at statistical cross-sections of society to assess the number of people living in poverty. Let's assume that they count 20 million people living in poverty. Two years later, they do the same analysis and note that there are still 20 million poor people. They tend to think that the financial conditions of the poor have not improved. This is called static analysis. In reality, their analysis fails to consider the upward mobility that our free society provides. Only a portion of the 20 million counted the second time were likely to have been counted the first time. Rarely does the media publish statistics on how many poor people were able to move out of poverty and become lower-middle-class or above. Consider the graphs found in Figure 4-1.

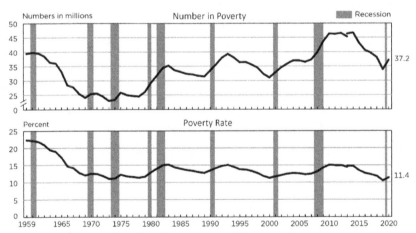

Figure 4-1: Number in Poverty and Poverty Rate: 1959 to 2019 (Population as of March of the following year)[21]

---

[21] Source US Census Bureau, "Income and Poverty in the United States: 2020," September 2021

As of 2019, the number of people in poverty was 34 million. That means we had roughly six million fewer people in poverty than in 1959, despite the country's population having more than doubled in the same period. As a percentage of the population, poverty was cut by more than half during the period shown, with the most significant percentage reduction occurring from 1959 to 1969. Find me a Marxist country that can match this performance.

If China is your answer, you would be wrong. According to the Brookings Institute, China claims to have eradicated poverty:

> To make this claim, the Chinese Government uses a poverty line of about $2.25 a day, in 2011 prices and adjusting for purchasing power. The World Bank believes that a threshold of $1.90 a day is appropriate for countries with per capita incomes of less than $1,000 or so, such as Ethiopia. For lower-middle-income countries such as India—with per capita incomes between $1,000 and about $4,000—it recommends a poverty line of $3.20 a day. For upper-middle-income countries like China, it reckons that a reasonable poverty line is $5.50 a day. In other words, the Chinese Government uses a poverty line appropriate for a country making the transition from low- to lower-middle-income, even though China is 10 times as wealthy.[22]

You're only poor in a Marxist totalitarian regime if the government says your poor. But since you live in a Marxist utopia, you are thrilled to make $5.50 per day. The CCP cooks its books any way it wants. There isn't a statistic or balance sheet that comes out of China that you can fully trust. Of course, the entire globe has been affected by the COVID-19 pandemic. So, it will be interesting to see revised poverty statistics as we emerge from the effects of the pandemic. Lower-income people have likely been drastically affected. Although as of this writing, the economy is posting more jobs than we can fill.

---

[22] Brookings Institute, "Deep-sixing Poverty in China," January 25, 2021

Employment statistics are clouded because of extreme government intervention with the free market.

Marxism Will Take Care of You

During the Pandemic, extended unemployment benefits were introduced as an offset to the government's shutdown of our economy—an action that resulted in the most significant transfer of wealth in world history. As the pandemic receded, extended government unemployment subsidies made it more lucrative for people to eschew employment and sit at home. This government largess was unprecedented and lasted far longer than it should have, which has triggered the worst inflation in 40 years.

Part of the grand Marxist plan is to introduce Universal Basic Income (UBI), where everyone receives a check from the government for doing nothing. UBI is another fiendish means of control designed to breed passivity and destroy free enterprise as Marxists peddle their myth that government can take care of everything for you. The losers will love this. True patriots, independent of party, abhor the concept. I'm convinced that extended benefits were essentially a test for the introduction of UBI during the economic shutdown. Progressives actually thought it was possible and desirable for the government to pay everyone to stay home. All in the name of controlling the spread of COVID. The deliberate stoking of fear was a very useful tool during the pandemic to justify a plethora of outlandish and ineffective policies designed to satisfy human impulses.

Leftists want you to believe that we are really no better than animals. Animals operate primarily on impulse. Animals act on what they feel is an immediate need. For humans, our emotional side is equally impulsive. Far too many people are conditioned to feel that they must receive immediate emotional remedies without first logically analyzing long-term ramifications. Leftists push the idea that immediate satisfaction of emotion is your right. They fan the fire of emotion and then claim they have the extinguisher. Marxists play on the people's emotions with the deftness of Itzhak Perlman playing a Brahms violin concerto on a Stradivarius. They stoke our fear so that we will be more likely to beg for government help. The more Americans looks to the government for every solution, the more we inch toward totalitarian control.

Capitalism is Not the Problem

Marx labeled capitalism as the root of oppression. His remedy was to place all capital into the hands of the government, thereby eradicating the free market economy. In truth, capitalism and the free-market economy lift people out of poverty. Capitalism has rescued more people from poverty around the globe than any other economic system. Marxism destroys all incentives and has never worked and will never work.

Referring back to Figure 4-1, you will readily see that between 1959 and 2019, the number of people living in poverty in the US declined by six million while the total population effectively doubled, as shown in Figure 4-2. This is due to the robust capitalist and free-market system we are fortunate to live under. Could a Marxist regime ever double its population while reducing its poverty rate?

Capitalism works best because of the built-in profit motive guided by controlled self-interest. When a capitalist society operates under healthy conditions, the capitalist must serve the needs of his customers, or a competitor will. The entrepreneur must innovate to solve society's needs. When combined with the republican principles of the rule of law and private property rights, the people flourish under capitalism.

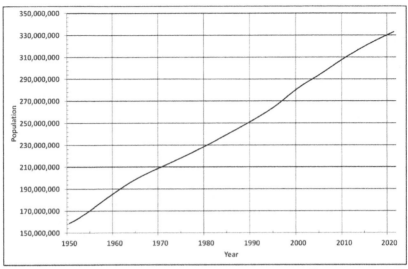

Figure 4-2: US Population by Year[23]

Clearly, capitalism as a system is not the problem. Collusion between politicians and big business is the problem. Herbert Hoover once said, "The only problem with capitalism is the capitalist." Warren Buffett, the legendary investor, evaluates businesses he buys partly in terms of the "moat" they have around them. The moat is the metaphor for the business' position relative to competitors. If the company has unique advantages such as scale, quality, product features, brand recognition, etc., the business is viewed as less assailable by a competitor. Therefore, it is said to have a strong moat.

Capitalists compete at a fever pitch. The game is driven by serving the consumer better while also defeating competitors. When it is working well, this is basically economic Darwinism, where the fittest survive. Businesses seek to establish the strongest moat possible. This is reasonable as long it is done in the spirit of healthy competition. Capitalism falls off the rails when monopolies emerge, and the government does nothing. The worst case is when politicians collude

---

[23] Source www.macrotrends.net cross-referenced to US Census Bureau data.

with big businesses to help them strengthen their moat through unnecessary regulation.

Prudent and minimal regulation of a free-market economy is needed to maintain societal order. For example, stopping pollution, breaking up monopolies, and prosecuting price-fixing are areas where the government should intervene to re-level the playing field and protect citizens. However, when politicians manipulate government regulations to widen the moat for the businesses of political allies, crony capitalism fails the public interest. Examples include:

- Massive bank bailouts and other actions taken during the Great Recession under the auspices of the Troubled Asset Relief Program, which allowed anyone the government selected to reach into the government till and unload their highest risk assets. This led to a massive consolidation of the banking industry, transferred exorbitant amounts of risk onto the taxpayer, and placed crushing regulations on small regional banks. Instead of shielding the public from the problem of banks being too big to fail, it created even bigger banks with less competition.

- Direct government intervention by crushing industries it doesn't like such as the domestic oil and gas industry as demonstrated by the political ping-pong game played with the Keystone XL pipeline and restrictions on domestic energy exploration.

- Excessive regulations and standards stifle competition by creating hurdles for smaller competitors. Many environmental standards are used for this very purpose.

- Tax abatements transfer business risk onto the shoulders of taxpayers.

- Subsidies of all types prop up businesses that would otherwise not be able to sustain themselves, specifically green technologies that just don't work.

- Favorable tax laws allow specific industries special treatment, such as professional sports franchises entitled to write off the depreciation of the franchise.
- Monopoly protection for specific industries such as cable companies and Major League Baseball.

By far the biggest and scariest collusion of them all is the increasing online censorship and cancel culture that is designed to silence dissenting opinions and disproportionately targets conservatives.

So, when people like Bernie Sanders, Alexandra Ocasio-Cortez, Edward Markey, and others rail against the evils of capitalism, there is a grain of truth buried in their rhetoric. As usual, the most effective Marxist lie is based partly on truth. What these diehard leftists don't tell you is that the left routinely conspires with big business for their personal enrichment and aggrandizement. They then point to the corruption and say they can solve the problems if only they were given more power. So, their gaslighted electorate obliges, and the issues never go away. They kick the problem down the road so they can continue to extract political contributions by repeatedly recycling the same racket.

Lest you think this author is a blind partisan, I can assure you that the right is frequently guilty of similar machinations. But at least the right is not trying to fundamentally alter the country's structure by invalidating our Constitution. It is not the right that seeks to confiscate firearms from law-abiding citizens. It is not the right that divides Americans by the color of their skin and continuously shovels the manure of low expectations into the faces of minorities they claim to serve. It is not the right that is systematically teaching our young people to hate their country. It is the Marxist left. The more we allow the left to consolidate government power, the faster America slides toward a destiny of tyranny.

Frederick Douglass referred to slavery as "irresponsible power." The overseer or slave master was accountable to no one. They could beat a slave and even murder one with virtually no fear of repercussion. Consider Marxism in terms of "irresponsible power." Under this heinous system, you are what the state says you are. You keep only what the state says you can keep. And you dare not ever speak against your master, or brutal repercussions will rain down upon you. Marxism is the ultimate in irresponsible power. Marxism is universal slavery. Now let's take a closer look at chosen tool for teaching America to hate itself.

CHAPTER 5

Critical Race Theory—The New Racial Hatred

"Stupidity intellectual and stupidity moral (for the one always means the other, as you will, with surprise or not, discover if you look)..."

—*Thomas Carlyle, 1850*

Critical Race Theory (CRT) is an ideology that divides everyone into two classes based on race. You are either an oppressor or part of the oppressed. If you're white, you are an oppressor. Any Person of Color (PoC) is part of the oppressed. It literally determines your social standing based on the level of melanin in your body. In case, you're wondering, melanin is the pigment that our bodies naturally produce and is the primary determinant of skin color. That's how ridiculous, shallow, and race-obsessed CRT purveyors are. According to the race hucksters, we're supposed to either feel guilty or oppressed depending on our level of melanin. CRT is the epitome of intellectual stupidity and only leads to moral stupidity.

Loudoun County, Virginia, has suddenly become ground zero in the battle against CRT. When I moved to Loudoun County and started my family 34 years ago, the county's demographics were very different. As more people from all colors and creeds moved in and

CRITICAL RACE THEORY—THE NEW RACIAL HATRED • 99

the county became much more diverse, can you guess what happened—NOTHING. Peace and harmony continued.

Folks still greeted each other on the walking trails and in the parks. We still had one of the safest counties in America. No single group was denying any other group their God-given rights of life, liberty, and the pursuit of happiness. I've found that if you're nice to someone, they are very likely to be nice to you in return. Most Loudouners just didn't care and still don't care about the level of melanin in someone else's body.

Despite sustained community harmony, our school system felt compelled to address some fictitious form of racism that is not even remotely prevalent. Our schools are now plagued by Marxist brainwashing that teaches our black children that they are oppressed victims, and white people are the responsible oppressors. The CRT charlatans also include so-called "brown" children in their oppressed categories trying to indoctrinate Hispanics and Asians into their misguided fold. This is a no-win situation for all races.

Don't allow yourself to be gaslighted. The sole purpose of CRT is to teach people to hate anything connected to "whiteness." Just by virtue of attaching something to whiteness, that thing can then be automatically diminished, discredited, and destroyed. Whether it is the Founding Fathers, our Constitution, our free market system, our businesses, sports, and yes, even mathematics as we know it, everything is tied to whiteness and is therefore racist.

CRT is hardly a theory at all in the scientific sense. When we hear the word theory, it automatically gives weight to a supposition. We frequently hear terms like the Theory of Evolution, The Big Bang Theory, and Theory of Relativity. Even the moderately informed are somewhat familiar with these grand descriptive systems used to interpret our physical world. So, the word theory has great weight in our consciousness.

The left loves to say, "Believe the science. Follow the science." Science, science, science. This carries weight because science is cast as objective and logical. I'm an electrical engineer by education. I could not agree more that when science and scientists are left to the purity of purpose such as inquisitiveness, experimentation, testing, and proof, science is objective and reveals the truth.

So back to this weighty word – "theory." Let's follow the science. In scientific reasoning, a theory is a set of principles that explain phenomena already supported by data. In other words, a theory is supported by evidence. Further, theories can and must be constantly challenged. Scientific theories are continuously tested. Parts are sometimes invalidated or reinterpreted based on new experiments and discoveries. The Big Bang Theory is an excellent example of this. The more we observe our universe, the more data we collect. The theory is made stronger as it is challenged or expanded as new bodies of information unfold. Parts may also be discredited as we learn more. This is good as long as facts in favor or against are used to support all adjustments.

Theories are not someone's wild guess. They are principles and systems of principles that explain things already substantiated extensively by data. Because theories are routinely subjected to testing, this rigorous scrutiny gives them gravitas. Theories have a high probability of being true because they are constantly challenged.

CRT does not merit theory status. Fundamentally, it has no basis in scientific research and data. It is all conjecture driven by an emotional argument based on half-truths and distortion of history. CRT's most apparent failure as a theory is the unwillingness of its proponents to subject it to scrutiny. Questioning the supposition that "whiteness" is an inherent characteristic of racism makes you inherently racist. On this basis, the theory can never be tested, and no observation can ever be made to test its validity.

Don't believe me? Try it. Try to argue with a CRT peddler regarding the absurdity of their claims and observe how they try to shut you down. They go immediately to their preferred weapon – shouts of racist, racist, racist! This zealotry begins to resemble cult indoctrination more than any honest intellectual attempt at discourse and scientific discovery. Any theory that cannot be challenged is not scientific at all. It is mere propaganda.

Derrick Bell is the widely recognized originator of CRT. He was the first tenured black law professor at Harvard University—the pinnacle of liberal learning. He died in October 2011.

The current leading peddlers of CRT-based propaganda and concepts derived from it are Robin DiAngelo and Ibram Kendi. They have each made millions in speaking fees, books, and "consulting."

I'm a consultant. So, I've often wondered what CRT consulting might be like. What exercises might a CRT consultant recommend to his clients to reinforce learning? How about this? Stand in front of a mirror and slap your face as hard as you can while shouting, "Bad, bad white person!" The harder you slap, the more effective the exercise is. You should try to slap the whiteness off your face. Steadfast commitment is essential. Anything less than ten slaps per session indicates a lack of commitment. Repeat daily or more if you feel yourself slipping into racist thoughts of any kind. If you're uncertain whether a thought is racist, do the exercise anyway as a preventative.

Shall we talk microaggressions? The recommended level of self-loathing is two slap sessions per day per micro-aggression. Obviously, if you engage in microaggression against a PoC, you've turned your thoughts into action. This is egregious. So, slap away! Yes, the self-flagellation promoted by CRT is just about as absurd as my fictitious CRT exercise. Let's take a closer look at our CRT hucksters.

Robin DiAngelo

According to the About Me page on her website, Robin DiAngelo has a Ph.D. in Multicultural Education and is a tenured professor at Westfield State University in Massachusetts. She is also an Associate Professor of Education at the University of Washington. Her proclaimed area of expertise is "Whiteness Studies" and "Critical Discourse Analysis," which supposedly trace how whiteness is reproduced in everyday narratives.

"Whiteness studies" and "how whiteness is reproduced in everyday narratives" are disturbing terms. They evoke a sentiment that being white is some kind of disease. I frankly don't know how DiAngelo can look at herself in the mirror every morning if that's how she feels about the cosmic randomness of her being born white. Maybe she routinely performs the self-beating exercise I just described.

This next part of her bio is truly precious. "I grew up poor and white. While my class oppression has been relatively visible to me, my race privilege has not." Huh? Did our "white supremacist" society overlook her when they were handing out white privilege cards? Her statement is very clever maneuvering, allowing her to simultaneously claim and reject victimhood. Typically, lefty propagandists crave to be labeled victims to gain "street cred." DiAngelo reaches for her share of pathos by claiming class oppression. It's her only option to gain a victim card. But because she makes millions as a race huckster, she has to stay true to her schtick by claiming that being white was part of her privilege even though she was raised in poverty.

I can't help but think that these leftist "Piled High and Deep (Ph.D.)" types are just too smart for their own britches. In America, wealth and privilege go hand-in-hand. If you're not wealthy, you don't have much privilege. You still have rights, but let's face it, our society rolls out the proverbial red carpet for those who have the "scratch." If you're wealthy, you have the means to live well—private schools, fine restaurants, designer clothes, private jets, etc. These are all societal privileges that must be earned. The harder you work, the more red-carpet treatment you can buy. I know of nothing that you can obtain by simply flashing your "white card."

Some of the most privileged people in the world are black. Have you noticed? Beyonce and Jay-Z, Lebron James, Robert Johnson, just about every star black athlete. And let's not forget the most privileged black couple on the planet—the Obamas. The list of privileged black people is long indeed and growing every day. Millions of American black people have achieved a level of success that is only dreamed of for PoC in other countries. I bet these successful Black Americans will also tell you that they worked their butts off to reach their level of success. Their leftist viewpoints may be cynical and wrong, but I don't doubt they worked hard to earn their privilege. Good for them. They should be grateful they live in America. But let's get back to Robin's twisted rhetoric.

DiAngelo is an "expert" at teaching her clients to be "less white." One of her trainings posted on LinkedIn and reportedly used by Coca-Cola is titled: "Confronting Racism: Understanding What It Means to Be White. Challenging What It Means to Be Racist."[24] In the training she states:

> To be less white is to: Be less oppressive, be less arrogant, be less certain, be less defensive, be less ignorant, be more humble, listen, believe, break with apathy, break with white solidarity

The training is the very definition of racism. Can you imagine the outcry if you substituted "black" for "white?" Imagine if someone

---

[24] As reported by Newsweek, Christina Zhao, February 21, 2021

told a black person to be less black. It's time to start suing companies that force their employees to sit through this garbage. These are blatant civil rights violations, and they won't stop until someone receives a massive payout in court.

Writing a book on any serious topic requires a great deal of research. So, I wanted to see firsthand what one of DiAngelo's lectures was like. Enabled by the glories of YouTube, I located a lecture on "White Fragility" that DiAngelo delivered on Thursday, June 28th, 2018, at the Seattle Central Library.[25] I forced myself to watch every excruciating second.

Early in the video, at the 4:35 mark, DiAngelo states that she likes to use humor and a bit of mockery in discussing white fragility. I find it only fitting that she be subjected to a bit of mockery herself. Mockery is a powerful tool for exposing pseudo-intellectualism. Nonetheless, I chose to hold back my jabs because her rhetoric is so ludicrous that it practically mocks itself. Follow this.

The central idea of white fragility is that white people just can't stand to confront their racism. However, fragility, she says, is not necessarily a weakness but a deliberate construct to maintain white superiority. White fragility is manifested every time a white person is forced to confront the meaning of "whiteness." The outward signs are defensiveness and argumentation. The unchallengeable premise for her argument is that being white is racist. To challenge the assumption simply demonstrates your white fragility. On this basis, there is no way to counter her argument because of deliberately constructed circular reasoning. If you're white, you're racist. If you argue, it simply proves you're racist. See what I mean? Self-mocking stupidity—piled high and deep (Ph.D.)

---

[25] URL for DiAngelo lecture on White Fragility,
    https://www.youtube.com/watch?v=45ey4jgoxeU

Surprisingly, I discovered an unexpected gem of profound truth in her presentation. The following is a direct excerpt from the transcript along with the time marks so you can easily hear it for yourself if you want to subject yourself to the torture of her lecture.

10:42	This book is intended for us,
10:44	for white progressives who so often,
10:47	despite our conscious intentions,
10:49	make life so difficult for people of color.
10:52	**I believe that white progressives**
10:55	**cause the most daily damage to people of color,**
10:59	and I define a white progressive
11:00	as any white person who thinks he or she
11:03	is not racist or is less racist or is in the choir
11:07	or already gets it. White progressives
11:10	can be the most difficult for people of color,
11:12	because to the degree that we think we have it,
11:16	we're going to put all of our energy
11:18	into making sure you think that we have it and none of it
11:22	into what we need to be doing for the rest of our lives.

The profound truth of her statement goes beyond her idea that progressives can't make any excuses for themselves even if they regularly self-loath. Every progressive policy is demeaning to black people. This topic will be explored much more deeply in Chapter 6. For now, let's press on with a few more nuggets from DiAngelo's lecture.

DiAngelo uses the story of Jackie Robinson as an illustration of how white people distort history to their advantage. She talks about how Jackie Robinson is celebrated every year for breaking the "color line" (commonly called the color barrier in baseball parlance) because he was exceptional. According to DiAngelo, this context exemplifies how white people put blacks down because no one until Robinson was good enough since blacks were considered inferior.

She recommends his story be retold more truthfully. "So, imagine if we told the story like this: Jackie Robinson, the first black man whites allowed to play Major League Baseball." But that is still only a misleading half-truth as well. Here's my more complete truth:

"Jackie Robinson, an extraordinarily talented athlete, was the first black man allowed to play Major League baseball. Branch Rickey, a religious white man, had the courage to take a stand against the evil of segregation created by Progressives. As the president and general manager of the Brooklyn Dodgers, Rickey was the catalyst that shattered segregation in baseball by signing Robinson to a Major League contract in 1947. Robinson would forever be celebrated for breaking the color barrier, and Rickey would go on to be a vocal civil rights activist. When good people of all races work together on a common cause, change happens."

Black people certainly deserve the majority of the credit for their enduring fight and advancements. No moral person denies the indignities they suffered throughout history and in particular the Jim Crow era. But lefties like DiAngelo are always quick to omit the efforts of white people to stand against what is wrong and set things right. I guess my telling of the story would quickly be called racist by DiAngelo and her ilk since Rickey was only doing what should have been the norm. Nonetheless, change happened because of two courageous men—one black and one white.

I've read training material from other race peddlers that rigorously lists every historical injustice perpetrated against blacks but conveniently omits "little events" like the Civil War, where hundreds of thousands of white men died to preserve the Union and end slavery. A war that also claimed approximately 32,000 black union soldiers. My point is that the race hucksters are guilty of their own biases because they aim to always paint all white people as oppressors. Let's look at another jewel from DiAngelo.

DiAngelo tells a story of a friend who paid a mere $25,000 for a house in New Orleans, but she also had to buy a gun because she didn't feel safe. DiAngelo's reaction: "I immediately knew they had bought a home in a black neighborhood." I guess there's no stereotyping at all in DiAngelo's automatic assumption. The story effectively states that the house is $25,000 because of the black residents in the neighborhood. What about crime? Was it the high crime in the area that made her friend feel unsafe? DiAngelo's answer is simply that white people equate black people with crime—just as she did.

DiAngelo's rhetoric is structured to ensure that white people can never claim to not be racist. The two screen shots from her training, shown at Figure 5-1, list all the statements white people make to assert their lack of racism. None of the assertions are deemed valid in DiAngelo's eyes.

Here's another favorite gleaned from the lecture. You can't claim to not be racist whether you have lots of contact or no contact with black people. There is no winning. Let's say you have to form an "equity team" in your company. If you don't ask any black people to join, you're racist. If you automatically ask a black person to join, you're racist because you assumed that the black person was interested in being on the equity team just because they are black. Is your head about to explode yet?

To sum up Robin DiAngelo's mentality, I'll share this quote from her lecture:

51:59   When I do a caucus group or something,
52:00   and the white people are afraid I might think they're racist,
52:04   I think you're racist.
52:05   I do because I think I am, too, right?

Figure 5-1: CRT Training Session

I can only conclude that people like her are either devious opportunists, or self-loathing mentally unstable people that enjoy constantly feeling ashamed. Well, this white man doesn't care what she or any other wokester thinks. All of their opinions are foregone conclusions based on circular logic. I would just shrug my shoulders and say, "Who cares?" But unfortunately, we can't. Whether it's corporate training or every level of education, millions of decent Americans of all races are being gaslighted by these twisted ideologues making big money by tearing down America.

You might want to challenge someone like DiAngelo with a question, "So what's the solution, oh wise and perceptive white fragility trainer?" She won't answer that question because it would break her circular reasoning. She even states in the lecture that she hates that question. Of course, she does. If she offered a solution, it would imply that white people could find a way to stop being racist. Curing racism is not her goal. Her goal is to place white people in a permanent state of shame and self-loathing. This guarantees her revenue stream for race peddling speaking gigs.

Ibram Kendi

Ibram Kendi was born in Jamaica. Not the country, but the Queens, New York neighborhood. Coincidently, the same neighborhood in which I was born and raised. Born to Carol and Larry Rogers, his birth name was actually Ibram Henry Rogers. He adopted the name Kendi after marrying Sadiqa Kendi. I guess Rogers was too white-sounding for his taste, and Kendi made him sound more authentically African. Kendi eventually earned bachelor's, master's, and Ph.D. degrees in African American studies.

I've digested more interviews of Kendi than I can stomach. Kendi is a master of twisting words and, thereby, thought. Here's an example. If you call someone a name or accuse them of being something they are not, the receiver takes it as an offense. If you call someone a racist, it is not pleasant. It's definitely not like saying, "Gee, that's a nice shirt you're wearing." Quite the contrary, the person being called a racist is insulted even if they genuinely are racist in the classic sense of the word. Racist is a negative word and a negative label. It's bad to be racist. Being on the receiving end of "racist" would feel belittling, especially if you don't deserve to be called racist. Being called racist does not enhance one's reputation; it lessens it. The term is therefore derogatory. Derogatory and belittling are the very definition of *pejorative* words.

Only a white-sheet-wearing, cone-hooded fool would smile and be glad to be called racist. Anyone else would be insulted and feel diminished. These days, racist is THE go-to leftist attack word. There are a few other "faves" like homophobe, misogynist, and Nazi. Still, racist is probably their top attack word because it is so automatically and universally divisive and making the label stick to someone virtually assures their destruction.

According to Kendi, calling someone racist is not a pejorative at all, and declaring it an attack word is a fabrication of white nationalists. Here's an excerpt from Mr. Kendi's interview with the Canadian Broadcasting Corporation (CBC) on February 15th, 2019.

> **Host:** When you call someone a racist, it is heard as an insult. How should I take it if someone labels me or something I say or do as racist?

> **Kendi:** The same way we should take it if someone labels something we said or did as mean. It's a descriptive term. It describes what we just said or did. ***It is not a pejorative term.*** That idea that "racist" is an attack word, a pejorative term, has been promoted by white nationalists. What's ironic about so many people who claim to not be racist is

that they can't even define the term "racist" in a way that everyone can understand.[26]

Where does one begin to respond to such twisted logic? First, let's agree on something. Yes, it is a descriptive term. It is, after all, often applied as an adjective. As a noun, it is a descriptive label. It is also very much a pejorative term because as I've established, one does not feel better, one's reputation is not enhanced, and one is likely to be insulted by being called racist. Therefore, it is most definitely a pejorative.

The impact of "racist" versus "mean" doesn't even compare. Equating the two is comparable to saying Hitler was mean. Saying Hitler was mean is a vast understatement. Evil is a more appropriate adjective. Mean and racist simply do not equate. Equating the two creates another convenient language tool that permits the race hucksters to gaslight the gullible. In the race baiter's world, the jump from mean to racist is very easy. If someone does something mean to you, and they have less melanin than you (less melanin means lighter skin), it must be racism. Maybe the mean person is just a jerk? But that can't be. It's racism.

Is racist an attack word? It has very much become so. Any disparity between black people and the rest of the country is racist. Any argument against any position held by a black politician or activist is racist. Just count how many times Obama and his minions played the race card during his administration. Challenging the validity of CRT is racist. Arguing with Ibram Kendi is most assuredly racist. The disproportionate spread of COVID-19 throughout black communities is due to racism. Instead, we should examine the COVID-19 issue by following the science—a favorite leftist catchphrase when it suits them. Once Kendi and the high priests of CRT label you

---

[26] Interview on CBC radio program "Out in the Open" with host Piya Chattopadhyay, Feb 15, 2019

racist, you are done. By definition, the word's destructive power over one's reputation makes it an attack word.

The end of his remark is truly precious. It hints that white people are ignorant because they can't even define what racism is in a way everyone can understand. Thankfully we have the learned Dr. Kendi to set us all straight through his twisted logic. I have no problem defining racism. It is "the belief that race accounts for differences in human character or ability and includes the belief that one race is superior to another simply by virtue of the color of their skin. Beyond simple belief, racism is also discrimination or prejudice based on race."[27]

I purposefully chose the definition from the American College Dictionary published in 1993 to also illustrate the bending of meaning. Tech companies can't be trusted because they are "all in" with social justice gaslighting. So, I wanted to compare the definition I've traditionally understood to what I would find on Dictionary Dot Com. The online definition tracks with the traditional definition except it adds "also called institutional racism." Sorry, these terms are related, but racism and institutional racism do not mean the same thing. It is not surprising that the online tech lords bend with the leftist winds.

Ironically, the word is so overused as an attack word that it is in fact losing its meaning and effect. If everything is racist, you will eventually not be able to recognize true racism when you see it. Just as crying wolf all the time will be ultimately ignored, being called racist will, in time, be dismissed as CRT peddlers are exposed for what they really are. Further, Kendi appoints himself as the keeper of the definition, "I define a racist as someone who's expressing racist ideas or supporting racist policies with their action or inaction." Sorry, that's not Webster's definition of the word or any other

---

[27] The American Heritage College Dictionary, Third Edition, 1993.

reputable dictionary, and no one gave Kendi the right to redefine our language. And conveniently, in his world, Kendi has the authority to determine what actions or inactions are racist. This ensures that anything he defines as racist must be treated as such.

The race hucksters' ploy is to reserve the right to apply the racist label to anything and anyone they want while at the same time denying access to specific terms for with people opposing ideas. For example, being "not racist" according to Kendi is impossible. "There's no such thing as a 'not racist' or 'race neutral' policy," he declares. People must be categorized as either racist or antiracist. You are not allowed to say you are not racist. You may wonder, "Racist and not racist are two valid possible states of someone or something. How can absence of racism not be a valid state?" Confused yet? If you are, welcome again to gaslighting. Confusion, alteration of language, and preventing access to words that express valid ideas are all part of the indoctrination.

On February 2nd, 2021, Kendi appeared on the TV program "The View" where the fawning hosts tossed him one softball question after another. He made this comment about educating our children:

> It is important for us to realize that when we teach our kids to be antiracist, when we teach that brown or black girl that there's nothing wrong with you because of the color of your skin, or when we teach that white boy that there's nothing right about you because of the color of your skin, when we teach America's history of racism, we are protecting our children.[28]

What a hideous thing to say. Did he misspeak? Should we give him the benefit of the doubt? Kendi does enjoy using twisted logic, but he is undoubtedly articulate, and you'll notice his lines are well

---

[28] Episode of "The View" aired on February 2, 2021, video posted to MindUnion.com for reference.

rehearsed if you watch his speeches and interviews. Sadly, there's no mistake. He said almost the exact same thing in a previous talk he gave at the New Roads School in Santa Monica, CA:[29]

> If you teach a white child there's nothing right about you because of the color of your skin and you teach a black child that there's nothing wrong about you because of the color of your skin, when that child comes around and tries to tease them and they're certain that there's nothing wrong with them because of the color of their skin, it's not going to land in the same way as a kid who's still struggling with their sense of self.

One can interpret these statements in two ways. Is Kendi saying that being white doesn't make a child inherently better while being black doesn't make a child inherently flawed? If this is his intent, I can certainly agree with the logic. The alternative interpretation is that we actually need to teach our children that you are okay if you're black, but there is literally nothing right about you if you're white. Since he expressed his ideas almost precisely the same way on at least two occasions, one can only take his words at face value. How is this not racist in the extreme?

Therefore, gaslight the kids. White children must be taught to hate themselves. There is nothing right about them because of the color of their skin. Shall we create generations of children with the self-esteem of pond scum? If, as a parent, you sit idly by while CRT slime oozes into your school system's curriculum, the result will devastate the psyche of vulnerable children. Vast swaths of our youth are being taught that because of the color of their skin, they are racist products. Many children grow up with self-esteem issues as they struggle through their formative years. Imagine adding the guilt-

---

[29] Santa Monica Daily Press (California) December 7, 2020 Monday, Clara Harter, Staff Writer

ridden ideology of CRT to their psychological burdens. This is sick. There is no other way to describe it. It is gaslighting in its rawest and most evil form.

America will never be united if we are forced to consistently observe and acknowledge the color of someone's skin. According to Kendi, aspiring to be color blind is racist because we fail to notice the "beauty of the rainbow." Another false analogy.

Being color blind with respect to race does not mean that you don't actually see the color of someone's skin. It means that you have reached a level of enlightenment where the color of someone's skin simply does not matter. To be color blind is to live the immortal words of Dr. Martin Luther King, Jr.:

> I have a dream that my four little children will one day live in a nation where they will not be judged by the color of their skin, but by the content of their character.

There is no starker contrast I can think of than King's words versus Kendi's words. Ask yourself, wasn't Dr. King advocating color blindness? Isn't the meaning essentially that what is inside a person matters much more than their exterior packaging? What is the higher state of human relations—living the words of Dr. King or constantly being forced to notice the color of someone's skin as Kendi advocates?

Kendi's view is that we must constantly acknowledge race. This shows a fundamental neglect of human psychology. Humans are attracted to sameness and are uneasy about difference. This is an ingrained biological fact. It is not a microaggression. Therefore, if we want unity, we should encourage everyone to focus on our sameness, not our difference. We need to teach our children that all races are far more alike than we are different. I made the point earlier that all humans are similar across 99.5% of their DNA. We are also pre-wired with a set of emotions and an inherent understanding of right and wrong. We all want the same things, which were captured perfectly in our Declaration of Independence—life, liberty, and the pursuit of happiness.

CRT doesn't cure racism, it encourages it. This warped ideology is a scam for profit specifically designed to pit the high-melanin groups against the low-melanin groups. Nothing could be shallower and more counter to Dr. King's core beliefs than CRT. Truly the highest state of social enlightenment we can attain is to live a life where we see each human being as a soul in a human body created by God, not as mere bodies arranged in some politically authorized leftist rainbow. Do you want to live by the words of Dr. King or Dr. Kendi? You must choose.

Masterful Marketing Strokes of the Left

The twisting of words and meaning is a core leftist art form, and so is slick marketing. Two such Masterful Strokes are the terms antiracist and Black Lives Matter.

Antiracist is a term that Kendi has popularized and defined in his own way. It is part of his shtick. You would think that an antiracist is simply someone who opposes racism. If that is your thinking, you are only partially correct. Anti-racist seems like a simple term. Using the basic rules of English, we seek the definition of the root word and then modify the meaning by adding a prefix such as "anti." Therefore, applying the definition of racist as you've seen above and modifying the word with "anti" one would conclude that to be anti-racist is to be against racism. Not so fast. You can't claim to be anti-racist unless you pass a few more litmus tests.

To be an antiracist is to also join the CRT movement. You must be actively working to implement anti-white policy. You must be willing to admit, believe, and declare that everything about America is racist and must be torn down simply because it was founded by white people. In other words, you must hate yourself for being white, and you must hate your country because it was founded by white people. If you cease to be an antiracist at any time, you are racist. Being antiracist and proving it means joining the CRT parade and staying in line. Just look the other way. No gaslighting to see here.

To reach your fully antiracist blossom, you must admit that present day America is racist. You must accept and confess your white guilt if you are not endowed with sufficient melanin. You must also be actively working to denounce racism everywhere it exists, as identified by the "Woke High Command" (WHC). Failure to do any of these things prevents you from securing your antiracist identity card. If you had previously secured an antiracist ID card, as issued by the WHC, you must promptly surrender it and accept your cancellation should you cease active denunciation of whiteness. That's just about how it works. What if you disagree that America is racist to its core, and you don't profess the debunked, propaganda of the 1619 Project? Well then, you guessed it, you are RACIST!

DO NOT DARE defend yourself by saying, "I'm not racist." According to Kendi, that is not a term you are allowed to use. It's a cop-out term that really doesn't exist. I'm sure you're scratching your head at this point. You might be asking a few questions like me. Aren't the words "not" and "anti" both negating terms? Aren't "not racist" and "antiracist" both opposites of racist? Merriam-Webster defines anything "anti" as "opposite in kind." So, don't both terms effectively mean that you're against racism? In Kendi's world, you are not allowed to say, "not racist." That's just a cover term for racists. You must claim your place as an active member of the CRT driven antiracist movement.

Black Lives Matter

Black Lives Matter was a slogan that emerged in the aftermath of George Zimmerman's acquittal in the Travon Martin shooting. The Michael Brown shooting in Ferguson, Missouri later spawned the Black Lives Matter movement. As the slogan gained widespread attention it provided the springboard for creating a national organization.

Figure 5-2: BLM Website Image

The name Black Lives Matter is pure marketing genius. Anyone who opposes the organization can easily be labeled racist by CAT-5 Marxist whack-a-doo. If you say I oppose Black Lives Matter, then you must think that black lives don't matter. BLMers are also full-on devotees of Critical Race Theory concepts. Don't believe it? Figure 5-2 is a copy of the image they proudly display on their website as of this writing.

Since the name of the organization is also a slogan, sympathetic hearts are quick to post the slogan on their lawns, store windows, and car bumpers. Leftist mayors like Bill de Blasio of New York, Muriel Bowser of DC, and Lori Lightfoot of Chicago emblazoned the public streets with the slogan. Never mind that tax dollars paid for that street.

So, while these displays are claimed to be empathy, they simultaneously provide free advertising to a deeply Marxist organization that hates America and uses race as a tool to annihilate its foundations. They are committed to bringing down the "oppressive American system." Any guesses on what they would replace it with?

I want to be clear that my critique of BLM is directed at the organization and its agenda, not the sentiment. Of course, black lives matter. All lives matter.

Let's review the pivotal events that occurred in Ferguson, Missouri, that gave rise to BLM. Michael Brown had just stolen a handful of cigars from a convenience store when the clerk tried to stop him. Brown and his friend Dorian Johnson shoved the clerk out of the way. Police were called. Officer Darren Wilson encountered Brown and Johnson walking down the middle of a street, unaware that Brown was the subject of the call.

Evidence presented at the grand jury investigation supported Wilson's account that the much larger Brown punched him and reached for his gun. The lie BLM perpetuated was that Michael Brown had his hands up and yelled "don't shoot" when Darren Wilson pulled the trigger anyway. Autopsy evidence proved that Brown did not have his hands in the air when he was shot. Nevertheless, "hands up don't shoot" became the rallying cry for BLM. People still believe the false narrative to this day although it was a total lie.

Every police shooting of a black person becomes international news instantly. What people see most is what becomes their reality. The statistical context and factual evidence are rarely provided because it does not support the corrupt corporate media's narrative.

BLM's founders are Alicia Garza, Patrisse Cullors, and Opel Tometi. Earlier versions of their website boldly professed that they are trained Marxists. They have since scrubbed this declaration from their website because it wasn't playing well to advertise their true ambitions. While BLM founders are quick to assert that the white man is the root of all evil, I've often wondered if they ever noticed the race of Karl Marx. Somehow this is the only white man whose ideology they embrace. Washington, Jefferson, and all the other Founders be damned, but Karl Marx, he's the man!

I can understand how the melanin levels of Karl Marx may have slipped past the attention of BLM's founders. After all, they are busy peddling racism, cashing checks to buy houses, and pursuing their demands with a fervor that I'm sure occupies most of their attention. So, I'll assume they just didn't notice that Marx was white.

Are you wondering what their demands were? Their stated pursuits have since been scrubbed from their website, which is now a much slicker propaganda site with toned down extremist language but still filled with massive distortions and deliberate lies. Their previously stated demands, I'm confident, are still at the core of their activism. They are just covering their intentions more cleverly.

> 1. Convict and ban Trump from future political office: We are joining Rep. Ilhan Omar, Rep. Ayanna Pressley, Rep. Cori Bush, Rep. Jamaal Bowman, and others who are demanding Trump be immediately convicted in the United States Senate. Trump must also be banned from holding elected office in the future.

Immediately convict? Really? We gave Charles Manson a fair trial. Can we get a little bit of rule of law for a former president? Clearly, BLM sees Trump as a threat to the advancement of Marxism. He has and will oppose the advancement of racist doctrines like CRT. I can see that BLM would naturally want to destroy him on these grounds. The irony is that black unemployment dropped to record low levels under the Trump economy. Opportunity abounded.

Conversely, under the Biden administration, black people will suffer huge setbacks through policies fully supported by the representatives BLM adores. Legions of unskilled migrants are flooding our nation daily. Whose jobs will these people take? Low-income American households of all races will suffer, but low-income black people will likely be hit the hardest. BLM might say that black lives might matter, but black financial advancement doesn't. Alignment with the four most extreme leftists in Congress essentially declares how the money will flow from BLM to pandering politicians playing the race card daily.

> 2. Expel Republican members of Congress who attempted to overturn the election and incited a white supremacist attack: More than half the Republican representatives and multiple senators stoked Trump's conspiracy theories and encouraged the white supremacists to take action to overturn the election. We are supporting Rep. Cori Bush's resolution to expel them from Congress for their dangerous and traitorous actions. We also support steps to bar them from seeking another office.

In the Marxist world, due process does not exist. I'll wait for all the facts to be made public on what exactly happened on January 6th. Bowing to Marxist demands without due process goes against rule of law, a core American principle.

> 3. Launch a full investigation into the ties between white supremacy and the Capitol Police, law enforcement, and the military: The Capitol was able to be breached and overrun by white supremacists attempting to disrupt a political process that is fundamental to our democracy. We know that police departments have been a safe haven for white supremacists to hide malintent behind a badge, because the badge was created for that purpose. We also know off-duty cops and military were among the mob at the Capitol on January 6th. Guilty parties need to be held accountable and fired. We are supporting Rep. Jamaal Bowman's COUP Act to investigate these connections.

This is purely, a racist, anti-police, and anti-conservative ruse. Yes, we need an investigation, but a real non-partisan investigation of the entire sordid event. But this will never happen if no one is watching the watchmen. I have no confidence that Nancy Pelosi and Adam

Schiff will rise above partisanship. It is far more likely that they will use the riot to destroy every political opponent they can.

4. Permanently ban Trump from all digital media platforms: Trump has always used his digital media platforms recklessly and irresponsibly to spread lies and disinformation. Now it is clearer than ever that his digital media is also used to incite violence and promote its continuation. He must be stopped from encouraging his mob and further endangering our communities, even after inauguration.

This is classic Marxist suppression of free speech. People like Maxine Waters and other leftist politicians have made extremely egregious statements that border on incitement of violence. Yet there's never any action against her or the left by social media platforms. Iran's Ayatollah is given a platform on Twitter. So are the Taliban and the Chinese Communist Party. But Trump must be banned.

5. Defund the police: The police that met our BLM protestors this summer with assault rifles, teargas, and military-grade protective gear were the same police that, on Wednesday, met white supremacists with patience and the benefit of the doubt, going so far as to pose for selfies with rioters. The contrast was jarring, but not for black people. We have always known who the police truly protect and serve. D.C. has the most police per capita in the country; more funding is not the solution.

For jurisdictions that have actually defunded the police or in other ways tied their hands, what comes to mind is the old quote from Dr. Phil McGraw, "How's that workin' for ya?" New York City's former mayor acted on the idea like other leftist mayors. "Bolshevik Bill" de Blasio disbanded the plainclothes unit of the NYPD. Crime subsequently soared with gun violence exploding. Lori "Lightweight" Lightfoot of Chicago "astutely" points out that generally violent crime is down—with one small footnote, murders and shootings are up dramatically. Through the end of October 2021, Chicago logged 717 homicides an eleven-year high. A person is shot in Chicago roughly every two hours.[30] Of course, minority neighborhoods are hit the hardest when these leftist mayors defund the police to please organizations like BLM. If you ask law-abiding citizens of these crime ridden neighborhoods, they clearly want more policing not less.

> 6. Don't let the coup be used as an excuse to crack down on our move-ment: In response to the coup, Politicians have already introduced the Domestic Terrorism Prevention Act of 2021. We've seen this playbook before. These laws are used to target black and brown communities for heightened surveillance. Republicans are already busy trying to create an equivalence between the mob on January 6th and our Free-dom Summer. We don't need new domestic terror laws, facial recog-nition, or any other new police power for the state. Our government should protect righteous protest and stay focused on the real issue: rooting out white supremacy. There are enough laws, resources, and intelligence, but they were not used to stop the coup. Our elected of-ficials must uncover why.

Surprisingly, I partially agree with this demand. BLM is partly correct. Even a blind squirrel finds a nut once in a while. The left will use the January 6th protests as an excuse to treat vast swaths of our population as domestic terrorists. I disagree that these initiatives will be solely used to target minorities. These initiatives will target everyone, but most likely conservatives of all races. As for the Free-dom Summer, rioting in cities across the country caused billions in property damage and theft and claimed the lives of at least fifteen

---

[30] Crime statistic website, www.heyjackass.com as of November 1, 2021

people, with countless cases of injuries to police and other bystanders. I guess freedom is the new leftist word for violence.

> 7. Pass the BREATHE Act: The police were born out of slave patrols. We cannot reform an institution built upon white supremacy. We need a new, radical approach to public safety and community investment. President Biden has already drawn on the BREATHE Act in his executive actions calling for racial equity screens in federal programs, investing in environmental justice at historic levels, and engaging with system-impacted communities. The BREATHE Act paints a vision of a world where black lives matter through investments in housing, education, health, and environmental justice.

This demand is primarily a comprehensive police defunding movement and an amalgamation of other leftist initiatives like disbanding Immigrations and Customs Enforcement, dramatically reducing the Department of Defense budget, and closing all federal prisons. [31]

Clearly, we do need lots of change to help inner-city black communities. What about starting with initiatives to improve the public education system, reducing fatherless families, and purging drug dealers from the streets? Unfortunately, the BLM agenda is a racism driven, America-hating agenda that will create more problems than solutions. All the while, BLM stays absolutely silent on the epidemic of black-on-black crime that is the leading cause of violent death in inner-city neighborhoods.

Social Media Drivers

Black people are routinely hunted in the streets. This is what the leftists would have you believe because it plays to their false narrative

---

[31] BREATHE Act initiatives

of systemic racism. Any loss of life is a tragedy in the universe's grand scheme. Even when a criminal is legally executed via the death penalty or the police are justified in shooting a criminal, the loss of life is the result of some human failure. It is unfortunate that circumstances culminated in death.

In May 2020, Ahmaud Aubrey was shot down in a suburban Georgia neighborhood by two white men who said they suspected he was a robber trying to break into homes. The two men involved in the shooting and an individual who recorded the incident on video were all subsequently charged with murder. Justice played out in the courts, and all three were found guilty. Before the arrests, Lebron James did not hesitate to tweet out his emotional inflammatory reaction:

> We're literally hunted EVERYDAY/EVERYTIME we step foot outside the comfort of our homes! Can't even go for a damn jog man! Like WTF man are you kidding me?!?!?!?!?!? No man ARE YOU KIDDING ME!!!!!

Any decent American would be disturbed by the video of the shooting, and I understand that a black man viewing the video would be particularly disturbed. But Lebron James has approximately 70 million followers on social media. While I'm empathetic to his feelings, he needs to consider the inflammatory nature of his words.

"Literally hunted," really? Can James please show us the body count that supports that? If his words were literal, then we would see millions of dead black people all across the country. The statistics do not support the rhetoric in James' tweet. NOT EVEN CLOSE. Some people may dismiss his language as hyperbole, but many take him literally and believe him. The damage his careless words inflict on our society is immeasurable because the emotional component is what people remember most.

If black people are being hunted in the street, it is certainly not the police doing the hunting. The numbers tell a very different story. In 2020, according to the FBI's Uniform Crime Reporting (UCR) database, 3,740 black people were murdered. In 3,210 of those cases, the offender was also black. If we were to analyze murders in Lightfoot's Chicago, we would find that pattern holding. Do these black lives matter? Does BLM care about addressing the root causes of black-on-black violence? Or do black lives only matter when a black person is killed by a white police officer?

Systemic Racism—Does It Exist?

When I conceived the general theme of this book, my point of departure was an observation that the country was descending into the grips of Marxism. The tactics employed by the left are clearly visible. As masters of the half-truth, many of the left's assertions regarding society's issues ring true to many people. The most effective and evil lie is the one based partially on truth. Therefore, I felt from the onset that each leftist lie, each cornerstone of their movement had to be analyzed objectively and logically to refute the assertions that proved patently false.

One cornerstone of the leftist movement is systemic racism. Does it exist in present-day America? As promoted by the left, the central premise of systemic racism is that everything about the American system is irredeemably racist. It is a system designed by white men, for white men, to the exclusion of all people of color. They conveniently omit that the design of the American system served as the podium upon which all civil rights leaders were able to stand. They stood on the shoulders of Jefferson and the concept that "all men are created equal."

I challenge any who thinks Marxism is the answer to point to a single law in existence today that specifically holds down black people or any other minority. Please point to a single statute that excludes anyone from the pursuit of happiness based on the color of their skin. I'll be waiting for your reply. The facts point to the truth. There are no such laws anymore.

In 1954, segregation in the educational system was outlawed when the Supreme Court handed down its decision in Brown v. Board of Education. The sixties saw a string of legislative acts that permanently extinguished Jim Crow laws that promoted legal segregation. In 1964, President Johnson signed the Civil Rights Act, making segregation and race-based discrimination illegal. In 1965, Congress passed the Voting Rights Act that prevented discrimination designed to keep minorities from voting. Finally, in 1968, the Fair Housing Act ended discrimination in renting and buying homes. These acts were made possible because of our Constitution, which was over time correctly interpreted by the Supreme Court.

In fact, today, the Federal Government and just about every state and local government directly favor minorities, which is opposite to the now-defunct Jim Crow laws. Governments at every level have minority contracting programs. We have the 8(a) Program at the federal level to provide competitive advantage to minority firms when pursuing federal contracts. Under the 8(a) program, minorities include Blacks, Asians (includes Indians), Hispanics, and American Indians—every so-called person of color. In essence, just about everyone that is assumed to have an above-average melanin level is now favored. There are numerous scholarships and grants set aside for minority students and financial aid available exclusively to minorities. Clearly, society has now gone to great lengths to compensate for the egregious wrongs of the past. So, where exactly is all the systemic racism that the race-baiters rail against daily? To answer this question, one needs to examine the history of systemic racism.

CHAPTER 6

The History of Systemic Racism

"Thus, by quartering ill policy upon ill principles, they have frequently promoted the cause they designed to injure and injured that which they intended to promote."

—Thomas Paine, *The American Crisis*, 1783

Democrat party roots can be traced back as far as 1792. Alexander Hamilton was a leading federalist who believed that the country should form a strong central government and a national banking system. George Washington and John Adams also favored this approach. In 1792, Thomas Jefferson and James Madison formed the Democratic-Republican party specifically to oppose the federalist ideas of Hamilton. The federalists then formally created the Federalist Party in opposition. By the early 19th century, the Federalists disbanded their party. The presidential election of 1824 consisted of four Democratic-Republican candidates with no opposition party. Since there was no electoral majority between the four candidates, John Quincy Adams ultimately prevailed when the House of Representatives selected him over Andrew Jackson.

This did not sit well with Senator Martin Van Buren. He formed a new political organization, the Democratic Party, to consolidate support behind his friend Andrew Jackson who subsequently defeated John Quincy Adams in the election of 1828. By 1832, Jackson's opponents formed the Whig Party.

Fast forward to the pivotal election of 1860. The slavery issue defined national politics throughout the 1850s. Abraham Lincoln was nominated by the newly formed Republican Party that opposed the extension of slavery in all new territories. The Democrats suffered a significant setback at their convention as they emerged without selecting a nominee. They convened a second time and nominated Stephen A. Douglas. He favored allowing each state and new territory to decide the existence of slavery within their borders based on popular sovereignty. Douglas's selection fractured the Democrats into a Northern Faction backing Douglas and a Southern Democratic Faction supporting John C. Breckinridge. The Southern Democrats wanted to keep all new territories open to slavery. The election of 1860 was contested among a field of four candidates. In addition to Lincoln, Douglas, and Breckinridge, John Bell also ran as the nominee of the Constitutional Union party formed from Whigs who did not join the Republican party.

Lincoln defeated Douglas soundly in the North while Breckinridge and the proslavery Southern Democrats swept the South. However, their electoral tally was not enough to overtake Lincoln, aided by Bell, who pulled crucial votes away from Breckinridge by winning three states, Virginia, Kentucky, and Tennessee.

After Lincoln was elected, secession followed, and civil war erupted soon after. The Southern Democrat power base created the Confederacy to preserve slavery. The Democratic Party will forever wear the label of the party of slavery. The Confederates were nearly all Democrats.

After the North defeated the Confederacy, reconstruction and reintegration of the South began. Lincoln had outlined a benevolent reintegration framework as eloquently expressed in his famous second inaugural address, "with charity for all and malice toward none." After Lincoln's tragic assassination, Vice President Andrew Johnson assumed the presidency.

Johnson was actually a Democrat senator from Tennessee who remained in the Senate even after Tennessee had seceded. Lincoln had chosen Johnson as his running mate in the hope of gaining support from Southerners who were against leaving the Union. Johnson gained popularity and eventual election to public office through his defense of the small farmer and white laborers severely impacted by the large plantation owners who thrived from slavery. In contrast to Lincoln, Johnson was a racist and bore no genuine concern for former slaves.

After Lincoln's death, Johnson somewhat followed Lincoln's framework of rapid reintegration without severe punishment for secession. However, he took an even more lenient approach promoting the idea that the Southern States should decide what was best for themselves. He also liberally granted presidential pardons to influential plantation owners and former confederate officials, allowing them to rapidly return to power. His lax approach toward former confederates and lack of support for the rights of freed blacks earned him the enmity of Republicans. He was also held in contempt by Southerners, who viewed him as a traitor for remaining in the Senate after secession. The embattled Johnson quickly proved to be a disaster for the entire nation.

The restoration of former Confederate Democrats to positions of power led to the implementation of Black Codes throughout the South that stifled the realization of true freedom for former slaves. Republican leaders like Pennsylvania Representative Thaddeus Stevens and Senator Charles Sumner of Massachusetts sought to vigorously counter the effects of the Black Codes. They pushed a bill to Johnson's desk that was intended to extend the life of the Freedmen's Bureau to help black people compete in the free market.

Under the leadership of Stevens and Sumner, Congress also passed the Civil Rights Bill of 1866. Shockingly, the racist Democrat Johnson vetoed both bills stating that he did not support blacks having the same property ownership and voting rights as whites.

Johnson's views appalled Republicans. Moderate Republicans who were lukewarm in supporting rights for black people became energized by Johnson's blatant racism. They joined Stevens and Sumner along with other more "radical" Republicans to override Johnson's veto. Subsequently, they passed the Fourteenth Amendment, which implemented three crucial provisions. First, it affirmed citizenship for black people and reinforced equality before the law for all citizens. Second, if citizenship rights were impeded in any way, states abridging those rights would lose representation in Congress. Third, anyone participating in insurrection by supporting the Confederacy could not hold public office.

The Republicans weren't finished. They subsequently passed the Reconstruction Act of 1867, which removed the right to vote and hold office for any leading former Confederates. This last Act created a power shift in the South from the former Democrat Confederates to Southern Unionists who supported the Union during the Civil War. Control of the South was also placed in the hands of the military through the establishment of five military districts that empowered the army to protect black property and rights.

Despite Johnson's efforts to thwart Republican initiatives, the nation was progressing toward equality. Southern states rewrote their state constitutions and ratified the Fourteenth Amendment. For a while, the situation for black people in the South was improving. Former slaves began to thrive in politics, though less so economically. Black people ran for and won many public offices, becoming sheriffs, judges, school board members, city councilmen, and legislators at the local and national levels. Economically, life was still a struggle as many turned to sharecropping, which resembled the old plantation life and often bound former slaves through less visible, yet still oppressive chains of debt as opposed to iron.

Southern Democrats who had their world turned upside down through legislative action were not about to give up easily. They turned to violence and intimidation. They formed organizations like the Ku Klux Klan to oppress black people wherever they could. Klansmen included more than just disaffected former Confederates. They included shopkeepers, ministers, and tradesmen who frequently donned their sheets and cone-headed hoods to beat, murder, and rape black people.

In the election of 1868, Ulysses S. Grant emerged as the Republican candidate against Democrat Horatio Seymour. The Ku Klux Klan had become a powerful terrorist force in just a few years. In 1868, their main focus was violence against Republicans and much more acutely against black people who would undoubtedly vote Republican if allowed to reach the polls. The Klan committed thousands of murders across the South as part of widespread voter suppression tactics.

Once again, extreme Democrat tactics backfired. Grant was elected and reinvigorated Northern Republicans passed the Fifteenth Amendment, "The right of citizens of the United States to vote shall not be denied or abridged by the United States or by any State on account of race, color, or previous condition of servitude." Grant's efforts in combating the Klan and enfranchising black people led to his landslide re-election in 1872.

By 1872, the strains for reconstruction were taking their toll on the nation. Violence and voter suppression tactics continued in the South. Grant would sporadically choose to intervene with federal troops. However, he was caught in a political vise between the forces in the North and South that favored states' rights and the forces that required protection of Southern Republicans and black people. When Grant intervened, he was criticized by both Republicans and

Democrats, who opposed constant federal intervention in matters internal to the states. When he did not intervene, racist violence would flourish, and the Republican cause would be damaged, nonetheless.

During Grant's second term, reconstruction began to rapidly lose momentum. Numerous scandals that engulfed members of his administration began to erode Grant's power base. Though his character was never directly questioned, the corruption of those beneath him began to sour the nation. Reconstruction was perhaps dealt a mortal blow by the Financial Panic of 1873, further weakening the focus on turning equal rights into reality. From 1873 to 1879, the nation slipped into depression, and much of the South fell into dire poverty. This allowed the Democrats to regain control of the House of Representatives, effectively ending the Reconstruction Era.

The election of 1876 significantly curtailed the Federal Government's ability to enforce the Thirteenth, Fourteenth, and Fifteenth amendments. The election rested on disputed vote counts in three Southern states. A compromise was reached that placed Republican Rutherford B. Hayes in the White House on the condition that the Federal Government would withdraw Union troops from all Southern States. Enforcement of the reconstruction amendments was effectively placed on pause.

At the end of reconstruction, Southern Democrats dominated state legislatures throughout the South. They began passing ever more restrictive laws known as Jim Crow Laws designed to segregate black people and curtail their political power. It was racism pure and simple, backed by the force of local law. Tactics to block black people from Congress proved highly effective for the racist Southern Democrats.

During reconstruction, black representation in Congress reached a peak of eight seats in the 44th Congress that convened from 1875 to 1877. Representation slowly dwindled until there were no black representatives left when the 50th Congress convened in 1877. The 51st Congress saw three black representatives elected, followed by one each in the 52nd through 56th, covering 1889 to 1901. As the progressive era dawned under Theodore Roosevelt, there was no black representation in Congress from the 57th Congress until 1929, when Oscar Stanton De Priest won a seat in Illinois. Black people were prevented from reaching any national office for 28 years. The Southern Democrats had succeeded in shutting down black suffrage, and any meager gains made during reconstruction were reversed in a little over ten years. In fact, no black people were elected to any Congressional office in the South until 1973 when Andrew Young won in Georgia.

Through 1933, no black man had ever held a Congressional Office as a Democrat. Twenty-three black men had been elected to the House and Senate from the end of the civil war until 1935 all as Republicans. From 1935 to the present day, black people elected to Congress have been overwhelmingly Democrats with few exceptions. It is as if someone threw a switch. The question is, "What happened in 1935? Why did the Republicans who were the pioneers in fighting for civil rights lose the black voter?" It's a threefold answer— migration to Northern urban centers, The Great Depression, and Franklin D. Roosevelt's New Deal.

The Great Migration

The onset of World War I created a shortage of industrial labor in urban centers. Southern black people that had been suffering under segregationist laws and oppressive violence began to head north to large, industrialized cities. The factory wages they could earn were three times what they could make working in the fields throughout the South. From 1910 to 1920, cities like New York, Chicago, Philadelphia, and Detroit saw extraordinary increases in the black population. This period became known as The Great Migration. While financial life improved for the descendants of enslaved people, racism still impacted them even though segregation didn't legally exist in the North. Redlining of neighborhoods and unwritten racist policies often prevented black people from intermingling with whites in residential areas. This situation, in turn, gave rise to concentrated black urban centers within major cities.

The Great Depression

When the depression arrived in 1929, The Great Migration slowed significantly. As poverty took hold across the country, Black Americans were hit disproportionately hard. Franklin Roosevelt was subsequently elected in 1933 and began his New Deal. He launched vast public works programs to alleviate unemployment and effectively created the welfare system to provide immediate relief for the poor. This positioned Roosevelt and the Democrats as the new center for sustenance among poor Black Americans.

Two other factors combined to capture black voters. Formerly enslaved people were beginning to die off. The younger generation, and their descendants, that had taken refuge in urban centers had not directly experienced the violence of the Klan or the lash of an overseer. They no longer directly connected their oppression to the source—Southern Democrats. As Black Americans resettled in large cities, they were courted and attracted to powerful Democrat political establishments in those centers. According to House records, "just nine black Republicans were elected to Congress between 1929 and 2017—about seven percent of the African Americans to serve in that time span."

Arthur Wergs Mitchell was the first Black American elected to Congress as a Democrat and served four terms in the House. Shortly after his election, he shared his personal view on gaining political office:

> I am not going into Congress as a Negro with a chip on my shoulder thinking I am of an inferior race and that every man's hand is against me. I am going in as an American citizen, entitled to my rights, no more, no less, and I shall insist on them. I'm going as the representative of all the people of my district.

The New Deal

Mitchell was an ardent supporter of Franklin D. Roosevelt and the New Deal. Mitchell tapped into the emotions of the poor as he took his seat in the 74th Congress, "What I am interested in is to help this grand President of ours feed the hungry and clothe the naked and provide work for the idle of every race and creed." At the nomination of FDR for a second term, Mitchell's position on the New Deal was clear. It addressed many of the problems faced by "America's largest and most neglected minority group." He also noted that the New Deal had created the best conditions for Black Americans since becoming citizens. The New Deal delivered millions of dollars to devastated black communities hit hard during the depression. Black Americans constituted between fifteen to twenty percent of the workforce for projects managed by the Public Works Administration (PWA).

Mitchell served honorably until the Chicago Democrat political machine turned against him in 1942. They withdrew support for him because he defied their orders to drop a discrimination lawsuit against a Chicago-based rail company. In Mitchell v. the United States, the supreme court ruled that black passengers had a right to the same accommodations as whites. This was an essential step toward the dismantling of Democrat supported Jim Crow laws throughout the South.[32]

Despite blacks turning en masse toward FDR and the Democrats, their "love" was unrequited. FDR remained ambivalent toward dismantling segregation in the South. He needed the support of Southern Democrats to stay in office and was not about to challenge them on their institutionalized racism where Jim Crow laws would remain entrenched for decades more. In the Northern urban centers, Democrats courted and captured black votes. Throughout the South, they continued to suppress their votes, oppress them financially, and murder them with impunity.

From 1890 to 1952, close to 200 anti-lynching bills were introduced in Congress and only three times did the bills pass the House of Representatives. Each time the bills were blocked in the Senate by Southern Democrats. The propaganda periodical, USA Today, deceivingly called them "Southern Conservatives," but they were not conservatives in the modern-day political sense. They were racist Southern Democrats fighting hard to "conserve" their vile Jim Crow world. In 1935, Sen. Richard B. Russell, a Georgia Democrat led a six-day filibuster to block one of the anti-lynching bills. While the present-day Leftist Democrats advocate for removing statues of Jefferson and denounce our Founding Fathers, they still proudly display Russell's name on the oldest Senate Office building.[33]

Let's step back to the early 20th century and examine Woodrow Wilson's "contribution" to race relations. Wilson was a profound and unapologetic racist. It must be noted that Wilson's dismissal of natural law and that "all men are created equal" gave him moral permission to institutionalize racism. He boldly segregated the civil

---

[32] United States House of Representatives Archives, Biography of Arthur Wergs Mitchell.

[33] As reported by The Frontrunner, "Senate Apologizes for Failure To Pass Anti-Lynching Bill," June 14, 2005

service in 1913 based on his core belief that blacks were racially inferior to whites. He instituted policies that made it difficult for blacks to get government jobs by requiring a photograph on their applications. This made it easy to identify and exclude black applicants. He even argued that the policy was good for blacks. Arthur Wergs Mitchell would later attempt to have this policy reversed by suggesting the use of a fingerprint for identification. His proposed legislation was blocked. Wilson's policies and public statements on race gave legitimacy to the infamous Jim Crow era.

Wilson even proved to be a two-faced flip-flopper in addressing Black American's quest for equality. While campaigning for office in 1912, he wrote a letter to Alexander Walters, head of the National Colored Democratic League, "should I become President of the United States they [Black Americans] may count on me for absolute fair dealing and for everything by which I could assist in advancing the interests of their race in the United States."[34] His empty promises garnered widespread endorsements from black civil rights groups. These endorsements undoubtedly translated into black votes, which helped him win the Democratic nomination and subsequently the presidency. His words were empty, but his deeds spoke volumes when he later segregated the civil service thereby placing Jim Crow on steroids. Subsequently, W.E.B. Du Bois wrote in an open letter, "It is no exaggeration to say that every enemy of the Negro race is greatly encouraged; that every man who dreams of making the Negro race a group of menials and pariahs is alert and hopeful."[35]

Wilson never reversed his racist policies though he finally spoke out against lynching and mob violence that often led to the

---

[34] "Civil Rights and the Making of the Modern American State," Megan Ming Francis

[35] W. E. B. Du Bois, The Crisis, September 1913; W. E. B. Du Bois, "My Impressions of Woodrow Wilson," The Journal of Negro History 58, no. 4 (1973): pp. 453–459

indiscriminate slaughter of black men, women, and children. He did so only after being cornered through political pressure generated by the NAACP and after making every attempt to ignore the bloodshed pervasive during his period. One must again ask, how much did his segregationist policies add fuel to the fire of racial hatred? His progressive ideology, on which present-day Leftist Democrats partially base their rhetoric, continues to damage America's national fabric.

Warren Harding, the Republican president who succeeded the racist Wilson, was much more receptive and genuinely concerned about improving conditions for Black Americans. He, unfortunately, died in office of a heart attack. Calvin Coolidge succeeded Harding and proved to be a courageous and outspoken supporter of racial equality. Coolidge even spoke out against lynching in his State of the Union message delivered on December 3, 1924. Harding had done the same before him by calling for Congress "... to wipe the stain of barbaric lynching from the banners of a free and orderly, representative democracy."

Still, no civil rights legislation was passed during the Harding and Coolidge administrations despite the Republicans having control of both houses and the presidency. The Southern Democrats were successful in blocking any legislation. One such example is the Dyer Anti-Lynching Bill.

In 1918, Republican Congressman Leonidas C. Dyer first introduced his bill to make lynching a federal crime. The bill was also designed to prosecute any local government official who refused to prosecute lynching offenses. He reintroduced his bill in 1922 and was able to usher its passage by a 230 to 119 vote margin in the House of Representatives. However, it never saw the light of day in the Senate, where a powerful block of Southern Democrat senators filibustered the bill and snuffed out any momentum the anti-lynching movement had gained. Their justification was the broadly advanced myth that lynching was a response to rape committed by black offenders. They also argued against the bill based on states' rights.

Anti-lynching bills were revived several times in the ensuing decades. The Costigan-Wagner Bill of 1934, sponsored by Democratic Senators Costigan of Colorado and Wagner of New York, suffered a similar fate as the Dyer Bill. Senator Robert Wagner tried again in 1937 and 1938, only to again be stymied by Southern Democrats.

In 1940, another anti-lynching bill was sponsored by Democratic Congressman Gavagan and Republican Fish. The Gavagan-Fish Bill passed the House with another overwhelming majority vote 252 to 131. When facing the threat of another Southern Democrat filibuster, then Democratic Majority leader Alben Barkley, tabled the bill and allowed it to die without a vote.

Where was the great FDR during the anti-lynching debates of the 1930s and 40s? Quiet and on the sidelines, though, his wife Eleanor publicly indicated her support for the Wagner bills. FDR never weighed in or lent his considerable political power to any of the bills. He prioritized his New Deal legislation and vast expansion of government bureaucracy over taking a stand against lynching. FDR was elected four times. He was the first to break the precedent that presidents should not serve more than two terms. FDR consistently courted the support of the Southern Democrats to maintain his power base and pass his New Deal programs. Supporting any legislation that specifically threatened that power base was just not something he seriously considered. Still, his New Deal work programs had mass appeal to Black Americans at a time of great economic distress. Many persisted in casting their votes for FDR while continuing their exodus from the Republican Party.

Republicans, on the other hand, often drifted away from their early championing of racial equality. Republicans sought to break the Democratic stronghold on the South by promoting candidates that appealed to the conservative nature of most Southerners while remaining neutral or silent on race issues. Nothing in Republican Party politics compares to the coordinated and systematic repression perpetrated by Democrats. However, Republicans did, to a degree, trade away their principles for an ill-advised power play and political expediency. This alienated many blacks and drove them further toward the Democratic Party that was also riding the wave of FDR's popularity.

One thing is very clear, Black Americans were steadily gaining influence in the political system. Their votes were becoming increasingly important. While this gave them some power to shape the national attitude on race relations, it also transformed the black voting block into a political football for the parties to wrestle over. The Democrats would eventually establish that chokehold on the black vote that they hold to this day. This warrants further inspection as we move forward in the timeline toward the reinvigorated Civil Rights Era of the 1950s and 60s. First, we must review landmark court decisions that initially damaged civil rights but then began to turn the tide in favor of equality for Black Americans.

The Supreme Court's Impact on Racial Equality

The Supreme Court has not always been the perfect interpreter of the Constitution, nor have they always been on the right side of history. One of their most notorious decisions was the Dred Scott case.

Dred Scott v. Sandford (1856) – Dred Scott and his family were slaves that had been transported from a slave state to the free state of Illinois. He was subsequently transported to the Wisconsin territory. The Missouri Compromise had established that slavery could not be extended to territories north of the 36º 30' parallel. This meant that Wisconsin was free territory. While residing in St. Louis, Scott and his wife later sued based on a Missouri statute that prohibited re-enslavement of someone who had been previously transported to a free territory.

Chief Justice Roger Taney, a Southern aristocrat, wrote the majority decision that re-enslaved Scott and his family. His decision was based on the principle that enslaved blacks were not citizens and could not sue in Federal court. He further held that the Fifth Amendment protected private property of slave owners, and slaves were property. This notorious decision also invalidated Congress's power to block the spread of slavery.

Plessy v. Ferguson (1896) – Even after the passage of three Constitutional Amendments establishing equal rights of former slaves, the SCOTUS ruled that racial segregation laws did not violate the Constitution as long as the facilities provided for each race were of equal quality. This established the "separate but equal" doctrine that also helped fuel the Jim Crow era. It is inconceivable how any court could justify laws barring entry to any facility based on the color of someone's skin. It would be another fifty-eight years until this bone-headed decision would be reversed.

The tide of court decisions eventually started turning in favor of equality through arguments based on the Thirteenth, Fourteenth, and Fifteenth Amendments.

Guinn v. United States (1915) – In 1870 the Fifteenth Amendment established that citizens could not be barred from voting based on "race, color, or previous condition of servitude." In 1907, Oklahoma passed a law requiring a literacy test in order to vote. Citizens could be exempted from a literacy test if they could prove that their grandfathers had voted, been citizens, or served in the armed forces. This law was cleverly designed to disenfranchise illiterate black voters who could not meet either the test or the exemptions. In Guinn v. United States, the SCOTUS struck down the Oklahoma statute as unconstitutional.

Buchanan v. Warley (1917) – The SCOTUS ruled that racial segregation in residential areas violated the Fourteenth Amendment and was unconstitutional. The Court's unanimous decision ruled that Louisville, Kentucky city ordinances that prevented the sale of property to blacks in white neighborhoods were unconstitutional because the ordinances interfered with individual rights to own property.

Moore v. Dempsey (1923) – The case centered on the death of a white man in connection with a shootout at a black tenant farmers union meeting in Arkansas. In the aftermath of the shootout, as many as 200 blacks were murdered by white vigilante gangs. Charges were brought against 122 black defendants, 73 of which were indicted for murder. In this landmark case, the SCOTUS ruled against mob violence in the treatment of defendants who had been beaten and coerced into confessing. Certain accused black citizens were not charged if they were willing to provide labor on terms dictated by landlords and also testify against other accused prisoners. The SCOTUS found the criminal trials were a complete sham and a wholesale violation of the due process clause of the Fourteenth Amendment. The Court also issued a writ of habeas corpus which compelled the lower courts to review whether the accused were justly imprisoned. After further legal proceedings reduced sentences for the accused, the Governor of Arkansas commuted their sentences. Eventually all the prisoners were released.

Brown v. Mississippi (1936) – In this case, the SCOTUS ruled that a coerced confession extracted by force is inadmissible as evidence because it violates the due process clause of the Fourteenth Amendment. In Kemper County, Mississippi three black tenant farmers were arrested for murder. The defendants were stripped, whipped, and beaten in an effort to extract confessions. Evidence presented at the ensuing one-day trial consisted solely of their confessions. SCOTUS ruled unanimously that such confessions were inadmissible and reversed the convictions. Incidentally, the Mississippi lawyer who prosecuted the case against the accused was John C. Stennis, who was later elected to the US Senate for thirteen consecutive terms. He was, of course, a Democrat and an ardent segregationist. Trial transcripts reveal that Stennis had full knowledge of how the confessions were obtained. The NASA Stennis Space Center in Mississippi is named after him.

Brown v. Board of Education of Topeka (1954) – The SCOTUS ruling in Brown v. Board of Education was in all likelihood the pivotal moment that ignited the Civil Rights Movement. Though numerous initiatives were certainly well underway prior to the ruling, the decision in this case legally ended segregation that had existed for decades in America's public schools. In the decision, the SCOTUS ruled that state sanctioned segregation was an inherent violation of the Fourteenth Amendment. The ruling had repercussions across all segregation in public facilities by establishing that "separate but equal is inherently unequal." Effectively, this reversed the Plessy v. Ferguson decision.

Last Gasp of the Former Confederacy

Even after Brown v. Board of Education, the Southern Democrats would not relent in their racist ways. In 1956, Congressman Howard Smith (D) from Virginia introduced the Southern Manifesto during a speech in the House of Representatives. Throughout the 1950s, Smith was instrumental in using his committee powers to kill civil rights legislation. Effectively, the Manifesto marked the last moment of defiance by sympathizers of the former Confederacy. It urged citizens across the South to use all legal means to resist the court ruling in Brown v. Board of Education. Approximately one-fifth of Congressional members signed the Manifesto—all from former Confederate states. Eighty-two representatives and nineteen Senators signed. Of the eighty-two representative signatories, eighty were Democrats, and two were Republicans. Of the nineteen Senators who signed, all were Democrats. Lyndon B. Johnson was a senator from Texas at the time and did not sign. John F. Kennedy was also in the Senate representing Massachusetts. Kennedy also did not sign, and neither did any representative or senator from the former Union States.[36] Let's take a look at a few select quotes from the Manifesto:

> This unwarranted exercise of power by the Court, contrary to the Constitution, is creating chaos and confusion in the States principally affected. It is destroying the **amicable relations between the white and Negro** races that have been created through 90 years of patient effort by the good people of both races. It has planted hatred and suspicion where there has been heretofore friendship and understanding.

I do not know what planet Howard Smith lived on before releasing his Manifesto. He somehow missed the thousands of murders and lynchings across the postbellum South and even in pockets of racial conflict in the North. Smith's argument hinged again on state rights and judicial overreach. He also noted that separate but equal schools had been the norm across the entire country since 1849. Unfortunately, that norm was a fundamental wrong that had now been righted. Nothing about black schools was ever equal to the norm in the rest of the country. Further, while we are a federation of independent states by design, the US Constitution supersedes the state constitutions when individual rights are trampled by misguided local policies.

Smith further claimed that the SCOTUS decision would destroy public schools. Our public-school systems are now indeed a disaster for all students, not just black students. Integration is certainly not what destroyed them. School segregation in the North existed as

---

[36] Clemson University, Strom Thurmond Institute, Manifesto Text and Signatories.

well. It was not simply a Southern problem. However, the Northern states tended to acquiesce to the decision though it would take years to achieve de facto integration.

The Southern Manifesto was a disgraceful event for the Democrat Party. While it was the last gasp of the former Confederacy as an obstacle to black advancement, the Democrats soon began to change their strategy for courting the black vote. During the John F. Kennedy and Lyndon B. Johnson administrations they would recast the image of the Democrat Party as champions of civil rights as if they had been the guardian angels of Black Americans since 1619. While everyone is entitled to redemption and turning away from evil, the Democrat reversal was really an exercise in opportunism. Given that the momentum generated by SCOTUS decisions would make equality for blacks an irreversible outcome, the Democrats seized the moment to lock them in as part of the Democrat power base.

The Civil Rights Era of the 1960s.

The 1960s were a tumultuous period in American history with plenty of triggers for social unrest. We had the Vietnam War, the steady advance of communism across the globe, the feminist movement, the sexual revolution, race riots, landmark civil rights legislation, and three horrific assassinations. The period would also be punctuated by more momentous court decisions that would put the final nail in the coffin of segregation.

There's an old saying, "Politics makes for strange bedfellows." Politicians of both parties have always tallied their support by factions and segments of the population. In the post-Civil War era, the South was dominated by white Southern Democrats determined to suppress Black Americans. As soon as they reascended to power in 1875, they did everything they could to stymie the advance of racial equality. Still, in 1933 large blocks of black voters, at the behest of the NAACP and the Urban League, jumped into bed with Democrats—the party that had enslaved them, oppressed them for decades, and would continue to do so until the present day.

With the election of JFK, elements of the Democrat party, mainly in the North, began to embrace the civil rights movement. They succeeded in hi-jacking public perception to recast their party as defenders of the black man. Was this a conversion of the heart or simply cold political calculus? In the case of JFK, I would say it was a combination of both. JFK and his brother Robert were, after all, politicians. Votes matter to politicians. Alliances and coalitions matter. But the Kennedy brothers also had an element of authenticity in their championing of equal rights for all races.

In 1960, Martin Luther King, Jr. was arrested in Atlanta following a sit-in. JFK called King's wife and Robert F. Kennedy was instrumental in securing King's release by calling the judge assigned to his case. These were very visible and influential actions in attracting the black vote in the run-up to the presidential election that same year. After his brother's election, RFK would also frequently meet with black leaders to understand their concerns and offer the administration's help.

In 1963, President Kennedy ordered the integration of the University of Alabama at Tuscaloosa. George Wallace, a staunch Southern Democrat, would not let that order go into effect without a fight. He decided to live out the words of Smith's manifesto from years earlier "to resist forced integration by any lawful means."

Wallace, the racist governor of Alabama, had taken his oath of office standing on the very spot where Jefferson Davis was inaugurated as President of the Confederacy over a century earlier. In his inauguration speech, Wallace unabashedly voiced his racism in an infamous line that was written for him by the leader of the Ku Klux Klan:

In the name of the greatest people that have ever trod this earth, I draw the line in the dust and toss the gauntlet before the feet of tyranny, and I say segregation now, segregation tomorrow, segregation forever.

In 1963, Wallace stood in the doorway of the auditorium at the University of Alabama in a self-serving political stunt to symbolically block the integration of the school. Kennedy had called up the National Guard to enforce the order, and Wallace's stunt ended in compliance.

In contrast to Kennedy, Lyndon Baines Johnson (LBJ) was a total fraud who only pushed civil rights to collect votes. He was a noxious racist who was unashamed to make his true thoughts known. In connection with the push for the Civil Rights Act of 1964, he supposedly said, "I'll have those niggers voting Democratic for 200 years."[37] Though some dispute this quote, it is actually very much within his character and speech pattern. He was well-known for throwing the n-word around like candy on Halloween. To Johnson, the tradeoff was lost votes in the South among the old guard Southern Democrats, in exchange for enough votes throughout most of the rest of the country and the black vote. These offsets, he calculated, would favor him.

Johnson still had to push the 1964 Civil Rights Bill among his own kind in the Southern States. MSNBC reporter Adam Serwer wrote the following in recounting the run-up to passing the Act:

In Senate cloakrooms and staff meetings, Johnson was practically a connoisseur of the word. According to Johnson biographer Robert Caro, Johnson would calibrate his pronunciations by region, using "nigra" with some southern legislators and "negra" with others.

---

[37] "Inside the White House: The Hidden Lives of the Modern Presidents and the Secrets of the World's Most Powerful Institution," Ronald Kessler, published in 1995

Discussing civil rights legislation with men like Mississippi Democrat James Eastland, who committed most of his life to defending white supremacy, he'd simply call it the nigger bill.[38]

Some of his defenders believe Johnson's language was part of political ploys to persuade fellow Democrats to support civil rights. However, it must also be noted that LBJ's voting record while in Congress from 1937 to 1957 was overwhelmingly anti-Civil Rights. Barrack Obama even noted this in a 2014 speech at the Civil Rights Summit. In 1957, LBJ suddenly became a civil rights advocate. It's much more likely that he was acting on political ambition and a well-computed political calculus more than any conversion of the heart. The SCOTUS was striking down discrimination with every case it heard. The writing was indeed on the wall, and Johnson could, at the very least, read it.

After the tragic assassination of JFK, now President Johnson pushed hard for the Civil Rights Bill to pass Congress in time for him to sign it before the election of 1964. He desperately wanted to steal the limelight from his opponent, Barry Goldwater, who was often portrayed as unsympathetic to the common man because of his strident small government rhetoric.

Small government did not appeal to black people. They had become accustomed to government intervention, though justified, as a means to right the wrongs of the past. Johnson's gambit ultimately worked, and he won the election of 1964. In the end, LBJ did the right thing for the wrong reasons. For the downtrodden, the grace of God sometimes arrives through the most unlikely conduits.

Meanwhile, the Republicans were following what was known as the Southern Strategy. This was a ploy to attract Southern Democrats who, excluding race issues, felt their party was drifting too far to the

---

[38] MSNBC Online Article, "Lyndon Johnson was a civil rights hero. But also a racist," April 11, 2014

left. Remember this was also the Cold War Era. The Southern Strategy also partly contributed to blacks moving away from Republicans who they began to view as abandoning their cause of equal rights. So, the power base of both parties was undergoing a realignment, and the political poles flipped. Black voters have been supporting Democrats over Republicans in a 90-10 ratio ever since.

The Great Society

Any discussion of LBJ's impact on black communities must include his Great Society and his War on Poverty initiatives. The statistics surrounding these initiatives are inordinately complex. Depending on who is performing the analysis and their perspective, LBJ's War on Poverty is either cast as a vital humanitarian success or an abysmal failure. In Johnson's rhetoric, poverty was to be combated like we fought and won wars in the past.

> On similar occasions in the past we have often been called upon to wage war against foreign enemies which threatened our freedom. Today we are asked to declare war on a domestic enemy which threatens the strength of our nation and the welfare of our people. If we now move forward against this enemy—if we can bring to the challenges of peace the same determination and strength which has brought us victory in war—then this day and this Congress will have won a secure and honorable place in the history of the nation and the enduring gratitude of generations of Americans yet to come.[39]

Years later, Ronald Reagan quipped, "We waged a war on poverty, and poverty won." There is definitely data to support Reagan's perspective. The data also shows that despite an ever-increasing total population, the percentage of poor, or the poverty rate, has remained

[39] Special Message to Congress, Lyndon B. Johnson, March 16,1964

relatively constant since the late 1960s. For now, I'll present the observable facts based on data I've been able to collect from reputable sources.

To begin the analysis, I'll repeat the graph from Chapter 4 for your ease of reference in Figure 6-1. In Chapter 4, this graph helped make a case for capitalism. I discussed how despite extraordinary population growth in the America over the same time period, we actually had about six million fewer people living in poverty by 2019 in the pre-COVID era than we did in 1959. The number of poor of course fluctuates with economic booms and busts. Notice how the number of unemployed rises with each recession and then falls during periods of economic recovery.

Only a robust free market society could devote the amount of money we've spent on assistance for the poor. Yet the problem persists, and the total number of poor continues to grow. Consider that every dollar removed from the economy by government spending is a dollar that has not been put to work in more productive ways. Out-of-control spending always acts as a damper on economic growth.

From 1965 to the present, we have spent in excess of $20 trillion on welfare and Medicaid programs combined. The War on Poverty has spawned over 122 government programs. The top thirteen of which constitute the bulk of the spending. Reports from the bureaucracies that manage these programs cast each of them as resounding successes. Can you ever expect a bureaucrat to say, "My program is failing. It should be canceled?" These programs are what you call self-licking ice cream cones that become job programs for those that run them. They are almost guaranteed to continue in perpetuity.

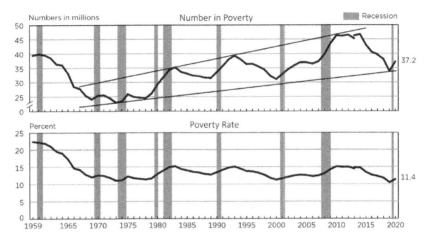

Figure 6-1: Number in Poverty and Poverty Rate: 1959 to 2019 (Population as of March of the following year)[40]

The chart in Figure 6-1 is also telling about the dubious results of the War on Poverty. In the period before the Great Society programs started having their effect, America underwent a period of tremendous economic prosperity. This was the post-WWII period of economic expansion. The poverty rate declined by about 11%. From 1965 onward, the poverty rate has been locked in a channel between 10.5 and 15% despite the trillions spent to eradicate it.

While the strength of our free-market system has been proven to lift people out of poverty, the statistics also show that our country maintains a permanent percentage of its population in poverty. As the population grows, so does the total number of people in poverty. With each recession, the number thrown into poverty by economic hardship also increases. The total number of poor in the country has been on a long-term increasing trend since the start of the Great Society programs.

---

[40] Source US Census Bureau, "Income and Poverty in the United States: 2020," September 2021

Further, statistics on economic mobility are even more complex. To unequivocally assert that welfare programs help people out of poverty, it would take a sustained longitudinal study of cohorts of welfare recipients to show that government assistance creates a floor from which people can rise out of poverty. There are indicators that recidivism is high among welfare recipients. In other words, people may get off welfare for a short while only to return because the root causes of their dependency have not been truly addressed.

In my research, I discovered an organization called Stand Together that had placed an advertisement on The Guardian website. The ad contained a thoughtful commentary on poverty that struck me as balanced and insightful written by people who work with the poor daily:

> On the micro level, the on-the-ground research from S+, in corroboration with findings from the Centre for Social Justice, has found five significant factors driving poverty today:
>
> - Chronic unemployment
> - Personal debt
> - Educational failure
> - Addiction and trauma
> - The breakdown of the family
>
> Major drivers of poverty rarely occur in isolation but are interconnected with one another. They stack together, compounding the complexity of the individual's scenario and increasing the barriers to escape.
>
> The opportunity to escape the cyclical poverty trap can only be initialized through a solution as layered and complex as the problem: personalized treatment (i.e., tailored case management), powered by local

knowledge of individuals and social entrepreneurs inside communities.

How can any massive, bureaucratic, wasteful government program generate sustained "tailored case management" when they consistently push one-size-fits-all solutions? The causes of poverty are only partly societal and mostly deeply personal.

For example, for those born into poverty and suffering early trauma, the difficulty of escape is compounded. A child who is molested or otherwise abused is likely to develop serious self-esteem issues and possibly much deeper psychological problems. The likelihood of then turning to drug and alcohol abuse increases along with a cycle of early sexual exploration that in turn leads to unwanted pregnancy. Still, everyone must own their decisions good or bad, but the government bureaucracy is not equipped to help someone heal from trauma as a step toward leading a productive life.

The breakdown of the family probably has the most significant impact on early childhood development and ultimate success in adulthood. The welfare system rewards out-of-wedlock childbirths. If a welfare mother with a child gets pregnant and has another child, she will receive more money. With each subsequent birth, the size of the check increases.

In November 2014, Thomas Sowell, opined on the impacts of liberalism on Black Americans in response to an article by Nicholas Kristof written for the New York Times. Sowell had first-hand experience with poverty and as a black youth growing up in Harlem. His thoughts and observations certainly carry weight:

Nearly a hundred years of the supposed "legacy of slavery" found most black children [78%] being raised in two-parent families in 1960. But thirty years after the liberal welfare state found the great majority of black children being raised by a single parent [66%].

Public housing projects in the first half of the 20th century were clean, safe places, where people slept outside on hot summer nights, when they were too poor to afford air conditioning. That was before admissions standards for public housing projects were lowered or abandoned, in the euphoria of liberal non-judgmental notions. And it was before the toxic message of victimhood was spread by liberals. We all know what hell holes public housing has become in our times. The same toxic message produced similar social results among lower-income people in England, despite an absence of a "legacy of slavery" there.

If we are to go by evidence of social retrogression, liberals have wreaked more havoc on blacks than the supposed "legacy of slavery" they talk about.

Fatherless households are more than five times as likely to live in poverty.[41]

One must ask if Black Americans would have been better off if they were just left alone after being freed. Frederick Douglass certainly thought so. Here was his response in 1862 to the question of freed slaves; what shall be done with them?

Our answer is, do nothing with them; mind your business, and let them mind theirs. Your doing with them is their greatest misfortune. They have been undone by your doings, and all they now ask, and really have need of at your hands, is just to let them alone. They suffer by every interference and succeed best by being let alone. The Negro should have been let alone in Africa—let alone when the pirates and robbers offered him for sale in our Christian slave markets—more cruel and inhuman than the Mohammedan slave markets—let alone by courts, judges, politicians, legislators and slavedrivers—let alone

---

[41] Source US Census Bureau, "Income and Poverty in the United States: 2020," September 2021

altogether, and assured that they were thus to be let alone forever, and that they must now make their own way in the world, just the same as any and every other variety of the human family. As colored men, we only ask to be allowed to do with ourselves, subject only to the same great laws for the welfare of human society which apply to other men, Jews, Gentiles, Barbarian, Scythian. Let us stand upon our own legs, work with our own hands, and eat bread in the sweat of our own brows. When you, our white fellow countrymen, have attempted to do anything for us, it has generally been to deprive us of some right, power or privilege which you yourself would die before you would submit to have taken from you.

Of particular interest is the foreshadowing of the results created by the welfare state in his statement, "When you, our white fellow countrymen, have attempted to do anything for us, it has generally been to deprive us of some right, power, or privilege..." Is that not really the aim of today's welfare state and victim mentality propaganda?

Malcolm X, the controversial civil rights activist of the 1960s, saw leftists for what they are—opportunists who began to use "help" in the form of social spending as the new shackles to keep black people under control, to ensure they think only about voting Democrat, and to prevent them from ever fully embracing the bounty of American citizenship. LBJ's goal of keeping Black Americans voting Democrat for the next 200 years has so far worked "to a T." Malcolm X held this view of liberals:

> There are many whites who are trying to solve the problem, but you never see them going under the label of liberals. That white person that you see calling himself a liberal is the most dangerous thing in the entire western hemisphere. He's the most deceitful. He's like a fox and a fox is always more dangerous in the forest than the wolf. You can see the wolf coming. You know what he's up to. But the fox will fool you. He comes at you with his mouth shaped in such a way that

even though you see his teeth you think he's smiling and taking [you] for a friend.

I do not agree with much of Malcolm X's rhetoric, but he certainly pegged the leftist playbook for what it is. Malcolm X and Thomas Sowell were on the same page on this particular issue. Sometimes people from opposing political angles see the same thing.

So, Where Is All the Systemic Racism?

To finally answer the question, we must define what we mean by a system. First, let's define the system as the governing structure created by the Constitution, modern law, and official government policy. If that is the definition of a system, then, as stated earlier, the answer is a resounding no—systemic racism does not exist. There is nothing codified in law today that even remotely promotes racism against black people. The Constitution has repeatedly been the framework that ultimately led to the proper court decisions supporting equality under the law.

But systems can exist in pockets beyond the Constitution. Systems can be formed by the foxes that Malcolm X railed against. Systems can be built around government institutions that are disguised as help, but in reality, are corrosive to the human spirit.

In the Antebellum South, blacks were enslaved and kept on plantations. In the Postbellum South, they were socially and economically oppressed. Many were forced to return to the plantations as veritable slaves due to indebtedness created by the sharecropping system. It can be said, that LBJ's programs created a third trip to the plantation, where too many remain today. This Third Plantation is not a farm in a rural setting, but the large pockets of urban poverty we see in our large cities. The Third Plantation is a political containment structure born out of LBJ's Great Society and War on Poverty.

The welfare and public assistance culture is a tool that the Democrat Party uses to contain black voters and ensure that they never drift away from the new plantation—the Democrat Party.

As I said earlier, a favorite ploy of the leftist propagandist is projection—accusing the opposition of the very things of which the left is guilty. They cast any shred of black adversity into a white crime, when in reality, the Leftist Democrats are the real criminals. A leftist defender might say, "Yeah, but Democrat Party history is not who the Democrats are today. That was then and today things are different." Well, my answer to this is that we must insist on intellectual consistency in any argument. To do otherwise is illogical. If according to the CRT propaganda, all white people bear the burden of past sins against black people, and all whites are guilty of those sins regardless of whether they committed those sins themselves, shouldn't the same logic apply concerning the history of the Democrats?

Let's pretend that this reasoning generates unbearable cognitive dissonance in all leftists. Democrat leadership suddenly and magically sees the light and withdraws all support for CRT. They admit that burdening present-day White Americans with the sins of the past is a fallacy. Therefore, we also cannot lay blame for the past sins of Democrats at the feet of present-day Democrats. At that point we'll at least have reached some level of intellectual consistency, but there is just one problem. The Democrat Party continues to oppress black people to this very day. So, yes. Systemic racism does indeed exist, but it's not our Constitution, it's not in our laws, it's not in our hearts. Systemic racism exists at the core of Democrat Party ideology driven by leftists as its sole purveyors.

If the Democrat Party were genuinely interested in helping black people, it would heed the words of Frederick Douglas. It would support replacing the failing public school system with school choice as the new centerpiece. It would reward two-parent households and remove incentives that create fatherless families. If the Democrat Party were genuinely interested in black people, safety would be a priority for crime-ridden black neighborhoods instead of supporting police defunding movements. If it were genuinely interested, it would not deliberately create a gaping hole in our southern border for unchecked illegal immigration that ruins job prospects for minorities. A genuinely caring Democrat Party would not permit the torrent of deadly drugs that disproportionately kill black people and is coming across that same porous southern border. If the Democrat party cared at all about black people, it would not promote abortion—another social ill that again disproportionately kills black people. If it cared in the least, black lives would matter to them for real.

But the truth is the Democrat Party has only contempt for black people. History shows that it always has. Joe Biden has such disdain for black people as individuals that he has the audacity to say things like, "I'll tell you if you have a problem figuring out whether you're for me or for Trump, then you ain't black." The left is rotten to the core, and today's leftist ideology embraced by the Democrat Party is simply the progeny of rot.

CHAPTER 7

Marxism on the March

"For as in absolute governments the King is law, so in free countries the law ought to be King; and there ought to be no other."

—*Thomas Paine, Common Sense, 1776*

Before the 2008 election, how much did you hear about racism? Racism appeared to be a thing of the past. It seemed like America had finally put to rest the egregious mistreatment of blacks. It appeared that we were well on our way to becoming a race-neutral society. Instead, society went off the rails. Here's a tale to illustrate the missed opportunity and what could have been.

An American Tale

Explorers discover a new land during an age driven by conquest and colonization. Through many tribulations, courageous pioneers escaping persecution carve out a new existence in a land of abundance. Evil would follow them to their new shores. Slavery, the ultimate debasement of fellow human beings, infects the new land like a plague just as it already had infected other continents for thousands of years before.

The new land courageously fights a war against overwhelming odds and becomes its own country. It is now free to establish its own just laws based on the concept of self-government and the laws of Almighty God—a concept unique in the world to this day. But evil would not relent.

Much blood would be shed to right the wrongs of the past. A great war and many fights would ensue until finally after 232 years, the new land achieved a society where the color of one's skin did not matter much at all. Though still not a perfect society, systemic racism was finally dead and rotting in the ground.

As a climactic symbol of healing, this now great country elects a man, half-black and half-white, to be its leader. He becomes a living symbol of healing. He declares that he is living proof of how far the country has progressed. On behalf of both races, he declares forgiveness and healing. The country is united in patriotic love, and the man is revered by all citizens as a wise and magnanimous leader.

Such a nice fiction. In real life, happy endings are most elusive.

The Obama Legacy

We now know all too well that events did not go down that way. Instead of wisdom and magnanimity, Barrack Obama proved himself to be power-hungry, greedy, and small. Almost from his first days in office, he began delivering divisive rhetoric based on race to pit Americans against one another. Instead of healing, he unleashed national division. The question is why?

Obama spoke early and often in his campaign about the remaking of America. "Hope and change" was his campaign motto. Hope in what? Change to what? Certainly, no member of the corrupt legacy media ever called his hand. We see the change Obama set in motion now unfolding before us. Instead of national unity, his legacy is the delivery of America into leftist control using race as the primary tool.

So, what drives a man like Obama? I can only speculate. No man can see into the heart of another. That is a power reserved for God. There are people in this world that crave power above all else. The prime motivating force is control over others. If I had to guess, I would speculate that Barry wants to be like Vlad. I would think that Barrack Obama wants the power that Vladimir Putin enjoys in Russia.

One event gives me a hint into Obama's psyche. You may remember a 2012 incident when Obama was caught on an open microphone whispering to the Russian President Dmitry Medvedev, who at the time was the placeholder president, while Putin was temporarily serving as prime minister. During this period, Putin was cunningly engineering an end-run around the Russian Constitution to help ensure his perpetual presidency. Medvedev was temporarily handed the reins of power. Here's how the exchange between Obama and Medvedev unfolded:

Obama: On all these issues, but particularly missile defense, this can be solved but it's important for him [Vladimir Putin] to give me space.

Medvedev: Yes, I understand. I understand your message about space. Space for you...

Obama: This is my last election. After my election I have more flexibility."

Medvedev: I understand. I will transmit this information to Vladimir.

The dialogue reveals a few interesting characteristics about Obama. First, he's a chatty fellow who doesn't know how to hold his tongue around potentially hot microphones that pick up his every word. Second is his duplicitous nature of saying one thing in public and doing the exact opposite when the cameras are off. At the time of the incident, he was approaching re-election. He wanted to appear tough on the Russians and strong on defense, but privately he was ready to give away the farm to please Putin. Third, his servile demeanor demonstrated through the comments hints at someone who admires Putin, views him as superior in stature, and wants desperately to be liked by him. This also hints at a desire to be like the man he admires.

Why does an American president need "space" to be granted by his supposed adversary? It's stupid to even ask for a favor like that as a precursor to crucial negotiations having geopolitical impact. This tells the adversary, "I'm in a bind and you can help me." If your adversary helps you, then you are psychologically in his debt. Right away, you owe him something. Indeed, a dumb setup for a negotiation. Asking for space places Obama in an inferior negotiating position. Obama felt psychologically smaller than Putin. Asking for space also means Obama likes Putin and feels comfortable asking for a favor. He thinks the feeling is mutual. This foolish and unnecessary banter reveals a telling layer of Obama's character. It would have been funny if like the soup Nazi on Seinfeld, Medvedev had replied, "NO SPACE FOR YOU!"

Remember how gaslighters project? They accuse their target of doing the very thing they are doing in secret. Leftist gaslighters always accused Donald Trump of having an unexplained affinity for Putin. This was a simple propaganda ploy with no basis in fact. The reality is that Obama has an unexplained affinity for the Russian strongman.

There once had been intermittent speculation of Obama possibly being nominated to the Supreme Court. The idea was akin to a juvenile progressive's erotic fantasy and not an actual probability. Obama loves power, money, and elitism. Being a supreme court justice is beneath his massive ego and would be constraining to his lifestyle. After occupying the most powerful office in the world as a chief executive, why would he want to be part of a group of nine? As we saw with President Biden's first opportunity to nominate a Supreme Court justice, Obama was never mentioned among the field of potential nominees. He is actually far more powerful and dangerous operating in the shadows through his cloak and dagger-style activism. After all, he is "Mr. Lead-From-Behind."

I suspect that Obama would gladly return to the presidency if only a piece of parchment didn't stand in his way. Should the Constitution be shredded by his leftist proxies, the road would be cleared for him to return. In the meantime, his influence remains profound.

The Biden administration is filled with Obama loyalists who maneuver Biden while they continue Obama's work in earnest. These people tolerate Biden and Harris, but they adore Obama with the devotion of cult followers. As USA Today reported, 75% of the top 100 aides in the Biden administration worked for Obama in some capacity.[42] What is the likelihood that they no longer communicate with the former president?

You'll find Valerie Jarrett at the center of "all things Obama." In March 2021, the Washington Post (WAPO) reported that Jarrett would join the board of the nonprofit Civic Nation as its chairwoman.[43] That article cites Jarrett as saying: "The gang's all back together again." She also added that she hoped the changes to Civic Nation would "expand the reach of what we can do." According to WAPO, "That expansion includes providing outside support to the new administration, which is stocked with its own cadre of Obama alums."

Another top Obama confident, Susan Rice, currently serves as Biden's Director of the White House Domestic Policy Council. She appears to be the perfect inside contact to act as Jarrett's touchpoint.

---

[42] USA Today article, "Biden insists his presidency is not a third Obama term; his staff picks suggest otherwise," June 16, 2021 by Maureen Groppe

[43] Washington Post article, "Obama alumni group reshuffles as the Biden administration launches," March 11, 2021, by Annie Linskey

The Barrack Obama connection to policies we're seeing from the Biden administration is evident. Former Obama aides formulate the policy for Biden to rubber stamp and then stumble through as he tries his best to regurgitate them at the presidential teleprompter.

The odds are close to zero that Joe Biden is driving the leftist juggernaut. Former Obama aides, who were hand-picked by and proudly wear the imprimatur of the former president, are the ones driving the bus. And they have help. Those aids aren't dreaming up these anti-American policies on their own either. The blueprint is being fed to them from think tanks funded by globalist elites such as billionaire leftist financier George Soros and possibly other participants in the World Economic Forum. All of this is done with the blessing of Barrack Hussein Obama who occasionally chimes in to give things a nudge. When he wants something done, he can just pick up his phone.

The Great Protectors of Democracy

In March of 2021, Biden issued Executive Order (EO) 14019 directing federal agencies to promote voter registration. Each agency was to formulate a plan to boost voter registration, promote vote by mail ballots, and provide election information. EO 14019 directs agencies to consider ways to expand access to voter registration and election information. This includes "soliciting and facilitating approved, nonpartisan third-party organizations and State officials to provide voter registration services on agency premises."

Who will approve these third-party organizations? What is the likelihood that the selected third parties will genuinely be nonpartisan? Who funds these organizations? Will our leftist "protectors of democracy" issue hundreds of millions if not billions of dollars in grants to these organizations to help ensure the leftists seize and retain power forever? Since these organizations will be performing these activities on "agency premises," the leftists will even provide the office space for their underhanded plans.

Within 200 days of the EO, agencies were expected to submit their plans. The plans were to be presented to none other than Susan Rice, Director of the White House Domestic Policy Council. The Obama team is really running the show at Pennsylvania Avenue while decrepit Biden dozes off at his desk in the oval office—if he's ever even there.

The justification of EO 14019 is of course racism, but the White House has also masked the EO as assistance for Americans with disabilities. The preamble to Biden's order reads as follows:

> The right to vote is the foundation of American democracy. Free and fair elections that reflect the will of the American people must be protected and defended. But many Americans, especially people of color, confront significant obstacles to exercising that fundamental right. These obstacles include difficulties with voter registration, lack of election information, and barriers to access at polling places. For generations, black voters and other voters of color have faced discriminatory policies and other obstacles that disproportionally affect their communities.

This is typical gaslighting and cherry-picking of history. Many laws and intimidation tactics were carried out to keep black people from voting in the past. That was then. Now, no such environment exists. Leftist gaslighters continue to use bygone racist conditions to pretend that people of color are still systemically oppressed, and their votes are suppressed.

Recent voting laws passed in Georgia and other states, are explicitly designed to make voting accessible while limiting opportunities for fraud. In other words, easy to vote, but difficult to cheat. The leftist position on such laws insinuates that people of color are somehow just too dumb to meet basic requirements like obtaining an ID required to cast a ballot legally. It is impossible to function in today's society without some form of identification. Even if you don't have a driver's license, it's easy to obtain a state ID at your local DMV.

Exactly what obstacles do people of color face? These are never discussed, but you are supposed to accept the dogma without question. When Georgia passed its Election Integrity Act in March 2021, it sparked a vicious reaction from the left. The law was tagged as the new Jim Crow simply because it requires an ID to cast a ballot and requires that ballot drop boxes be secured. Compared to Biden's home state of Delaware, Georgia's law actually provides broader access to the ballot. If Georgia's law is the new Jim Crow, what shall we call the laws in Biden's home state? Laws like the one passed by the Georgia Legislature limit voter fraud, and that is what the left hates.

Woke corporations quickly condemned the Georgia Law. Coca-Cola, headquartered in Atlanta, condemned the law with CEO, James Quincey issuing this statement in his official capacity:

> We want to be crystal clear and state unambiguously that we are disappointed in the outcome of the Georgia voting legislation. Throughout Georgia's legislative session we provided feedback to members of both legislative chambers and political parties, opposing measures in the bills that would diminish or deter access to voting.
>
> Our approach has always been to work with stakeholders to advocate for positive change, and we will continue to engage with legislators, advocacy groups, business leaders and others to work towards ensuring broad access to voting is available to every eligible voter in our home state.
>
> Additionally, our focus is now on supporting federal legislation that protects voting access and addresses voter suppression across the country. We all have a duty to protect everyone's right to vote, and we will continue to stand up for what is right in Georgia and across the U.S.

However, at its shareholder meetings, Coca-Cola requires an ID to gain entrance and to cast a vote as a shareholder. But the almost sacred right to vote for our elected officials deserves no such protection.

Delta Airlines also headquartered in Atlanta followed suit with its own condemnation. Major League Baseball moved its All-star game from Atlanta with a population that is 51% black to Colorado with a population that is 71% white because that really helped hardworking black Americans. Stacey Abrams, former candidate for Georgia Governor, and perennial leftist activist, encouraged these responses to the detriment of her own constituents and fellow black citizens. Leftists are all about power. They really don't care at all about you, and they certainly care a whole lot less about black people. To the left, the average Black American is nothing more than a pawn.

Then there is House Resolution 1 (HR1), also known as the "For the People Act of 2021." This is the left's most brazen play of all in trying to use the power of the Federal Government to cement their own grip on power. It is an exceedingly shameless tactic designed to crush all commonsense protections legally enacted by the states as part of their Constitutionally granted powers to administer elections. It is so shameless it should be named the "Screw the People Forever Act."

HR1 essentially makes permanent all the worst illegally implemented modifications to voting processes that many states enacted during the 2020 election under the guise of COVID protection. HR1 would make voting by mail, same day voter registration, and vote harvesting permanent options.

The Screw the People Forever Act would also weaponize the Internal Revenue Service as a partisan organization that could deny nonprofit status to organizations engaging in political activity. If you recall, the IRS was already once weaponized against conservatives.

In 2012, Lois Lerner, Director of the IRS' Exempt Organizations Unit targeted conservative organizations by either denying them tax exempt status or simply slow rolling their applications until they could no longer influence the election. Of course, she was never criminally charged because Obama's justice department hacks only found her culpable of "mismanagement, poor judgment, and institutional inertia." How convenient. HR1 would now make her corrupt actions legal and authorized by law.

Lastly, HR1 would ban all state voter ID laws by simply allowing individuals to sign a paper stating that they are who they say they are. No ID needed. Interestingly, under the COVID chokehold that leftist mayors and governors placed on their citizens, patrons of public establishments had to show their vaccination cards and some form of ID to do simple things like having a meal in a restaurant. But voting? No ID…no problem. I'm so thankful we have leftist ideologues to protect our democracy. Aren't you?

As of this writing, HR1 was passed by the House but does not have the votes to pass in the Senate. The bill is stalled and hopefully never sees the light of day again.

Follow the Money – The Left Gets Rich

Like HR1, the Build Back Better (BBB) plan was a key plank in the leftist scheme to ensure they maintain control forever. Also known as HR 5376, Nancy Pelosi and her loyalists in the House passed their outrageous multi-trillion dollar "social infrastructure" bill. The bill was an orgy of spending that would make a drunken sailor look like a prudent fiscal steward. Fortunately, it did not survive in the Senate. Two Democrat senators somehow discovered their inner voice of reason and took a stand against the bill– Joe Manchin (D-WV) and Kyrsten Sinema (D-AZ). Their refusal to support the ghastly bill gave the Republicans enough votes to stop the

insanity. Their resistance to spending trillions more in an inflation-
ary environment for extreme leftist pet programs that the American
taxpayer does not need, has at least pumped the breaks on America's
accelerating fall toward Marxism.

If passed, this multi-trillion-dollar behemoth would have extended the poisonous tentacles of big government in ways that
would forever change American Society. For example, $88B in addi-
tional funding for the Internal Revenue Service would increase that
agency's budget by 70%. This coupled with another leftist proposal
to require banks to monitor all transactions as low as $600 would
give the government a dangerous level of control over the lives of
every American. If you think the left was quick to weaponize the IRS
against political opponents before, imagine what the IRS could be
used for with this kind of power.

BBB would also have created a total takeover of daycare. Since
clearly the existing leftist monopoly on public education is not
enough, the care of newborns to age five would be placed in the
hands of the state providing a mechanism for the earliest possible
indoctrination of highly impressionable children.

The bill would have provided billions in assistance to illegal al-
iens, fund every conceivable green energy scheme, and created massive new environmental regulations that would choke industry and
dramatically increase the cost of energy for everyone. BBB would
have immensely expanded the welfare state providing billions to
people without any requirement for work. This was a backdoor attempt at establishing the Marxist dream of Universal Basic Income
(UBI), where everyone receives a basic amount of money from the
government for doing absolutely nothing.

BBB included a back door for the start of reparations by establishing a $775 million program to make payments of up to $500,000 per
farmer, rancher, or forest landowner determined to have experienced discrimination in Department of Agriculture farm lending

programs before January 1, 2021. How discrimination of that sort could be proven would likely defy the powers of Sherlock Holmes.

Since the housing debacle of 2008 was not a sufficient teachable moment for our leftist dimwits in Congress, they decided to include additional extreme meddling in the housing market once again. It may sound harsh, but there's a reason why low-income people can't get a mortgage—they can't make the payments. The only way to fix this problem is to create opportunities for low-income people to increase their earning power. This simple concept escapes the leftist do-gooder. So, they baked another mortgage scheme into the BBB because they learned absolutely nothing from the resulting 2008 financial crisis.

The bill would have provided "such sums as necessary to support payments to economically distressed borrowers." In addition, BBB would have provided the following:

- $6.8 billion for a new down payment assistance program to provide free down payments to first-time and first-generation homebuyers,
- $4 billion for federally guaranteed 20-year mortgages for "first-time" and "first generation" homebuyers,
- and $76 million for a program to increase access to small-dollar mortgages.

You may be wondering, why waste the "ink" on discussing a bill that was killed in the legislative process? Answer: the discussion sheds light on the vast corruption of our leftist leaders, and also because this legislative zombie will surely rise from the grave if the American public and our few remaining sane legislators do not maintain their vigilance. Remember, Marxists are relentless. As I write this, leftists in Congress are busy chopping up their moonshot bill into smaller pieces and trying to tuck parts of it into other unrelated bills under consideration.

Profligate spending damages America in many ways. The first and most obvious is the massive expansion and consolidation of government power, leading to the tightening of leftist control on virtually every aspect of society.

Then there's the destructive effects on the economy. Such massive spending creates some jobs in the short run, but these are not jobs that add to the nation's Gross Domestic Product (GDP) as efficiently as those created by the private sector. In effect, jobs created by government spending are a form of national overhead. The majority are a net cost to the economy. The hiring binge required to enact trillions in spending causes competition for labor with the private sector leading to worker shortages in just about every sector of the economy and driving up costs everywhere.

Further, trillions of dollars suddenly flooding the economy ignite inflation, which as of February 2022 is currently running at 7.2% annually. This is devastating to middle and lower-class Americans. One dollar you hold today will be worth just 69 cents within five years. Inflation is our debtor government's best friend. The government borrows today and repays the debt with cheaper money tomorrow. To you, inflation is your worst financial enemy.

Lastly, such vast sums are unmanageable. The public cannot possibly ever receive an accounting of where every dollar is spent. Insane spending levels are fertile ground for corruption, and that's the way our crooked politicians like it. While devastating to the average American, government largess always favors the elites. For example, money is often funneled to friends through nonprofits and Non-Governmental Organizations (NGOs) who may receive a grant under some ill-conceived leftist program. They spend a fraction of the money on the specific cause, pay high salaries to their friends, and make political contributions back to leftist candidates who run for re-election and start the cycle of corruption all over again. The word "grants" appears 631 times in H.R. 5376.

Accountability for results is typically not a requirement under grant programs. Even when the nonprofit or NGO is "pure in spirit" and is trying to actually make a positive impact, how exactly is success measured? Often the government imposes heavy administrative requirements that consume portions of the grant money just to pay for people to do the reporting. Some reporting is essential, but is progress toward the ultimate goal being measured or is activity the only thing being measured? Too often, it's the latter—measurement of activity. This is why so many billions are wasted on social programs that, at best, have only a marginally positive effect while often having many unintended consequences. The Great Society initiatives are a prime example.

The political machine doesn't really care about solving problems. It cares about keeping the river of cash flowing. Nonprofits and NGOs that feed at the government trough are an industry. Thousands of people are employed at these organizations with the primary goal of perpetuating their own existence. Perpetuating their existence means ensuring that politicians who support their quixotic causes remain in office. The best way to ensure their own survival is to funnel money back to the political campaigns of leftist politicians. And the machine goes 'round.

The Age of Propaganda

"The point about the press is that it is not what it is called. It is not the popular press. It is not the public press. It is not an organ of public opinion. It is a conspiracy of a very few millionaires, all sufficiently similar in type to agree on the limits of what this great nation (to which we belong) may know about itself and its friends and enemies."

—G.K. Chesterton, *The Tyranny of Bad Journalism*, 1917

Free people do not welcome Marxism overnight. They must be groomed. First, they are deceived. Then they are gradually subjugated and ultimately controlled. These goals cannot be achieved without a complicit and corrupt media that abets the left by distorting some facts and deliberately suppressing coverage of other facts and events that may prove damaging to the left. Welcome to the Age of Propaganda.

Deceit

What we saw decades ago in Nazi Germany and the Soviet Union was nothing compared to the power of propaganda in the internet age. The left has managed to control the narrative across vast segments of the legacy media as well. When you channel-surf between newscasts on major networks, you see the exact same stories with ubiquitous punch phrases and key points. It's all scripted.

Leftists have become highly effective in suppressing the truth. We see increasing evidence that cancel culture and online censorship are driven by Big Tech in collusion with Leftist Democrats. Their tools for advancing deceit are indeed formidable. Through these tools they deceive by promoting self-loathing and fear.

Self-Loathing

In Chapter 2, I covered all the most common ways that gaslighting leftists deceive Americans. To reduce America to a state of self-loathing, they have chosen race as the wedge. If people would take the time to investigate the actual statistics, they could quickly demolish all leftist lies about America. For example, in 2021, 60 police officers were killed in the line of duty, with 314 officers shot. Conversely, police killed 1,055 people of all races with only 15 being unarmed.[44] If you believed the media hype, you would think that police are shooting unarmed citizens, particularly black men, simply for sport. Statistics also show that police officers are less likely to use deadly force against black suspects.

Meanwhile, according to the last published report by the CDC in 2017 on the leading causes of death for young black males, homicide topped the list. For ages 1-19, 35.3% of deaths were due to homicide. For ages 20-44, homicide again tops the list at 27.6%. The vast majority of these homicides are committed by other black men. This is a sad but true statistic. Do these black lives matter to Black Lives Matter?[45]

---

[44] Center on Media, Crime, and Justice at John Jay College

[45] CDC Report on Leading Causes of Death – Males – Non-Hispanic black (https://www.cdc.gov/healthequity/lcod/men/2017/nonhispanic-black/index.htm)

Leftist lies are strengthened by the cult of celebrity when people like Lebron James, Cher, Kareem Abdul-Jabbar, Will Smith, Alyssa Milano, Jeff Daniels, Rob Reiner and many, many more all mindlessly repeat the racism claptrap. Then there is the Prince of Racism himself, Colin Kaepernick, who, during his biographic documentary, compared the NFL to modern day slavery. Believe it. I'm not capable of making up such stupid suppositions.

Every year the NFL holds what it calls the Combine to evaluate potential players before the draft. Players are assessed using various physical measures related to their football abilities. Apparently, poor Colin felt that this is comparable to a slave market. Again, the motivation can only be one of two things—deliberate deceit for personal gain, which would make him evil, or extreme stupidity. I'm sure he'll never sit down with an honest intellectual to debate the shaky foundation of his claims. He would be exposed in seconds.

Here's the reality. The Combine is more akin to a job interview for athletes where if they impress enough scouts, the athletes stand to make tens of millions of dollars. Everyone is there voluntarily. When I compare this to the descriptions of real slave markets provided by Frederick Douglass, if I were the descendent of slaves, I would feel deeply insulted by Kaepernick's comparison. And indeed, he denigrates every descendent of former slaves with his self-serving, attention-seeking behavior. I wish Kaepernick could somehow go back in time and trade places with one of Frederick Douglass' contemporaries. He would then precisely know what it means to be enslaved.

People routinely swallow garbage like Kaepernick's bio doc because they have very limited knowledge of true history, and too many Americans have limited capacity for critical thinking. Critical thinking is increasingly being deleted as a goal of education and replaced with rote memorization of facts the system wants children to know to pass a standardized test. No critical thinking required.

Our school systems have ensured that the minds of our youth are made dim by the very people entrusted with educating them. Most kids are not even aware of current events. If they were, they would know that the great social justice warrior, Kaepernick, has received millions from Nike, one of China's leading benefactors of slave labor. The same can be said of the NBA and Lebron James. Do you see any problem with their value system? Does anyone in the corrupt legacy media ever call them on their hypocrisy?

Corporate pandering plays right into the hands of the leftist propagandists. Many Fortune 100 corporations have jumped onto the leftist bandwagon by supporting and promoting CRT-based material and donating millions to BLM and other "social justice" organizations. Corporate pandering to leftist causes is a significant corrupting influence on our American foundation. When leftists push, woke CEOs quickly support their false narratives, as we saw earlier with the Delta Airlines and Coca-Cola examples regarding the Georgia voting law.

Our fashionably woke corporations are on the frontline of promoting the self-loathing dogma that America is a racialized society founded on racist principles. Employees are routinely subjected to humiliating training that supports the typical CRT narratives of white supremacy, often forcing employees to confess their white privilege and encouraging white employees to "cede power to persons of color." Such training has taken place at prominent corporations such as Bank of America, Lowe's, American Express, Verizon, CVS, Walmart, AT&T, and many more. Even the "House of Mouse," The Walt Disney Corporation, was recently exposed in whistleblower documents brought to light by reporter Chris Rufo that showed the company believes America was founded on systemic racism.[46]

Major defense contractors have launched CRT-based programs designed for executives and employees to admit and atone for their white privilege. This is really concerning since our defense companies build the weapon systems that keep America safe against aggressive rival superpowers. What happens when their workforce starts believing that America is a reprehensible country?

Of course, American professional sports leagues continue to be major outlets reinforcing the hate America messaging. The NBA, Major League Baseball, and the NFL have all dived headlong into the social justice arena, donating millions to leftist organizations and permitting on-field displays of solidarity with the deceptive social justice movement.

The divisions sown into our social fabric by the corrosive race-based ideology are even institutionalized through Environmental Social and Governance (ESG) standards driven by mammoth Wall Street firms such as BlackRock. While claiming to not be "woke" investors, they create a rating system for the world's largest corporations, similar to how the Chinese Government oppresses and controls its citizens every day using social credit scoring. BlackRock and many other financial institutions are beginning to score corporations based on their adherence to ESG standards as BlackRock defines them.

For example, BlackRock pushes ESG initiatives in the name of good capitalism. Blackrock manages trillions of investment dollars through a plethora of funds that hold stock in major corporations. They often gain multiple seats on corporate boards, thereby giving them direct management influence. They use their extraordinary financial and corporate governance power to push companies toward

---

[46] "Unmasking Woke Capitalism," By Chris Rufo, November 21, 2021

investments in often dubious green technology, while BlackRock holds investments in that very same green technology. When a major corporation receives a poor ESG assessment by BlackRock, it may be denied access to vital capital needed to fund its growth and operations. In effect, this is corporate blackmail and conflict of interest. Environmental activists have even proposed initiatives to deny access to capital for the entire oil industry. ESG is the tool they will use to destroy it.

Similarly, for the social portion of ESG investing, if corporations don't toe the line and launch equity, diversity, and inclusion programs, they can be punished by firms such as BlackRock. There is nothing wrong with promoting an inclusive race-neutral culture within a corporation. We have laws that prohibit discrimination. The vast majority of Americans support workplace cultures that value all employees equally. The problem is that companies often claim to create that culture by launching programs that advance the tenets of CRT. These are humiliating brainwashing programs that create division instead of unity among Americans.

To further anchor self-loathing culture into the world's economic structure, the World Economic Forum (WEF) wholeheartedly endorsed CRT. The WEF is a global organization of the ultra-wealthy elite. It is very much an oligarchy club. They are a group of self-proclaimed masters of the universe who claim to know what is best for you and me. Each year they put their phony climate concerns aside to fly to Davos, Switzerland on their private jets so they can formulate their schemes and plans on how to manipulate us lowly proles. I like to think of them as the Devils of Davos.

Capitalism and free-market societies are not without problems. No economic system is perfect. However, crony capitalism is the real problem, not the foundational principles of capitalism. The real problem is the collusion of the government ruling class with large corporations and society's elites. After all, those in power seek only to accumulate more power, thereby preserving and propagating their hegemony. The WEF is the ultimate club whereby billionaires and world leaders can collude to the determinant of the rest of us.

The WEF has been quietly implementing a plan called the Great Reset that seeks to rewrite the rules for the global economy. They are laying the groundwork through a well-organized network of global elites each tasked with attacking a particular area of western society. The Great Reset is essentially socialism for the entire globe. Their goal is to implement the Chinese system of capitalism for the chosen elites and socialism with total population control for the rest of us. They are steadily implementing their social credit system at the corporate level through ESG investing. As their plan advances, you can expect that to be broadened to states, cities, and individuals. You may dismiss this as an unfounded conspiracy theory at your own peril. Just research Claus Schwab and do your homework. He's really been quite open about the strategy and has written a book on the subject.[47]

The Great Reset also seeks to exploit the COVID-19 crisis to keep in place the societal controls and powers that western governments usurped in the name of keeping us safe. We can expect them to exploit any other world crisis that may arise to push their socialist agenda forward. While the WEF has endorsed CRT as a valid theory that claims to expose the racist underpinnings of modern western society, the WEF hypocrites say absolutely nothing about the atrocities being committed by the Chinese Communist Party (CCP) because they are all making money in China.

The CCP is literally committing genocide against multiple non-Han minorities. Among them are the Uyghur Muslims who are routinely enslaved, imprisoned, raped, and tortured. There is substantial evidence that forced organ harvesting and sterilization is also

---

[47] "What is the Great Reset," by Michael Rectenwald, Imprimis, December 2021

occurring on a systematic scale. Human Rights Watch estimates that the CCP has imprisoned as many as one million Uyghurs in concentration camps. The WEF hypocrites do not care. But somehow, in their minds, it is right to deceive western societies by encouraging self-loathing.

Recently, Chamath Palihapitiya, an American tech billionaire investor of Indian descent, caused a stir when he said he just "doesn't care about the Uyghurs." He cloaked himself in false moral superiority when he dared to draw moral equivalence between America and China. "If you're asking me, do I care about a segment of a class of people in another country? Not until we can take care of ourselves will I prioritize them over us," Palihapitiya said. His basis was the thousands of minorities who are incarcerated in the US for what he termed "ridiculous crimes."

Palihapitiya is also a part owner of an NBA franchise. The NBA is very popular in China, and anyone associated with the NBA pays the price if they dare speak out against the CCP. I'm sure he was not about to upset his business interests by offending his communist business connections. He even took it a step further. He chose to hand them a public relations victory by effectively denouncing America. This makes his comments even more contemptible.

I could not confirm if Palihapitiya is a member or even attends the WEF, but you can only imagine the ties that members of the WEF have to China. What's a little bit of slavery and genocide between business partners? Let's turn a blind eye and keep the money flowing. There are billions at stake, and we mustn't upset the Chinese. Lesson learned—when you dance with the devil, his stink rubs off on you.

CRT gaslighting now has the imprimatur of the most powerful billionaires on the planet. They have no credibility in taking a stand against western racism when they display intellectual duplicity by tearing down the west while remaining oblivious to Chinese slavery and genocide. They were either originators of self-loathing CRT ideology or saw it as another opportunity to advance their agenda of recasting the western world into global socialism.

Fear

Instilling fear in a population drives anxiety and causes people to blindly turn to their government for solutions. To create widespread fear, leaders need a powerful bogeyman that captures the nation's attention. The COVID-19 pandemic provided a golden bogeyman that allowed western governments to seize broad emergency powers and trigger vast wealth transfers to the global elite. The media-hyped mass hysteria surrounding the pandemic allowed governments to implement lockdowns, curtail the rights of peaceful assembly and freedom of religion, and alter election laws without legislative involvement.

In the early days of the pandemic, knowledge was scarce, and people were right to be afraid. Initial lockdowns billed as "two weeks to stop the spread" and essential to "flatten the curve" to prevent hospitals from being overrun with cases became protracted restrictions on freedom. The early restrictions were indeed instituted under the Trump Administration, but after Biden took office, the tactics quickly shifted toward oppressive mandates. The Biden Administration waged a campaign of deceit to stoke fear at every opportunity and force people to take COVID vaccines whether they needed them or not.

To this day, Democrats, who claim to be the party that follows science, ignore crucial pieces of science regarding the pandemic. Those with natural immunity are far more protected against reinfection with severe COVID than those who are simply vaccinated and have never had COVID. Despite the facts, the CDC practically ignores the value of natural immunity and forces everyone to get vaccinated and follow unnecessary restrictions.

The CDC has ignored nearly all therapeutics that thousands of doctors have used to cure COVID patients using cheap repurposed drugs. Instead, they push a one-size-fits-all solution of vaccinating the healthy while restricting the sick to its sanctioned death protocol. Not only have they ignored the science of therapeutics, but the Biden Administration has colluded with Big Tech and Big Pharma to silence anyone who publishes an alternative point of view on treatment or vaccine effectiveness. The media happily censors our most prominent expert frontline doctors who present any opposing viewpoints.

The CDC continues to push a COVID treatment protocol that ignores early intervention and instead places patients on a downward spiral that ends with a lonely death isolated in an intensive care unit with a ventilator tube shoved down one's throat. The CDC is complicit in the death of hundreds of thousands of Americans through what is best viewed as incompetence and, at worst, willful neglect to advance the left's authoritarian control agenda. The media has a full share of the blame as well.

The CDC's own data shows that the population segments most vulnerable to dying from COVID are the elderly and those with one or more comorbidities. Comorbidity is an underlying adverse health condition such as obesity or a compromised immune system. Ignoring all logic, the CDC persists in waging a campaign to require vaccinating children as young as five when the CDC's own data shows that healthy children are not at risk of dying from COVID. Injecting children with a vaccine they do not need is simply criminal.

Everything I've stated above regarding COVID treatment is fact. You can verify it by examining the CDC data and reading studies performed by reputable scientists whose voices have been suppressed. Their observations, documented successes, and scientifically valid studies have been shunned by journals that refuse to publish their papers. Look up interviews with Dr. Robert Malone, Dr. Peter McCullough, and Dr. Richard Urso. These men are genuine experts, not the progressive bureaucrats of the CDC. Courageous physicians have been successfully treating COVID patients while the nation has been forced to follow the dictates of Dr. Anthony Fauci, who hasn't seen a patient in thirty years.

Through the collusion of government and media, the deliberate stoking of fear, has led to a form of insanity known as mass formation psychosis. This is also known as the madness of crowds. It is the manipulation of people into focusing their attention exclusively on a particular leader or event. This leads to a form of hypnosis whereby the leader can then steer the population toward a specific goal. Mass formation psychosis is how the German people were groomed into persecuting Jews and acquiescing to genocide during the 1930s and 40s. In America's case, the goal is subjugating the masses, turning people into sheep, to advance control that can then be used for subsequent political purposes. Once deceived into self-loathing and agitated with fear, the people are ripe for subjugation.

Subjugation

For Marxism to take complete control, a fearful population that has also been brainwashed into self-loathing must now be subjugated. Multiple tools are available to the left in accomplishing this part of their agenda. I'll cover the three most potent: economic manipulation, crime, and weaponization of government.

Economic Manipulation

The first head of state of the former Soviet Union and devout Marxist, Vladimir Lenin, once stated, "The way to crush the bourgeoisie is to grind them between the millstones of taxation and inflation." An economically distressed population is significantly weakened in its ability to resist the creep of totalitarian control. Their resources are drained, and their spare time to support resistance movements is diminished as the demands of basic survival increase. What do we have today? Out of control inflation and an administration that is considering tax increases.

In its extreme application, this grinding of the population leads to people standing in line for hours just to buy a loaf of bread. Such was life in the Soviet Union. Such is life today in North Korea and Venezuela. The totalitarian regime implementing this tactic may then let the people rise very slowly as a safety valve against triggering broad social unrest and potential revolution. This is the game that the CCP has chosen to play. They realized long ago that communism removed all incentives to succeed. They allow just enough success to maintain power by grafting capitalist structures into their totalitarian regime. If you rise too much, too fast, they can always slam you down hard. Just ask Jack Ma —if you can find him.

Is it a coincidence that the Marxist Democrats have triggered massive inflation and seek to increase taxes on anything that moves? Their reckless spending has created the highest inflation since 1982 while they seek to raise taxes across the entire economy. These are classic Lenin-style tactics designed to punish the population, all under the guise of taking care of us. Charlie Munger, billionaire investor and long-term business partner of Warren Buffett, recently remarked that inflation is "a very serious subject, you could argue it is the way democracies die." He added that our current inflation problem "is the biggest long-range danger we have, apart from nuclear war."

Crime

When I last visited Italy in 2017, I had a conversation with a relative who told me how the right for Italians to defend themselves had been severely limited by their laws. He told me that you can be prosecuted if you kill someone who has broken into your home. You can only defend yourself if the criminal strikes first and then only with sufficient force to run away. Should you beat him to death with a frying pan, you are going to jail. I was floored. At the time, America hadn't declined to that level just yet. I remember wondering, "Why would any government do this? How could it possibly be good for society?"

The answer has now come clear to me. Crime is a tool for subjugation. When a citizen is prevented from defending himself, it breeds passivity and submissiveness. Deliberate facilitation of crime is one reason behind the defund the police movement. It is also why George Soros and his ilk have spent $100s of millions to elect district attorneys and prosecutors who refuse to prosecute crimes committed by leftists. In turn, these Soros-owned attorneys aggressively prosecute those who dare resist by exercising their constitutional right to self-defense. Two cases jump to mind.

First, during the height of the "mostly peaceful protests," as the leftist media called the BLM riots of 2020, a St. Louis, Missouri couple, Mark and Patricia McCloskey, stood in front of their home holding weapons to defend their property against BLM rioters. According to news reports, 300 to 500 rioters had invaded their gated community and began threatening residents. It is alleged that the rioters had demolished a fence and ignored no trespassing signs. Even though Missouri law allows homeowners to use force to defend their homes, the Soros-owned prosecutor Kim Gardner filed charges against the McCloskeys. Kim Gardner was subsequently disqualified from the case because she circulated emails that tried to leverage her prosecution of the McCloskeys to raise campaign donations. The McCloskeys subsequently settled the case and later received a full pardon from the governor.

Then there is the controversial Kyle Rittenhouse case. Rittenhouse is a young man who watched BLM rioters destroy the town of Kenosha, Wisconsin. According to his stated purpose, Rittenhouse brought an AR-15 rifle for his own protection and entered the riot zone to render aid and defend property. He was subsequently attacked by rioters and acted in self-defense when he shot three people, killing two of them. Incidentally, all three men who attacked Rittenhouse were white and had substantial criminal records.

Kenosha's District Attorney Mike Graveley, Democrat, made sure that charges were brought against Rittenhouse. Despite the incident being one of the most prominent cases ever in Kenosha, Graveley was nowhere to be seen during the trial. He threw two of his Assistant DAs, Thomas Binger and James Kraus, into the lion's den because he likely knew the case was very weak from the start. Despite evidence that Rittenhouse had clearly acted in self-defense in all three shootings, the leftist playbook requires Rittenhouse to be charged.

Binger and Krause led a prosecution effort that can best be described as inept. They committed numerous acts of prosecutorial misconduct during the trial including withholding evidence from the defense. They also filed a false charge against Rittenhouse which the judge promptly dismissed.

Meanwhile, the media had savaged Rittenhouse. They labeled him a white supremacist, a racist, and a right-wing extremist who went looking for trouble by crossing state lines with an illegal firearm. None of which was true.

The prosecution of Rittenhouse should never have happened. It was a clear case of self-defense, but it was essential for the left to charge someone who had the courage and will to defend himself.

Even though Rittenhouse was acquitted of all charges, the effect of this unjust prosecution is chilling in the context of self-defense. Meanwhile, where are all the prosecutions of Antifa and BLM rioters who devastate communities and beat people to death? The Department of Justice under Attorney General Merrick Garland has been consistently dropping charges against rioters who attacked police and tried to burn down a federal building.

Criminals are allowed to run rampant, destroying people's livelihoods and beating into submission anyone who resists. This is by design. Criminals are the street army of the left who are then shielded from prosecution by the two-tier justice system implemented by leftist prosecutors. The tactic also conditions the public to be passive, so when the jackboot of the Marxist state comes down on someone's neck, there will be no resistance.

Crime is also helpful to the left for the taking of property. There's direct theft such as the wave of smash-and-grab crimes that is sweeping Democrat-controlled cities for example. But there is a less visible effect of crime on real estate values. When crime takes hold of a neighborhood, property values plummet. Small property owners then relinquish their properties for pennies on the dollar or are forced to abandon their property altogether. The properties are then scooped up by well-connected developers who can afford to sit on them until they collude with politicians to clean up an area. The area is redeveloped, gentrified, and the developers make millions. Along the way, they reward the politicians with fat campaign contributions. Crime is indeed a most useful tool for the left.

Weaponization of Government

Prosecutorial abuses demonstrated by the McCloskey and Rittenhouse cases are also examples of the weaponization of government. When the left develops two standards for prosecution, it tips the scales of justice in its favor. Conservatives get the book thrown at them while leftists receive a slap on the wrist or no slap at all. These dual standards encourage crime and are also tools for directly punishing political opponents.

The IRS is another powerful tool for political retaliation. As discussed earlier in the Lois Lerner case, the IRS can indiscriminately use its powers to favor any political cause it chooses. The IRS can also selectively enforce its auditing power to audit political enemies while turning a blind eye to the abuses of those it favors.

The IRS can certainly make life miserable for people, but its powers hardly compare to the FBI and the intelligence services. These agencies can spy on anyone they want to. All they need is a reason, which can readily be supplied through the trend of definition inflation. The definition of what constitutes terrorist activities seems to continually expand. Just like calling someone a racist activates social scorn, when the government labels someone a terrorist, a vast machine of surveillance and prosecution can be activated.

Immediately after the 9/11 attacks, fear among the American population was at a fever pitch. We wanted security at virtually any cost. We sacrificed many of our rights for that sense of security. The 9/11 attacks are a prime example of how the tool of fear was used to expand government powers.

Back then, terrorism seemed to be clearly defined. A terrorist was anyone who would commit extreme acts of violence to advance a political cause. Terrorists were clear-cut tools of what the Department of Defense calls asymmetric warfare. This type of warfare is usually waged by weaker forces that employ guerrilla tactics against civilian targets. We knew who the enemy was back then—Islamofascists who had a clearly stated goal of "death to America."

So, in response, we fashioned the PATRIOT Act. The official name is Uniting and Strengthening America by Providing Appropriate Tools Required to Intercept and Obstruct Terrorism (USA

PATRIOT) Act of 2001. Never underestimate a bureaucrat's ability to fashion a catchy acronym. During the height of the war on terror, the PATRIOT Act was useful in combating real terrorists. It was passed with broad bipartisan support as the nation was eager to strike back at those who had killed nearly 3000 Americans. The PATRIOT Act gave the government broad surveillance and data collection powers.

As of May 2020, portions of the PATRIOT Act containing sunset provisions have technically expired when President Trump threatened to veto their extension. Does this mean that your civil liberties are now secure against government abuse? Hardly. Much of the collection and surveillance apparatuses that agencies became accustomed to using are still very much intact. Those systems and programs are not going to just dry up and disappear. Further, the government uses massive open-source analysis methods driven by powerful artificial intelligence and machine learning algorithms capable of analyzing petabytes of information available on the public internet. This can be done without any warrant but can still be a valuable tool in monitoring individuals and maintaining the powers of the surveillance state.

The secret Foreign Intelligence Surveillance Court established under the Foreign Intelligence Surveillance Act of 1978 is also still very much in operation. The court rarely denies a warrant request. Attorneys for the government present their reasons for requesting warrants, but no attorney is arguing against issuing the warrant. This court, commonly known as FISA Court, was at the center of the Russia collusion hoax that the Clinton Campaign created to undermine President Trump. There is mounting proof that the FBI presented false evidence to the FISA Court while also withholding key facts in obtaining surveillance warrants to spy on the Trump Campaign in 2016.

When Trump was elected, leftist groups were screaming that Trump would use the PATRIOT Act to attack minorities, leftist organizations, political enemies, and anyone critical of his policies. Nothing of the sort occurred. Instead, the Obama Administration had already weaponized the court and intelligence services against Trump. I'll say it again, gaslighters project. They accuse their opponents of the very act of which they are already guilty.

At present, the Biden Administration is eager to expand the tools developed under the auspices of the PATRIOT Act. They continually seek to inflate the definition of "domestic terrorism" and seek to apply it to any person or group that opposes their policies.

According to the Legal Information Institute, Title 18 U.S. Code § 2331 defines domestic terrorism as activities that:

(A) involve acts dangerous to human life that are a violation of the criminal laws of the United States or of any State;
(B) appear to be intended—

(i) to intimidate or coerce a civilian population;
(ii) to influence the policy of a government by intimidation or coercion; or
(iii) to affect the conduct of a government by mass destruction, assassination, or kidnapping; and

(C) occur primarily within the territorial jurisdiction of the United States;

Paragraph B(ii) above is a very broad definition that gives the government extreme latitude to activate its antiterrorism machinery. Parents shouting at a school board meeting are now being investigated as domestic terrorists despite the denial, under oath, by current Attorney General Merrick Garland. These are people fighting for parental rights against draconian leftist measures in our schools such as institutionalized application of racist CRT ideology, sexually inappropriate material, pushing of transgenderism, and the baseless mask mandates forced upon children during the pandemic. Contrast the actions of concerned parents to the violent BLM and Antifa protests of 2020. Which do you think more closely fits the definition of domestic terrorism?

Any organization that is tagged as racist can subsequently be labeled "white supremacist" and from there called terrorists. We see this strategy unfold on a grand scale in Canada when the communist loving Premier Justin Trudeau unleashed emergency powers designed to combat terrorism against the peaceful truckers who wanted oppressive COVID mandates dropped. Trudeau's tactic foreshadows America's future. The pattern is identical.

In contrast, BLM and Antifa protestors who attack police, destroy property, burn down police precincts, and attack courthouses are somehow excluded as terrorists when the terrorism definition much more clearly applies especially since they are committed to the destruction of the Constitution. They are excluded because these organizations are Marxist tools.

The domestic terrorism push is gaining momentum as the administration pursues the creation of new domestic terrorism laws that resemble what Trudeau has at his disposal in Canada.

Recently, the Justice Department created a new domestic terrorism unit. This will surely expand as all government bureaucracies do. They will continuously seek to amplify their powers while our rights are diminished and our ability to protest government oppression evaporates. The genuine interest of the Leftist Democrats is crushing all political dissent. The target of their domestic terrorism push is all conservatives and, in particular—Trump supporters. This is why it is vital to the left's agenda that the January 6th assault on the Capital be cast as a domestic terrorism incident and an insurrection. This would give Democrats the moral high ground to clamp down on Conservatives with full force.

The January 6th incident was originally a peaceful rally that escalated out of control and evolved into a riot. There is absolutely no excuse for smashing doors, knocking down barricades, and illegally entering the Capitol. Every American will agree that the breach of the Capitol was abhorrent behavior. That said, the hyperbole spun by the Biden Administration and the leftist media has been absolutely ridiculous—"worse than the 9/11 attacks", "worse than the civil war." These hyperbolic claims are ludicrous but essential to the left's scheme that lies at the heart of their Congressional hearings and investigation.

The initial investigation by the FBI did not consider the event a terrorist act. That has changed. In subsequent testimony before Congress, FBI Director Christopher Wray clearly sought to frame the event as domestic terrorism perpetrated by extremists.

Title 18 U.S. Code § 2383 regarding rebellion or insurrection reads as follows:

> Whoever incites, sets on foot, assists, or engages in any rebellion or insurrection against the authority of the United States or the laws thereof, or gives aid or comfort thereto, shall be fined under this title or imprisoned not more than ten years, or both; **and shall be incapable of holding any office under the United States.** (Emphasis added)

The last phrase in bold is why the left wants so desperately to paint the riot as an insurrection. If they can connect Donald Trump to inspiring insurrection, he could be permanently barred from office. Further, anyone who provided "aid or comfort" could also be investigated and possibly charged. Did you send a donation in support of the rally? Did you sell water bottles to the protesters? Were you simply present cheering the President? Were you a Trump

194 • AMERICAN GASLIGHTING

supporter in any way? You could be investigated and possibly charged. This would be the ultimate weaponization of government against half of the country who voted for Trump.

Somewhere between 700 and 850 people have been arrested in connection with the riot. As of this writing, only 11 have been charged with sedition. These charges came nearly one year after the event. On January 14th, 2022, news broke that Stewart Rhodes, founder of a right-wing group known as the Oath Keepers, and ten others had been charged with sedition in connection to the riot. Convicting them of sedition will be a stretch. Connecting this small group to the larger rally and Donald Trump will be an even bigger stretch. However, a conviction of this group will be spun by the leftist media to cast the whole sordid event as an insurrection.

There are many very peculiar twists to the events of January 6th. All will eventually be examined in courts of law. If the January 6th riot was an insurrection, it will be viewed as history's most poorly planned insurrection. There is no evidence that anyone brought a firearm into the Capitol. There is also evidence of FBI plants seeking to incite violence in the crowd. Video of the scene also shows a crowd gathered on the Capitol steps and simply waving flags and shouting in protest. For no apparent reason, someone, maybe Capitol Hill Police, perhaps someone else, lobbed at least one flash-bang grenade into the crowd igniting the crowd's anger. Events turned insane from then on. Since when are flash-bang grenades used for crowd dispersal?

The only person shot was Ashli Babbitt, a US Air Force Veteran. There were so many officers on that day that acted with extreme restraint in the use of deadly force. One heroic officer, Eugene Goodman, courageously led rioters away from the Senate chambers. He never drew his weapon despite being pursued by an angry mob. Sadly, Capitol Hill Police Lt. Michael Byrd did not have the same level of restraint when he shot Babbitt. Byrd was behind a barricaded door; he had an escape route through the House Chamber. He chose to shoot an unarmed woman. Considering that no other officer did the same under a much more imminent threat than Byrd, his decision seems excessive. We can't ever truly know what influenced him to pull the trigger. While I can't question his motives, I must question his discipline. After several investigations, he was cleared of wrongdoing. There are two things for certain. First, the situation was chaotic. Second, he's very fortunate the victim was white.

I want to be clear that the breach of the Capitol was a national embarrassment, but it was not a planned insurrection. The decision to mount a rally in such a highly charged environment was as irresponsible as it was stupid. By January 6th, the jig was up. Stolen or not, there was no way that Biden's election would be overturned. Sometimes one must know when to back off, but that is not in Trump's nature. For all the good he did during his time in office, his presidency will forever be tainted by this sordid event. Conversely, if it is discovered that the FBI or any other agency secretly incited violence, there should be hell to pay for those officials. We'll see if justice is possible.

There are thousands of hours of video being held in secret by investigators under the control of the Democrat leadership. The truth will ultimately win out, but it will take years. This much is certain, any investigation driven by Nancy Pelosi will have far less interest in the truth than in pursuing the singular goal of destroying Donald Trump. If she succeeds, you can rest assured that his supporters will also forever be labeled as extremists and will come under ever increasing surveillance by a corrupted justice system. Meanwhile, the left will exploit these events through the media to suppress free speech and peaceful resistance to leftist oppression.

CHAPTER 9

The Left's Obsession with Death

"Woe unto them that call evil good, and good evil; that put darkness for light, and light for darkness; that put bitter for sweet, and sweet for bitter."

—*Isaiah 5:20*

In a totalitarian regime, life is cheap. As power shifts ever increasingly to the left in any society, control over the lives of its citizens increases. As that power eventually evolves to total control, life becomes cheaper and cheaper. If a dictator can control what you do and say, what you think, or how much you earn, why not also control who lives and who dies.

Vladimir Lenin orchestrated the Bolshevik Revolution in 1917 that led to the establishment of the Soviet Union. Though in the minority, his group seized the advantage in a country devastated by WWI by unleashing a tide of terror that secured his grip on power. He boldly declared, "The goal of socialism is communism." In other words, appear to take care of the people so you can establish a totalitarian government. Communism is the full implementation of Marxist ideology. The state owns and controls everything. Under

Lenin, a wave of murder swept across Russia until the state achieved that control.

As noted earlier, there really is no difference between Marxists and fascists. The distinctions are marginal at best and mostly fiction. Both ideologies result in total control by the state. These ideologies have resulted in the deaths of over a billion people across the globe in just the 20th century. Mao once said, "Political power grows out of the barrel of a gun." Throughout the 20th century, mass murder has been the tool of choice for dictators to gain and hold power. Mao proved to be an "overachiever."

The following totals from "top performers" reflect total deaths caused by the actions of brutal leftist dictators. These include direct murders, deliberately triggered famines, and civilian and military casualties resulting from war: Mao Zedong, 60-80 Million, Joseph Stalin, 20-23 million, and Adolf Hitler, 20-30 Million. The left is sick. Under the guise of total care comes total control and eventually murder on a mass scale.

The Abortion Death Cult

Since leftist ideology views life as cheap, abortion on demand, unrestricted, and at any point during pregnancy is readily accepted as moral. This is the left's goal in western society. Do you really think the left supports a policy of abortion on demand because they care about you? Abortion is actually about power and greed. Of course, the left shrouds their arguments in honeyed words to describe abortion—words like choice, healthcare, and rights. These euphemisms are all lies.

Choice is their most common euphemism in referring to abortion. Choice dehumanizes the whole process. A woman is not ending a life. She is simply making a choice like selecting shoes from her well-stocked closet. In truth, by promoting abortion propaganda and its culture of death, the state is advocating the choice of who lives or dies. The conveniently hide that the demographics of abortion tilt dramatically against black people. As a percentage of pregnancies, they are much more affected by abortion than the rest of the population. In fact, racism is at the root of Planned Parenthood as you will soon see.

Abortion as healthcare is another euphemism the left loves to use. Abortion is simply cast as a medical procedure like all other procedures. It is performed by a compassionate doctor who wants only the best for his patient—that only applies to the patient who can speak and express her needs. The defenseless patient, the one who is also the recipient of the doctor's "healthcare," is poisoned, violently dismembered, and cast into a pile of medical waste or sold in pieces in the name of a "higher purpose" — research.

There is another useful component to the healthcare euphemism. As the government gains increasing control of the healthcare system, which is very near total control at this point, it will soon become apparent to society that a leftist government cannot fund unrestricted healthcare for all. It will have to be rationed. Abortion reduces the number of people that must be cared for in the healthcare system. Abortion is the earliest tool for healthcare rationing.

The euphemism of abortion as a right is the basis of all legal battles currently ongoing in our courts at multiple levels. The Constitution grants no such right, and it is certainly not a natural right. In fact, a stronger case can be made that abortion is the ultimate denial of rights. It is a summary execution in the womb of the most defenseless and innocent class of Americans. The only "crime" that the unborn is accused of is being unwanted through no fault of their own.

Roots of the Abortion Industry

Margaret Sanger is the founder of the Clinical Birth Control Research Bureau, an organization that eventually evolved into Planned Parenthood. She was a fervent proponent of birth control from multiple perspectives: feminism through the liberation of women as a mere procreative tool, general population control based on the fear that overpopulation leads to mass starvation and the general inability of the world to sustain population increases, and most controversially, eugenics, the concept that inferior humans should not reproduce.

Many pro-life advocates view Sanger as a proponent of abortion. Throughout her career she cleverly covered her support for abortion as birth control. She was most definitely a birth control and contraception advocate. While she sometimes portrayed herself as an opponent of abortion, her eugenics-based policy views could easily evolve into unfettered abortion. Her rhetoric also reeks of totalitarian style population control. In her book, *The Pivot of Civilization*, she refers to abortion as a crime. However, she also wrote:

> To create a race of well born children it is essential that the function of motherhood should be elevated to a position of dignity, and this is impossible as long as conception remains a matter of chance. We hold that children should be: 1. Conceived in love; 2. Born of the mother's conscious desire; 3. And only begotten under conditions which render possible the heritage of health. Therefore, we hold that every woman must possess the power and freedom to prevent conception except when these conditions can be satisfied.

"Create a race of well born children" sounds a bit Nazi-esque. Sanger was very much a eugenicist who believed that the human race should be culled to leave only the superior elements of the species.

Certainly, a dangerous platform for public policy. Who decides which parents are entitled to procreate? At one point, she also endorsed the idea of a birth permit that would authorize parents to have a child.

Her advocacy also begs the question, what if her three criteria could not be met? What then? Planned Parenthood has answered that question. Simply redefine abortion as a form of birth control and healthcare then the pseudo-noble intentions of Margaret Sanger would become perfectly aligned with the modern baby killing machine.

The Eugenics Angle

The objective of eugenics is to "cull the herd." Preventing procreation of people with undesirable or weak genetic characteristics eventually leads to extinction of those characteristics. In theory, one could eliminate entire genetic lines or enhance other desirable lines. Such is the purpose of animal breeding. Sanger saw eugenics as a way to eliminate hereditary diseases, or the "feeble minded" as she called them, and black people. WHAT? Yes, black people. Was Maggie a racist?

In collaboration with Dr. Clarence Gamble, Sanger launched The Negro Project. She dispatched one of her trusted lieutenants, Florence Rose to organize the project throughout the South. In a letter dated to Gamble, December 10th, 1939, Sanger wrote:

> Miss Rose sent me a copy of your letter of December 5th and I note that you doubt it worthwhile to employ a full time Negro physician. It seems to me from my experience where I have been in North Carolina, Georgia, Tennessee, and Texas, **that while the colored Negroes have great respect for white doctors, they can get closer to their own members and more or less lay their cards on the table which means their ignorance, superstitions, and doubts.** They do not do

this with the white people and if we can train the Negro doctor at the Clinic, he can go among them with enthusiasm and with knowledge, which, I believe, will have far-reaching results among the colored people. His work in my opinion should be entirely with the Negro profession and the nurses, hospital, social workers, as well as the County's white doctors. His success will depend upon his personality and his training by us.

The minister's work is also important and also, he should be trained, perhaps by the Federation as to our ideals and the goal that we hope to reach. We do not want word to go out that we want to exterminate the Negro population and the minister is the man who can straighten out that idea if it ever occurs to any of their more rebellious members.[48] (Emphasis added)

Note in bold, first the low opinion she has of black people as ignorant and superstitious. And in the last paragraph how the scheme cleverly seeks to enlist the help of black ministers to help provide top cover for their true intent.

As early as April 1923, Sanger's position on the eugenic benefits of birth control was well publicized. Sanger's opinion was revealed in an article published by the New York Times and republished by the American Birth Control League.

"Birth Control is not contraception indiscriminately and thoughtlessly practiced. It means the release and cultivation of the better **racial** elements in our society, and the gradual suppression, elimination, and eventual extirpation of defective stocks–those human weeds which threaten the blooming of the finest flowers of American civilization."

---

[48] Letter to Dr. Clarence Gamble from Margaret Sanger, December 10, 1939, obtained from Smith College Library

Who in the American South could possibly have been viewed as "defective stocks" and "human weeds" in both 1923 and 1939?

Elements of the left, as usual, provide cover for Sanger. The Wikipedia article about her practically canonizes her. The article frames her involvement with black communities as the efforts of a typical white liberal savior. It notes how her work was praised by prominent civil rights activists including W.E.B Du Bois, co-founder of the NAACP, and even Coretta King, wife of Martin Luther King, Jr.

New York University's website articles treat the damning excerpts from her letters as taken out of context. She really meant to express concern that her joint efforts with Gamble would be misinterpreted as wanting to exterminate the black race. This argument is dubious.

The evidence I've shown here indicates the opposite. She viewed the prolific reproduction of the lower classes both black and white as a considerable threat to the human race. Incidentally, in 1947, Clarence Gamble would later become a founding member of the Human Betterment League of North Carolina. This is an excerpt from a New York Times article regarding the damage that group did:

> Wealthy businessmen, among them James Hanes, the hosiery magnate, and Dr. Clarence Gamble, heir to the Procter & Gamble fortune, drove the eugenics movement. They helped form the Human Betterment League of North Carolina in 1947, and found a sympathetic bureaucrat in Wallace Kuralt, the father of the television journalist Charles Kuralt.
>
> A proponent of birth control in all forms, Mr. Kuralt used the program extensively when he was director of the Mecklenburg County welfare department from 1945 to 1972. That county had more sterilizations than any other in the state.
>
> Overall, about 70 percent of the North Carolina operations took place after 1945, and many of them were on poor young women and racial

minorities. Nonwhite minorities made up about 40 percent of those sterilized, and girls and women about 85 percent.

The program, while not specifically devised to target racial minorities, affected black Americans disproportionately because they were more often poor and uneducated and from large rural families.[49]

Gamble directly assisted in the implementation of a program to sterilize black women.

In 2019, over 618,000 babies were killed in the womb. The left is committed to maintaining this death machine. What must also be understood is that today's abortion industry is a de facto eugenics machine. According to the most recently available data from the CDC, 132,878 black babies were killed. That is 38.4% of all reported abortions where the race is identified. That is an estimated 23.8% of all abortions though black people comprise only 13% of the population.[50] For the leftists, black baby lives don't seem to matter.

Planned Parenthood is running away from Margaret Sanger's legacy faster than Usain Bolt sprints out of the starting blocks in a 100m dash. They have removed her name from their flagship death factory in New York City and seek to remove her name from an honorary street sign in lower Manhattan. Only the left is entitled to be excused for their own past. Maybe Planned Parenthood should pay reparations to all its victims.

The Abortion Money Machine

When Margaret Sanger formed her contraceptive program, she relied on private donations. The government did not play any role

[49] "Thousands Sterilized, a State Weighs Restitution," by Kim Severson, New York Times, December 10, 2011

[50] Number of reported abortions, by known race/ethnicity and reporting area of occurrence — selected reporting areas, United States, 2019, www.cdc.gov

for a long time until the welfare state took hold in the 1960s. Today, the government spends billions on contraceptive programs. The money is spent through government programs run by non-profits and NGOs. Organizations like Planned Parenthood and MSI directly receive government funding. The latter used to be called Marie Stopes International until, like Sanger, Stopes was found to be a racist eugenicist.[51] Stopes was also a Nazi supporter who praised Hitler.[52] So MSI dropped its founder from its formal organization name.

According to a Government Accounting Office (GAO) report covering a three-year period from fiscal years 2016-2018, Planned Parenthood Federation of America, MSI, and International Planned Parenthood Federation received $1.8 billion in taxpayer funding.[53] Did all of that money go toward abortion? No. But money is fungible. Money paid in grants can easily be rerouted to fund abortion. Planned Parenthood generates over half a million dollars from abortion every day.

In the 2019-2020 election cycle, the Planned Parenthood PAC donated $746,595 to Democrats and $0 to Republicans.[54] Clearly, Planned Parenthood knows who butters their bread. I'm sure records would show that the Planned Parenthood Federation did not directly donate a single dollar to anyone. Donations are all made through their PAC, but the name is a leftist siren call. Their prominence is certainly enhanced by the injection of federal dollars into their coffers each year.

---

[51] The Project Gutenberg EBook of "Radiant Motherhood," by Marie Stopes

[52] "Marie Stopes: Women's Rights Activist or Nazi Eugenicist?" by Palash R. Ghosh, International Business Times, October 18, 2012

[53] GAO-21-188R Health Care Funding

[54] Planned Parenthood PAC Contributions to Federal Candidates, OpenSecrets.org, (https://www.opensecrets.org/political-action-committees-pacs/planned-parenthood/C00314617/candidate-recipients/2020)

Abortion activists love to say that the government has no place in the womb. The activists mean that the government should not pass laws to stop abortion. If the government has no place in the womb, shouldn't that also be true for abortion funding? According to the left, it seems that government only has a place in the womb if a baby must be ripped out of it using taxpayer funds. At the very least, the government should have no role in abortion and thereby provide no funding at all to organizations that perform it.

The Ultimate in Leftist Gaslighting

It is no surprise that the further left you look, the more support you find for abortion. Abortion is a powerful tool for the left. First, it's big business. It's a multibillion-dollar death machine that provides financial feedback loops to leftist candidates. Blood money from dead babies doesn't bother the left at all because life is cheap in the leftist's world. And that is the second angle. If totalitarian ideologues can decide it's okay for babies to be killed in the womb, what about any other vulnerable citizen? What about the elderly and infirm? If the most defenseless is expendable, anyone can ultimately be labeled as expendable.

The left also knows that abortion keeps people in psychological slavery. This helps ensure that they don't stray from the party. I'm sure there are plenty of Republicans that have also had abortions. There are Republicans that call themselves pro-choice. But the left is by far the champion of abortion on demand. Once a woman has an abortion, she can easily become psychologically committed to believing that she has done the right thing. She must therefore be an advocate for other women to do the same. Abortion philosophy helps them fall into natural alignment with the left.

Some of these women become the most ardent activists like Alyssa Milano. She has revealed that she had two abortions in 1993 within months despite being on birth control.[55] Milano claims that the country is so "f'd up right now" because of restrictive abortion legislation being passed in states like Texas. Milano advocated for women to "go on a sex strike" in protest. Good luck with that, but I could see how it would be good advice for young, unmarried women with no support structure. After all, abstention is the only foolproof way to prevent pregnancy.

In the wake of Amy Coney Barrett's nomination to the Supreme Court, Stevie Nicks chimed in with her admission.[56] "If I had not had that abortion, I'm pretty sure there would have been no Fleetwood Mac," Nicks said. "There's just no way that I could have had a child then, working as hard as we worked constantly. I would have had to walk away." Sorry Stevie, you chose personal convenience over the life of your baby. You just took the easy way out for yourself. It's not like Fleetwood Mac was working on a cure for cancer, and millions would have died had you not sacrificed your baby. Even then, abortion would not have been morally justifiable.

However, Stevie persists in rationalizing her decision, "I knew that the music we were going to bring to the world was going to heal so many people's hearts and make people so happy. And I thought, 'You know what? That's really important. There's not another band in the world that has two lead women singers, two lead women writers.' That was my world's mission."

I've enjoyed Fleetwood Mac's music. When I happen to hear their music now, I can only think about the self-focused decision Stevie Nicks made. Her logically absurd rationalizations demonstrate a hugely distorted view of her own self-importance. Stevie's rationale is based on an argument for the supremacy of personal convenience;

---

[55] "Alyssa Milano reveals she had two abortions in 1993 within months: 'It was my choice,'" USA Today article, by Cydney Henderson, August 19, 2019

[56] "Stevie Nicks on art, aging and attraction," Interview with The Guardian, by Jenny Stevens, October 14, 2020

the primacy of social status derived from being part of the world's only band with two women lead singers and songwriters; and audience appreciation of musical performance being more intrinsically important than letting a baby live. Her unborn child did not get the chance to live, but at least she received a "consolation prize" from Stevie. She wrote the song *Sara* while imagining what her child might be like. Sad indeed.

It seems that Stevie has some regret deep down inside her and the rationalizations help her cope with her decision unlike other female abortion proponents who boast of their abortions like a badge of honor. It has to be psychologically very difficult to profess regret for abortion. To do so is effectively an admission of manslaughter.

To anyone who has had an abortion, performed one, supported the abortion movement, or assisted in any way, I offer this advice. Seek forgiveness from the Creator. God's grace heals all—even the most egregious sin. I pray for you, and I pray for our country.

We hear many sad stories about crisis pregnancies such as a 10-year-old rape victim. Cases such as these are the hard cases where compassion and common sense must prevail. The left heavily publicizes these cases to undermine common sense pro-life arguments. The public must also be made aware that hard cases such as the one just mentioned comprise only 3% of abortions. This includes rape, incest, maternal health, and birth defects while 97% of abortions occur for social or economic reasons.[57]

The public should also know that a baby's heartbeat begins at three to four weeks after conception, and the baby's organs are fully formed by the end of the eighth week. Given this information, is it too harsh to call abortion killing or manslaughter? I'd wager that many of the screaming hysterical pro-abortion female protesters you see don't even know these basic facts.

---

[57] "10 Facts About Abortion," Human Life International

You also never hear that support is indeed available for women in a crisis pregnancy. You are actually more likely to hear the opposite: there is no support structure for women in dire circumstances. That is simply not true. Adoption is always an option. Why not reach out for help? Why not channel government money to support groups willing to care for and place unwanted children? Why doesn't the government make it easier for couples to adopt American babies instead of having to traveling to Russia and Asia, where adoptions have less red tape? Why does the left insist that white couples shouldn't adopt black babies? Instead, the whole system makes death the easy way out. That cannot possibly be healthy for any society.

Abortion is the "freedom" that the sexual revolution has gifted to us—an American national scourge, just as slavery was. Abortion is also a global scourge, just as slavery still is in many countries. Can we ever heal our nation's moral fabric while living under this cloak of darkness? America overcame slavery; maybe we can find the moral fiber to eliminate abortion to the greatest extent possible and be a light for the rest of the world too.

CHAPTER 10

Operation Push Back

"There is nothing in the way of your liberty except your own corruption and pusillanimity; and nothing can prevent your being free except your-selves."

—Henry Grattan, *Speech in the Irish Parliament, 1790*

If you want to preserve our treasured rights, you will have to push back against the forces acting in concert to erode our freedoms. These forces are not a joke. They are extremely powerful coalitions composed of politicians from both parties and wealthy elites. Not all politicians advocate for Marxist-leaning controls, and not all billionaires are evil, but sifting out the devils from the angels is difficult. Despite these forces, as a more emboldened society, America can withstand the onslaught of tyranny and reverse it if all patriotic citizens regardless of past party affiliations engage.

Understanding the Political Landscape

I encourage you to listen to JFK's inaugural speech. It could easily have been written by Ronald Reagan. The stark contrast between JFK's speech and the modern Democrat party highlights how far left they have drifted.

At least half of the country is very much aware of what the Democrat party has become and understands that the country has veered way too far left under their fog of propaganda. These voters must remain highly engaged to maintain conservative-leaning voter turnout. The other half of the country persists in voting Democrat.

A big slice of the traditional Democrat vote, about 30%, is virtually irredeemable. This is the committed hardcore base who support leftist ideologues and are intellectually cemented in their big government, centralized control ideology. However, there is a segment of Democrat party voters that is redeemable. This segment is beginning to wake up to the facts. These are people whose families have consistently voted Democrat, and they simply continue voting blue because they can't psychologically identify as Republicans. Conservatives must dialogue with them and persuade them that the Democrat party of their mothers and fathers no longer exists. Together, we must work at every level of government to elect freedom-loving leaders who believe in our Constitution and are not woke but awakened to what is truly happening.

Every single elected public office is important. From the president down to school board member, every office is a target of value to the left. Every elected Democrat will work in favor of the woke agenda. They'll even hijack the local office of dog catcher if it's an elected position.

Some may say, "My Democrat senator is not a leftist radical. Why should I stop voting for him or her?" Senators like Manchin (WV) and Sinema (AZ), for example, were instrumental in scuttling Biden's Build Back Better (BBB) agenda. Their states are what the pundits call purple states that can swing either Republican or Democrat. Their true reasons for torpedoing BBB are probably obscured. However, the polls indicated strong opposition to BBB in their states. Despite Biden having lost West Virginia by nearly 40%, Manchin still votes party line about 95% of the time. Biden barely won Arizona, but Sinema has voted party line about 98%. Senators Warner and Kaine of Virginia are frequently touted as moderates by legacy media. Yet Kaine has voted party line nearly 100% of the time, and Warner has scored a perfect 100%.[58]

The leftists control the Democrat party. Along with all the Obama retreads serving the Biden administration, they are clearly shaping the Democrats' anti-liberty agenda. Re-electing so-called moderates simply keeps radical Democrats in power as the majority party. The leftists dominate the moderates within the Democrat ranks to the point where deviation from party orthodoxy puts one's life in peril. Just ask Joe Manchin. Republicans must retake the Senate and the House. If the country does that, we are home free, right? Let's not be naïve.

Republicans do not represent a perfect answer but certainly a better answer. It is really core beliefs that matter most—being conservative versus merely Republican is crucial. Do you think the Devils of Davos aren't busy buying Republicans as well as Democrats? I'm sure they are trying. The challenge is this. When the Democrats are in power, they advance the leftist agenda vigorously, but when the Republicans are in power, they either don't have the political strength to undo previously implemented leftist legislation, they lack the courage, or they too are somehow benefiting. We must elect committed conservatives, and they must be held accountable. Regardless, the dividing line between the party ideologies is clear. Leftists and Marxists dominate the Democrat part. This is not good for anyone.

According to a Rasmussen poll published in January 2022, 76% of Democrat likely voters who are familiar with The Great Reset advocated by the WEF favor the concept with 43% strongly in support. Conversely, 76% of Republican voters and 59% of voters not

---

[58] FiveThirtyEight.com, a property of ABC News and the Disney Corporation, https://projects.fivethirtyeight.com/biden-congress-votes/

affiliated with either party oppose The Great Reset.[59] The Democrat party is not only the party of slavery, but they have also positioned themselves as the party of global socialism.

You should be wary of all politicians because a sincere one is as common as unicorns and mermaids. After all, they are experts at telling people what they want to hear. When the right is in power, they must be held accountable to adhere to conservative principles. However, when the left is in control, you can be assured that your freedoms are for sale. Who would you rather have in office, someone who is blatantly against personal liberty or someone who at least says they are in favor of liberty and may actually be telling the truth? Vote for the right. At least you have a chance.

Thinking Clearly

If you don't exercise, your body goes soft, and you lose strength. If you don't exercise your thinking powers, doesn't your brain go soft too? Of course. The brain is an organ that needs nourishment and exercise, just like the rest of your body. If you were fortunate enough to have received an education emphasizing critical thinking, you are probably in decent shape, but you still need to keep up.

To build your thinking ability, you must become a skeptic who doesn't assume anything in politics is true unless properly tested and investigated through logically structured questions and answers. While maintaining a permanent state of skepticism, you should never lose sight of the fact that objective truth does exist. Leftist gaslighters would have you believe that all truth is relative. They twist statistics and frame reality with language structure that obfuscates the truth. Objective truth has a remarkable quality. It stands like a mighty pillar that can never be destroyed, even able to withstand the

---

[59] Heartland/Rasmussen "Great Reset" poll, January 5, 2022

most violent storm. Truth requires no energy to remain standing. Lies, on the other hand, require constant maintenance. The liar must constantly invent new lies to cover the previous lies hence the centuries-old aphorism, "Oh what a tangled web we weave when first we practice to deceive."

In the Marxist world, truth is whatever the state propagandist says is true. Facts don't matter to leftists because they consistently invent an alternate reality that suits their narrative. They act as if the American public is stupid. A quote attributed to Robert A. Heinlein tells us, "Ignorance is curable, but stupid is forever." This has often been restated as "Ignorance is curable, but stupidity is permanent." Many in America are becoming stupid. Their inability to engage in critical thinking renders them so.

When a muscle is not exercised, it atrophies. When unused for prolonged periods, the muscle will reach a point of no return. So it is with the brain. If it has never been exercised, it won't develop. Eventually it slips from ignorance into a permanent state of stupidity. Marxists need to create as many stupid people as they can in order to thrive. This is why they are working like busy beavers to destroy our school systems, substitute indoctrination for education, and perpetually stoke our emotions using fear and hatred.

You need tools to become a clear thinker. Just like weights are your tools for exercise at the gym, books are the tools to exercise your mind. You must be willing to make the investment. Critical thinking requires questioning, and the best person to learn from is the most skilled questioner in all of history—Socrates, the philosopher. To sharpen your critical thinking, you should familiarize yourself with the Socratic Method. This sounds like a deep, complex academic study that some may view as irrelevant. The truth is quite the opposite. The Socratic Method is a simple, systematic way to examine any issue and test it for logical consistency, which is a crucial test of truth. Truths never cancel or conflict with each other. If two statements are in direct conflict, one or both are not true. Establishing a method for increasing the probability of knowing the truth was the culmination of intellectual development in the ancient world.

The best book I've discovered that explains Socratic Method in a clear, easy-to-understand format is *The Socratic Method: A Practitioner's Handbook* by Ward Fransworth. The book describes how the Socratic Method can be easily mastered and put into practice by anyone.

Socratic Method is the basis of legal training. It is the chosen method that lawyers use to get at the truth, and that should be your goal as a critical thinker. You can see how Socratic questioning is vital to legal cross-examination. Lawyers and police interrogators use persistent logical questioning to trip up witnesses or suspects as a way to uncover contradictions. When someone is telling the truth, they can repeat it over and over with little effort. When someone is lying, they have to remember the lies they told. Therefore, simple relentless questioning to discover conflicting information helps analyze everything the media and the government tells you whether it's coming from left or right leaning sources.

Understand the Basics of the Human Mind

In your quest to become a clear-thinking skeptic, you should also understand two fundamental psychological phenomena that nearly everyone occasionally suffers from. These are confirmation bias and cognitive dissonance.

Confirmation bias is a tendency to seek only information consistent with one's deeply held beliefs. It is captured perfectly in the lyrics of *The Boxer* by Paul Simon:

A man hears what he wants to hear and disregards the rest.

Confirmation bias is an obstacle to truth-seeking and impedes authentic Socratic questioning. Socrates maintained that humility was essential to seeking truth. He believed that one should never be wholly convinced that they are wise and have all the answers. The humble truth-seeker is also not afraid to have his beliefs questioned. This willingness to be questioned makes one stronger. If one of your deeply held beliefs is proven wrong, you are better off. Why would you want to go through life believing something that's untrue? In contrast, if your deeply held belief withstands questioning and is shown to be consistent, it is likely to be true. Therefore, you know you are on the right track.

History has shown us that as power becomes concentrated in the hands of the few, the more violent and oppressive society becomes. Therefore, how could Marxism, which depends on totalitarian control, possibly be better than the freedom we have typically enjoyed in western civilization? History has provided the questioning and the answers, but our ignorant youth, who refuse to believe the old who lived through it, must be taught these lessons anew. They must learn through reasoning and not experience because the experience will be irreversible this time.

When exploring a topic, you must guard against confirmation bias. You may have formed an initial opinion, but you should be open to the possibility that your view could be wrong. When I started writing this book, I freely admit that I entered the project with the deeply held belief that systemic racism did not exist. As I completed the research, that opinion changed. Systemic racism is not codified in our laws, nor is it currently prevalent in our culture. However, it is practiced through specific misguided policies that create more harm than good, all in the name of helping poor minorities. I also concluded that these policies are purposefully promoted by the left—namely, the Democrat party. I welcome the debate to prove this wrong.

Cognitive dissonance results when one is presented with material that directly contradicts one's deeply held belief. It is a sense of inner discomfort that arises in dealing with contradiction. Cognitive dissonance can also result when one is shown to have behaved in a manner that they profess to hate.

Cognitive dissonance does not necessarily mean that the new information is true, and your beliefs are false. The dissonance is an alarm bell that two conflicting statements can't both be true. An adjustment must be made. You either reject the new information as false, or you adjust your beliefs. Cognitive dissonance is healthy skepticism when sifting through propaganda.

Psychologists contend that people are opposed to inconsistencies and usually seek to resolve them because they need to resolve the uneasy feeling of contradiction. I interpret this as an inner desire of most well-meaning people to want to live in truth. Of course, this naturally excludes liars who deliberately obfuscate the truth to manipulate others. For example—Marxists.

People react to cognitive dissonance in a variety of ways. One way is to attack the source of the conflicting information. This is the classic ad hominem attack. Discrediting the source discredits the information. If the information cannot be trusted, then my belief is assumed correct, and I can go on believing what I believe. This is the primary method by which leftists deal with evidence that exposes them. It is also their purpose to attack everything connected to white people. The Founders were all white. White people are evil. Therefore, our Constitution is evil. The argument is false, but they persist because dupes readily fall for ad hominem arguments.

Another way people deal with cognitive dissonance, is to simply ignore the new information. This resembles a child that pretends to not hear or see a parent when they don't want to follow instructions. I call it the "I don't see you; I don't hear you" response. This attack shuts down the source. Censorship is the left's chosen tool to implement "I don't see you; I don't hear you."

Mature, open-minded people resolve cognitive dissonance by adopting a new belief when clear evidence becomes available that their previous belief was wrong. They can also refute the new information if they follow a logical thought process that disproves the information. Censoring the proof or unjustly discrediting the source are evil leftist tactics.

The first test in engaging with a redeemable mind is to confirm that the person is willing to alter their beliefs if proof can be provided to do so. This tells you if you're dealing with a logical, open-minded person. If so, you're likely to engage in constructive dialog. However, don't be surprised if, even after the eloquent and airtight logical defense, your dialog partner responds, "I hear what you're saying, but I can't change how I feel." Really, they're saying, "I refuse to change what I believe." People hate to admit they're wrong, and transformation usually doesn't happen in one conversation.

Learn to Argue Effectively

Argumentation does not necessarily mean confrontation. Argumentation is a reasoned debate. It is a good thing. Many people think that arguing is bad and avoid it. The word has acquired negative connotations, often equating the conflict of ideas as a step toward physical confrontation. This can undoubtedly be true among hyperemotional extremists. For most reasonable people, arguing without giving offense is a constructive process. Unfortunately, conservatives are frequently censored and canceled when they dare to express ideas that do not conform to the leftist gaslighting narratives. This is a crucial indicator that leftists cannot defend their positions with logic. They must, therefore, shut off debate. If you care to protect and save your country, you must push back. Here are some ideas.

Don't Self-Censor

Most people whose minds are gripped by leftist thoughts are most often not evil or insane. If the right never converses with people on the left, we can never hope to persuade people away from leftist principles. Likewise, if you're a centrist and don't see where the left is leading the country, you may want to keep an open mind. The challenge is that we live in an environment where speaking against leftist positions you don't believe can get you canceled.

You may have encountered the leftist at work who never shuts up about how awful and fascistic conservatives are or how evil capitalism is. If you happen to be a conservative, you may be reticent to engage in conversation. If you don't speak up, you are self-censoring. You've put a sock in your mouth while the leftist has the advantage of total freedom to speak. Forget phony white privilege. What the left is creating is leftist privilege. They are creating an environment where only leftist orthodoxy receives airtime.

You must refuse to self-censor to push back against leftist nonsense. When a lefty spouts some nonsense with which you disagree, simply state, "I can't go along with that." Stop right there and pause. Let the heavy silence hang in the air. The conversation may end right there, or someone may ask why. If they ask why, simply ask questions in return. Don't try to lecture people with facts. Asking questions as a method to draw the facts out in the open is far more effective and less confrontational. Here's an example.

During the height of the COVID pandemic, shutdowns of "nonessential" portions of the economy were the government's go-to response. People's livelihoods were systematically and deliberately wiped out. The government began throwing bundles of cash out of helicopters to pacify the masses. We were told this would help tide people over until we could reopen. Often, the paltry sums that trickled down to individuals didn't even pay one month's rent. While on a consulting engagement during this time, an upper west-side New York lefty I encountered spouted her opinion, "They ought to just pay everyone to stay home." They being our Federal Government. I simply replied with a question, "How would the math on that work out?"

Lefties seem to think that the government has its own supply of money. The government should just give everyone enough to live on indefinitely. Lefties fail to realize that government funds ultimately always come out of our pockets, whether the government prints more of it or raises taxes to collect it. My simple question rebutted her nonsensical position without directly contradicting her. Not surprisingly, the discussion ended there because she knew there was no logical defense for her original statement.

In another situation, I used a more direct approach. I was coaching a presentation team in pursuit of a federal contract. Typically, in these presentations we include a slide with photos and bios of each presenter. One participant in the virtual meeting interjected, "There are too many white guys on this slide." That's a comment I frequently hear, and it offends me. I responded, "That is a tired line that I hope to never hear again. Your purpose is to win the deal. To win the deal you need to find the strongest, most qualified presenters without regard to how they are packaged." The silence on the phone was a bit unnerving. I thought I might get fired, but nothing happened. I made my point that hopefully influenced someone's thinking. These stories are small acts of resistance, but they are essential in letting people know that not everyone is mindlessly succumbing to leftist dogma. Courage, like fear, is contagious.

Stick to One Topic at a Time

If you've ever engaged in a political argument, you've probably experienced the constant drifting from one issue to another while the conversation becomes increasingly heated. This can happen very quickly when one party starts arguing by analogy. An analogy is a comparison of one thing to another. They begin by saying, "That's as if..." or "that's just like." When you hear those phrases, an analogy is coming. Quickly the argument drifts toward arguing about the analogy until another analogy is presented, and so on. After a while, you can't even remember what the initial discussion was about. Meanwhile, everyone grew angrier and more frustrated.

Analogies are not necessarily proof that something is true. Analogies are useful in providing context by comparison. For an analogy to be proof, the analogy must have substantial similarity to the original argument. For example, earlier I used the analogy, "Just like weights are your tools for exercise at the gym, books are the tools to exercise your mind." That is a strong analogy. Since one can't lift weights with the mind (unless you're Yoda or Luke Skywalker), reading is a valid tool for strengthening the mind. A good analogy supports the argument. A weak analogy is a distraction that causes conversations to veer off course and shift topics.

Analogies are frequently the basis for legal arguments. The purpose is to establish consistency under the law. If a previous case is decided a certain way, similar subsequent cases must be decided the same way. Unfortunately, not every judge is an intellectual giant, and frequently courts rule based on weak analogies. In the case of activist judges, they accept a weak analogy to suit their needs. This causes the law to drift off course too.

The Hypotheticals Trap

Hypothetical arguments are usually a rhetorical trap designed to catch the target in an inconsistency. They represent a situation that could happen, not something that actually exists. You are cautioned to handle them with care. One possibility is to dismiss the validity of a hypothetical because it is unrealistic. The person presenting the hypothetical may be deliberately proposing a situation that is so extreme and unlikely but is using the situation to undermine an argument that is generally sound except for the extreme and unlikely case.

Avoid Ad Hominem Attacks

As mentioned, this is a favorite argumentation technique of the left. It is a sign of weakness. The person using the tactic doesn't have enough logic to support their case. Therefore, they must engage in slander and character assassination to make themselves appear like they are right. Conservative philosophy has truth and reason to its advantage. There is no need to slander your opponent to prove your point. Besides, I don't know many people who are persuaded if you call them an idiot in the middle of an argument.

Avoid Argument by Exception

Earlier, I made the point that no one is starving in the streets in America. The statement is a generalization that is not meant to be absolute. In a nation of well over 330 million, it is quite possible that last year someone died from starvation on the street. That does not prove the generalization wrong. If you found a thousand cases of starvation, then I might have to reconsider the statement. However, the left loves to find the handful of exceptions and hold them up as proof that a policy they don't like is invalid. They then use the exceptions to evoke pathos and trigger emotional responses that obscure clear thinking.

Public policy must be built around the concept of the greatest good, for the greatest number, for the greatest duration. That's the best government can do. Stamping out racism, for example, is an admirable goal. Is it achievable? No. Odds are that there will always be some small segment of idiots in the country that is racist. That doesn't mean that we should strangle our freedoms with legislation aimed at trying to achieve the impossible. Besides, in this example, stamping out racism is a ruse of the left. They are the purveyors of racism and love to use it as a tool to divide society.

A Recap for Arguing with a Leftist

How do you argue against something that doesn't make any sense? Simple answer: ask questions. Many leftist arguments are fraught with contorted logic flaws that leave one gob smacked. You may often find that their rhetoric is cloaked in complex sentence structures, sophisticated words, circular logic, and obtuse references that give their positions an aroma of lofty rhetoric and intellectual superiority. The leftist often sounds eloquent until you stop to examine the substance of what they actually said. The stream of pseudo-intellectual nonsense that spews from a typical leftist activist can be shockingly nonsensical as we saw with the circular logic of CRT peddlers.

If you find yourself engaging in political discourse with a leftist, I suggest a series of questions to prime the conversation. The following questions will help you determine if you're dealing with an idiot, a propagandist, or a redeemable mind willing to have a good-faith conversation.

"Do you simply feel that way about your position, or do you have concrete rational arguments to support your point that you can share?" If there is any clue that the person is a complete "feeler," it is unlikely that you will persuade this person with facts. These are people moved by zealotry fueled by inflamed passions. Reason will never penetrate the conversation. If you persist in your discussion, the most likely outcome is extreme emotions with little actual communication.

"I realize that people often feel very passionately about your topic. Are you willing to have a calm, friendly conversation because I'm interested in what you have to say?" This question sets the table for what will hopefully be an exchange of ideas. It also opens the door to reciprocity. I'm willing to listen to you; are you willing to listen to me?

"In general, when you are presented with a new set of facts that prove a point, are you willing to change your position on any given topic?" This is persuasion priming. People like to think of themselves as rational decision-makers, because logic has the quality of objectivity and correctness. If you discuss a specific point with a leftist friend, and you blow a hole in their position, you will create cognitive dissonance. We all enter discussions with a set of beliefs. Your goal should be to present facts that they must acknowledge. Reasoning that controverts their belief creates the disquieting mental state as previously discussed.

You should always strive to create cognitive dissonance when dealing with obtuse leftist arguments. Sadly, you would think that people who experience cognitive dissonance would accept new facts and abandon a false premise or belief. Unfortunately, that often does not happen. People tend to resolve their dissonance through rationalization. They begin fitting the new facts to their deeply held belief instead of modifying their belief to fit the facts.

If you are making a case for conservative viewpoints, I consider it your duty to argue with truth and logic. Conservative thinkers don't need propaganda to sustain their principles. Natural law is in our favor. If conservative thinkers begin to propagandize, they undermine the entire movement. Conservatism is aligned with our Constitution, which is, at its core, a benevolent document meant to preserve our freedoms. Truth is the only defense required.

Social Media and Woke Culture

Social media is seductive and addictive by design. One sampling makes you want more. It has lured billions of people into its snare by providing an outlet for expression and a means for social connection. Anyone with a keyboard in theory has a voice that can be amplified. People love the ability to share their life's details with friends as well as their opinions. Without self-restraint, social media becomes like eating bacon at every meal. It feels good, but it's not healthy. Despite its good qualities, social media has morphed into the ultimate propaganda tool. Change must happen.

Social media companies are effectively the new town square. In the old days, people could literally stand on a soap box and shout their beliefs to anyone who would listen. The town square was a public place where the government could not suppress free speech. Because social media companies are not government owned platforms, they can choose to shut down anything they don't like. This is the current legal argument they hide behind when censoring opinions with which they disagree. While hiding behind this legal shield, they can also secretly collude with political organizations to sway public opinion hence becoming a powerful propaganda tool and leftist government proxy. Only a very thin veil separates them from the government currently in the hands of leftist Democrats.

Social media's sharing features were also designed with the specific and more shrouded purpose of collecting every piece of data possible about its users. As Mark Cuban stated, "When a service is free, you are the product." The social media giants collect everything. If you search for something, Google records it. If you visit a website, your internet service provider records it. If you send an email, using a free service, you can bet that artificial intelligence algorithms are mining the content. Do you carry a smartphone everywhere you go? Your location is tracked to within three meters. Social media has also morphed into a government surveillance platform. The tech giants know more about you than you.

It's clear that the social media giants are not interested in honest public discourse. People who voice their traditional values and speak out against the woke agenda are routinely censored. Mark Zuckerberg doesn't give a damn about you. Jack Dorsey's handpicked successor at Twitter doesn't give a damn about you. Parag Agrawal, the new CEO, has essentially said that controlling the popular narrative is more important than your First Amendment right to free speech.

These social media companies, including Google, YouTube (owned by Google), Instagram, and LinkedIn, are working in lock step with leftists to suppress your rights to free speech. They have become tools of the totalitarian left. They regularly banish conservatives and suppress messaging they disagree with. The list of blatant ideologically driven censorship is long and well documented. Even the wealthy are trolled and attacked if they speak against leftist orthodoxy.

Here's the solution. Social media companies must be legally reclassified as a public town square. Under this classification, the definition of prohibited speech becomes very narrow. Essentially, anything you can legally say in the middle of Times Square, you should be able to say on social media without restriction.

Pull the Plug on Woke Sports

Drew Brees, former quarterback of the New Orleans Saints and a likely shoo-in for the NFL Hall of Fame became a target for speaking his beliefs. In June 2020, Brees made these comments during an interview with Yahoo Finance in the wake of George Floyd's death and the flag kneeling fad that swept through the NFL:

I will never agree with anybody disrespecting the flag of the United States of America or our country. Let me just tell you what I see or what I feel when the national anthem is played, and when I look at the flag of the United States. I envision my two grandfathers, who fought for this country during World War II, one in the Army and one in the Marine Corp. Both risking their lives to protect our country and to try to make our country and this world a better place. Every time I stand with my hand over my heart, looking at that flag, and singing the national anthem, that's what I think about, and in many cases, it brings me to tears, thinking about all that has been sacrificed. Not just those in the military, but for that matter, those throughout the civil rights movements of the '60s, and everyone, and all that has been endured by so many people up until this point. And is everything right with our country right now? No, it's not. We still have a long way to go, but I think what you do by standing there and showing respect to the flag with your hand over your heart, is it shows unity. It shows that we are all in this together, we can all do better and that we are all part of the solution.

I am personally deeply offended when someone kneels during the Anthem. When I heard his comments, I was thrilled that someone of his stature and reputation dared to stand up and voice his opinion on the issue. His remarks seemed well-reasoned and heartfelt. He acknowledges that not all is right in our country, and we have work to do. He also states that the sacrifices our flag represents includes civil rights heroes. There is nothing remotely wrong with the core message in his statement. His opinion is simple, disrespecting the flag is not the way to protest.

Within days of his comments, Brees was cowed into submission by a torrent of comments from teammates and an onslaught from the leftist blogosphere. He issued this apology via Instagram:

I would like to apologize to my friends, teammates, the City of New Orleans, the black community, NFL community and anyone I hurt with my comments yesterday. In speaking with some of you, it breaks my heart to know **the pain I have caused.** In an attempt to talk about respect, unity, and solidarity centered around the American flag and the national anthem, I made comments that were insensitive and completely missed the mark on the issues we are facing right now as a country. They lacked awareness and any type of compassion or empathy. Instead, those words have become divisive and hurtful and have misled people into believing that somehow, I am an enemy. This could not be further from the truth and is not an accurate reflection of my heart or my character. This is where I stand:

I stand with the black community in the fight against **systemic racial injustice and police brutality** and support the creation of real policy change that will make a difference.

I condemn the years of oppression that have taken place throughout our black communities and still exists today.

I acknowledge that we as Americans, including myself, have not done enough to fight for that equality or to truly understand the struggles and plight of the black community.

I recognize that I am part of the solution and can be a leader for the black community in this movement.

I will never know what it's like to be a black man or raise black children in America, but I will work every day to put myself in those shoes and fight for what is right.

I have ALWAYS been an **ally**, never an enemy.

I am sick about the way my comments were perceived yesterday, but I take full responsibility and accountability. I recognize that I should do less talking and more listening...and **when the black community is talking about their pain, we all need to listen.**

For that, I am very sorry, and I ask your forgiveness. (Emphasis added)

His apology could well have been written by a BLM spokesperson. The bolded text highlights typical BLM-inspired language that also appears in CRT-related literature. Brees may have a ton of courage on the football field, but when it comes to defending his principles, he proved himself to be "noodle-spined." The social media attacks on him were effective in censoring his beliefs.

Millions of Americans would likely agree with his original comments. Millions of Black Americans would also be among those in support. The flag is a national symbol to be treated with reverence. Kneeling in protest is disrespectful—full stop. Those who do it may have a right to do so. Those who oppose the act and are offended have the equal right to say so. They should not be forced to live in fear of censorship or cancellation. It is not racist to say that.

Had Brees stood by his remarks, he would have become America's quarterback. I would have become a fan. Instead, the entire NFL kneeling controversy and the subsequent embracing of kneeling by Major League Baseball has driven me and many other fans away from watching any professional sports. I watch none of it. I have not seen a Super Bowl or World Series since 2019. It is actually very liberating.

In the fall of 2019, the Washington Nationals won a dramatic World Series capping a magical season. Due to the pandemic, the following season's opening day did not occur until July 23, 2020. All players participated in a compulsory social justice pregame display in a premier season-opening matchup between the Nationals and Yankees. They all kneeled before the National Anthem while holding a long black cloth to symbolize solidarity. All were wearing "Black Lives Matter" T-shirts. These gestures not being enough, in the second game, two Yankees players knelt during the Anthem. I have not watched a baseball game since and won't for the foreseeable future. When wokeness dies, I might return. But for now, baseball is dead to me and many others. Their TV ratings are sinking to historic lows.

The NFL has committed to donating $250 million to social justice organizations over 10 years. Hundreds of thousands have so far filtered into groups that are working toward defunding the police.[60] Did you notice the heavy police presence at the last Super Bowl? Why would they support defunding the police for crime-ridden communities whose law-abiding citizens need police protection while welcoming all the police protection they can buy for their main event? Major corporations have donated money to BLM, including Apple, Amazon, and Facebook. While undisclosed amounts have made it to BLM, you can bet it is in the millions. BLM has been totally opaque about where the money has gone. Its refusal to be transparent along with reports of malfeasance have led to Amazon suspending donations to the BLM Global Network Foundation.

Vote with your TV remote. Stop watching all professional sports that support leftist ideology. Unless you're a total sports addict, you won't miss it. You can fill your time with more worthy pursuits, and you won't be giving money to organizations that enjoy insulting you by implying that you're racist.

Stop Canceling Women

The left has repeatedly accused the right of waging a war on women. Of course, the left's accusation is their response to conservatives resisting the unfettered killing of babies in the womb. Opposition to abortion is what the left frames as a war on women. Reality, of course, paints a very different picture. It is the left that is waging a war on women. Starting with what is indisputably the ultimate cancellation—death. Half of all babies aborted in America are

[60] "NFL funding 'defund the police' groups through 'Inspire Change' program," by Peter Hasson for FoxBusiness online

females. In other countries like China, it's even more than half because males are favored over females. Therefore, a female baby is more likely to be aborted.

The left is also eager to recognize transgender women as real women, as we are seeing in the case of the Penn State swimmer. The biological man who calls himself Lia Thomas has been embraced by the NCAA by allowing him to compete against women. As a male swimmer, he was ranked 462 after three years of competing as a man. As a female imposter, he is now ranked first. Something is seriously wrong.

Even Caitlyn Jenner, the former Bruce Jenner, thinks allowing biological males to compete against women is a bad idea. Ultimately, every single female sport will be infiltrated by a biological male if this trend is not reversed. Women who have trained all their lives to excel in their sport will be denied an opportunity to stand on the podium as champions. If an adult man decides to live as a woman, that's his choice. The psychological issues behind gender dysphoria are complex and should be addressed by competent medical professionals free from political and social coercion. However, the failure to protect women's sports will erase all the progress women have made in achieving equal opportunity in athletics.

The left is steadily canceling the very word woman. Woke legislators in Congress have started introducing terms like "birthing persons" in place of women. In 2020, the independent news site Devex.com published an opinion piece titled, "Creating a more equal post-COVID-19 world for people who menstruate." This prompted Harry Potter creator, J.K. Rowling to tweet the following:

'People who menstruate.' I'm sure there used to be a word for those people. Someone help me out. Wumben? Wimpund? Woomud?

Rowling, who is a self-professed feminist, has been outspoken against the idea of erasing biological gender in direct opposition to the left's concept that it is a mere construct assigned at birth by a sexist, patriarchal society. Her follow-up tweets include the following statements:

> If sex isn't real, there's no same-sex attraction. If sex isn't real, the lived reality of women globally is erased.

> I know and love trans people but erasing the concept of sex removes the ability of many to meaningfully discuss their lives." [I respect] every trans person's rights to live any way that feels authentic and comfortable to them.

> At the same time, my life has been shaped by being female. I do not believe it's hateful to say so.

Rowling is now targeted by the left for cancellation. She has received an onslaught of criticism for communicating common sense. The Harry Potter cast, all of whom would not enjoy the wealth and status they have without Rowling, has called her out as transphobic. She was excluded from a 20th-anniversary event celebrating the Harry Potter franchise. The left eats its own when strict adherence to woke orthodoxy is breached.

Fight Cancel Culture

Stop doing business with "woke" corporations to the greatest extent possible. I recognize that it is difficult to completely free oneself from the tentacles of these corporations, but you have to try. After being an American Express cardholder for over 20 years, I closed my account when I learned that they were teaching anti-capitalism and CRT in their internal employee training. I've stopped watching nearly all professional sports, I watch very little television, and I rarely go to the movies because almost all of it is garbage with embedded leftist ideology in nearly every script.

The willingly woke corporations respond to the "squeaky wheel" principle. They cave into small but very vocal activist groups, just like Disney in their response to Florida's Parental Rights in Education Bill. The bill is designed to prevent the teaching of sexually explicit material to children below the fourth grade. In my view, it doesn't go far enough. I don't understand why schools teach any sexually explicit material at any age.

Further, the bill requires schools to notify parents if Joey gets on the bus in the morning but starts feeling like a Judy while he's at school. Florida public schools are now required to notify parents instead of merely reaffirming Joey's clouded mind without telling the parents. The bill is really about parents' rights. However, leftist propagandists deceptively dubbed it the "Don't Say Gay Bill" because they are liars.

When the Florida Legislature passed the bill, the vocal left targeted Disney for not mounting strong opposition to the bill. Disney's CEO quickly responded with a groveling apology tour on social media. Disney, which is supposed to be a purveyor of family-friendly content for children, now promises to include more "LGBTQ-friendly" material in all of its releases. Meanwhile, thousands of Disney's own employees who disagree sit in silence and in fear of losing their jobs if they voice any opposition to their woke masters.

Stop watching professional sports and any NCAA events that support fiascos like the Lia Thompson scenario. Cancel your Disney subscriptions. It's time to impose tangible financial losses on woke corporations that do not reflect your values. It's time to turn off this garbage. It's time to stop self-censoring.

Never Apologize for Your Righteous Beliefs

When you know you are right, never apologize. If you misspoke, clarify your statement but don't retract the core message. Groveling before the woke gods won't buy you any mercy anyway. They will attack you until you apologize and then destroy you regardless. You may as well go down standing for what you believe. Mercy is a virtue. The left has no virtue. Therefore, the left is merciless.

Maybe Brees could have expressed the opening of his statement better. His phrase, "I will never agree with…" is what left him open to social media lynching. He probably still does not believe in disrespecting the flag though now he has humiliated and censored himself at the feet of the woke Nazis. He had to prostrate himself and declare that we are a systemically racist country for the heat to subside. In essence, he had to reaffirm the tenets of the left in his apology.

In contrast, Rowling stands firm in her view that gender is a biological fact. So far, she has held her ground, and kudos to her. To people that can think clearly, gender is a biologically determined, inalterable fact established at conception. Women are unique and different from men. That is reality and thank God for that.

I've presented a broad view of typical leftist lies. When you are confronted with the lies of CRT and the 1619 Project, for example, push back. Do not accept responsibility for a sin that is not yours. How could you possibly be responsible or bear any guilt if you never enslaved anyone? How could you be an oppressor if you treat everyone fairly in your daily affairs? If you know you're not racist and never commit racist acts, how could you possibly be racist simply because Ibram Kendi says you are? Don't succumb to stupid. Think clearly.

Reclaim Your Child's Education

Parents must ensure that their children are able to withstand leftist indoctrination. Parenting requires an extraordinary focus and investment of time to instill traditional values and cultivate critical thinking skills from an early age. You can no longer count on our schools to teach thinking skills.

Our education system has reached the melting point, and your children are now political pawns. It has become a failed system that is more focused on supporting bureaucracy, perpetuating propaganda, and collecting union dues than on creating well-educated citizens. Public schools are actively robbing children of their innocence by exposing them to perverted sexual content, such as teaching them that watching porn is a perfectly normal pastime. Public schools are now nothing more than leftist mind control camps. It is time to reclaim our education system or check out altogether.

Instead of defunding our police, we should consider defunding the public school system and giving education vouchers to parents. I recently learned that most public school systems receive funding based on headcount. The more students, the more money they receive. Therefore, if you can check out, you will be pulling money out of the corrupt public education apparatus.

If you can afford it, send your child to a private school. But don't think you're safe just because you're paying for private education because private schools have also been infiltrated with leftist ideology. However, since parents directly pay tuition in a private education setting, you are likely to have more influence over the curriculum than you might have in the mammoth bureaucracy of the public school system. You are also much more likely to shield your child from the worst of the brainwashing in a Catholic school or other religious schools, and your child may also receive some lessons in virtues and morality.

Homeschooling is another option. This too places more burden on parents. Despite that, interest in homeschooling and the number of homeschooled children is rising. Support structures are emerging, and parents are forming co-ops to share the task of educating children. Expect this option to grow as innovations emerge while traditional public education declines.

Our universities have mainly become perverse breeding grounds for anti-American ideology. The university is supposed to be the setting where no question is out of bounds, and sharing diverse perspectives is the foundation for learning. But diverse perspectives are limited only to opinions that oppose traditional values and are consistent with America-hating woke ideology. All other views must be left at the campus gate.

Don't assume that the degree program your child pursues provides any protection against woke ideology. The left's propaganda has infested prestigious universities like Harvard and Yale and also penetrates programs that you think would be somewhat immune to irrational thinking such as medicine, law, and engineering. Even the Journal of the American Medical Association (JAMA) has started publishing woke articles that frame the delivery of medical care in racial terms.

The greatest caution of all is to not let your children pursue a B.S. degree in some worthless field like communications or gender studies. In this case, B.S. does not stand for Bachelor of Science. If you allow your child to pursue this type of curriculum, the result will undoubtedly be indoctrination, not education. Do not hesitate to put your foot down. You are better off handing your child $50,000 in cash and a one-way ticket to the French Riviera. They will learn more, and it will cost you less.

Become Politically Active

Running for political office is an arduous commitment. It is particularly challenging when running for low-level local offices or even state legislatures. Often the pay is low, but the time commitment is substantial. However, these positions have more direct impact on your daily life than the president. Local politics shapes communities which ultimately shape the nation. The left has thrown hundreds of millions of dollars at local office races. They understand that the way to transform a country is to transform each county. This is how they advance their soft on crime agenda for example.

George Soros has put several attorneys general and prosecutors in his pocket who are purposefully soft on crime in jurisdictions across America. These include crime-ridden Chicago under the jurisdiction of Kim Foxx, who received $2M in support through a Soros-funded PAC. George Gascón of Los Angeles County received $2.25M for his reelection. Larry Krasner, District Attorney of Philadelphia, received $1.5M in campaign advertising. Buta Biberaj, Commonwealth Attorney for Loudoun County, Virginia, received $861,000 from a George Soros-funded PAC.

The left pushes these radical candidates as criminal justice reform advocates. Their revolving door approach to prosecution has led to skyrocketing crime. The soft on crime policies of ideologue prosecutors has directly led to the murder of innocent citizens by criminals who were released from custody after elimination of cash bail. Leftist prosecutors have blood on their hands when that happens, but that does not stop them from implementing their idiotic agenda without shame or remorse. Skyrocketing crime is just one impact of corrupt prosecutors. The emergence of the two-tier justice system that drops the hammer on conservatives and distributes get-out-of-jail-free cards to leftists has also weaponized your local prosecutor's office.

In June 2021, Scott Smith was arrested for disorderly conduct at a Loudoun County School Board meeting. He was there protesting his daughter's rape by a supposed transgender student. The biological male, by school policy, was permitted to use the girl's restroom where he raped Smith's daughter. Smith's heightened emotional state was understandable. When the school board tried to silence him at a public meeting in their effort to suppress the rape incident, Smith refused to leave and was arrested for disorderly conduct by Loudoun County deputies.

In an extremely rare instance, Buta Biberaj chose to personally prosecute this minor offense and had the nerve to request jail time despite her otherwise anti-incarceration, soft on crime ideology. Smith's attorney was dumbstruck that a disorderly conduct charge would even go to trial, let alone require jail time. In August 2021, Smith was found guilty of two misdemeanor charges of disorderly conduct and received a ten-day jail sentence, which was suspended contingent upon one year of good behavior. Biberaj also wanted him to submit to anger management training. I guess you're not entitled to be angry when your child is raped by a "gender-fluid" pervert.

I have no insight into Smith's political leanings, and frankly, they are irrelevant. Still, at the time, the Loudoun County School Board, run by progressive radicals, was under political assault from conservatives for their leftist indoctrination agenda. Their agenda included a CRT-driven curriculum, sexualization of children, introduction of pornographic material into schools while banning classics like To Kill a Mockingbird, and most egregiously allowing biological males to use girls' bathrooms. Biberaj was eager to send a message to conservative activists. Attempting to jail Smith was the ticket.

Biberaj is a leftist tool who willfully implements the two-tier justice system. This is what leftist funding buys for American citizens. The purchase of prosecutorial power is one of many chosen weapons

238 • AMERICAN GASLIGHTING

for suppressing freedom. They refuse to prosecute existing laws when it suits them while also using the full force of law enforcement to hammer conservatives whenever they have an opportunity.

Of course, Soros' political donations influence an increasing number of elections. It doesn't stop at local offices. His network of PACs is widespread and far-reaching. Defeating Soros' billions seems daunting, but money doesn't always win elections. Conservatives have often won elections while being massively outspent by the left. To win, we must tell the truth unabashedly, and we need just enough money to get that message out. Hard work, a solid message, and adherence to real justice wins votes. People are growing tired of a failing economy, political corruption at all levels, and radical agendas like the indoctrination of children in our schools. Many Democrat voters are waking up and starting to realize that their party is infested with communist cockroaches.

Saving Our Country

I boldly assert that the salvation of America lies in embracing conservatism. We must separate political philosophy from party labels. We must analyze what is best by comparing political philosophies. Leftist philosophies lead to loss of liberty and cheapen human life. Rightist philosophies readily align with our Founder's intent for America. They enhance liberty and value life.

The conservatism of which I speak is an unwavering commitment to the rule of law and the upholding of the Constitution as a well-reasoned static framework which can only be changed through legislative action and assent of the people. It is not a relic of the past, but rather a timeless framework that protects us from tyranny. If we could just start from there, we would negate the entire progressive movement that seeks to dilute the Constitution into a mere collection of suggestions to be reinterpreted at the whims of activists.

Now, how do philosophies line up with parties? Where do we find conservative politicians? The answer to these questions determines how one should vote if you can embrace my position on conservatism's alignment with our Constitution.

Do we find conservatives in the Democrat party? If you find an honest, true conservative that happens to be a registered Democrat, by all means vote for him or her. I don't see any. Not one. Are conservatives clustered under the Republican banner? The answer is yes. Do we have corrupt gaslighters who claim to be conservative under the Republican banner? Again, the answer is yes.

Like most things that are not aligned with leftist orthodoxy, conservatism is maligned in the media with hyperbole and propaganda. Conservatism is not fascism like the left would have you believe. The fascism claim is pure gaslighting. Conservatives are nationalistic, but not fascistic, which as I've established is a socialist philosophy. Conservatives believe in limited government, which is the exact opposite of fascism.

A core belief of conservatism is that the greatest amount of personal freedom is attained when one exercises self-restraint. This is a key component of what our Founders meant by self-governance. The first level of self-governance begins with restraining one's own impulses and desires that when left unchecked become damaging to oneself and society.

You may exercise the freedom to take drugs, but your freedom will quickly turn to slavery because you abandoned self-restraint. You will become a slave to your addiction. You may exercise the freedom to engage in promiscuity, but then you become a slave to disease, possibly unwanted pregnancy, and then possibly abortion. Self-restraint is a companion principle of conservatism.

Lack of self-restraint creates a yearning for solutions to problems created by poor decisions. This yearning causes people to turn to big government as the answer. This is the final stage to surrendering freedoms and sadly where vast segments of American society currently reside.

Conservatives must organize to push back against the gaslighting of America. We must support genuine conservative candidates and leave no election for any political office unchallenged. I encourage you to engage in all future election cycles to push the left out of office at every level as much as possible. After all, conservative apathy is at least partly responsible for ceding so much ground to the left.

Consider running for office. America needs virtuous leaders more than ever. If you can't run for office, support someone who will. Volunteer to work on campaigns and support committed conservative candidates.

I repeat that the Republican Party is not pure. It is far from perfect, but that should not stop you from joining the revolt against leftism. Conservatism is your best hope. You can be a voice for change and keep Republicans honest and keep them from succumbing to swamp style behavior.

If you're a Democrat and want to stick with Team Blue, maybe you can talk sense to those who will listen and get them to turn away from hardcore Marxist tendencies. But, good luck with that. It's much more likely that you'll be shunned rather than heard.

And for goodness' sake, vote! Do not let any talk of rigged elections stop you from casting your vote. If you become indifferent, the left wins. Stand up and fight if you love your country. The alternative is—well, by now you know.

Epilogue

As American Gaslighting moved to the final stages of editing and publication, the political landscape continued to evolve. There is so much more I wish I could cover, but the writing would never end, and the book would never be published. As we went to press, the Supreme Court handed down a momentous decision on abortion. The poorly reasoned 1973 Roe v. Wade decision that claimed a Constitutionally protected right to abortion was finally overturned. States are now free to enact whatever abortion restrictions they want. There will also be states that permit abortion on demand at any point during pregnancy. I also expect states like California will act quickly to establish themselves as abortion centers for the nation.

In other developments. Obama has reemerged as the propagandist-in-chief. DHS, under the leadership of the disgraceful Alejandro Mayorkas, attempted to launch a disinformation board that bears a disconcerting resemblance to Orwell's ministry of truth. The premier woke cinematic cesspool, Netflix has practically imploded as their subscribers desert them in droves. And Elon Musk attempted to purchase Twitter with the stated goal of restoring free speech on the platform though the transaction appears to have fallen apart. The left has descended into spasmodic apoplexy. Hope springs eternal.

One of the primary tests of truth is consistency. There is only one version of the truth but lies have infinite versions and are often logically inconsistent. Leftists are perennial liars. Their rhetoric is devoid of intellectual consistency. In American Gaslighting, I have laid bare the history of the American left. The left now owns the Democrat Party—dragging it steadily towards full-blown Marxism. Their politics is rooted in racism and erosion of our Constitutional freedoms. They preach that America is irredeemably racist and must be dismantled because of its past sins. Yet the actions of the Democrat party were principally responsible for perpetuation of racism, which they continue stoking to this day. Shouldn't the Democrat party be labeled as irredeemably racist, dismantled, and replaced with something that at least has some trace of virtue? At least, we would achieve intellectual consistency.

The truth about politics is that both parties analyze and poll the electorate in terms of demographics. But only the Democrats frame nearly all issues in the context of race. You, the voter, are nothing but a racial category to them. Each category is carefully propagandized and pitted against other classes. They then control their messaging to pretend that they care about your needs with no real intent to ever solve any problems. They create a myth that communities exist solely based on melanin levels. They claim that these communities speak with one voice, but this is not true. Self-appointed voices who claim to represent the Black community, the Hispanic community, or the Asian community are mostly frauds. But these artificial melanin-based special interests are fracturing as leftist lies are exposed.

Values create communities in a far more meaningful way than melanin levels. Every citizen is an American first and must begin to think and act in the spirit of American individualism with the freedom to exercise their right to life, liberty, and pursuit of happiness. Adherence to the rule of law and belief in the American Dream create the community that matters most—The American Community.

The left's community messaging has been extremely damaging and diabolically successful among Black Americans. Black people do tend to vote 90% Democrat. I find it a bit ironic that the people whose ancestors were once enslaved can swing the nation's politics away from the threat of Marxism thus saving us all from impending slavery. Republicans would be well-advised to make a concerted push for welcoming Black Americans home to the Republican party—the party that fought for their rights and freedom.

So, I offer an open letter to my fellow citizens of African heritage. Everything in it has been said before by black scholars, intellectuals, and prominent authors who broke free from the mental shackles of the Democrat Party and Marxist philosophy. These courageous black thinkers have been ridiculed by the left as Uncle Toms, house negros, and somehow, no kidding, "black white supremacists." As certain as the sun will rise tomorrow, I will be called racist for voicing the same ideas. I make no apologies for speaking the truth because I know where my heart is.

Dear Black Citizens of America,

For many of you, the history of your ancestors in America is a painful story. No one denies that. As a country, America ultimately had to correct its past mistakes. Our country fought its bloodiest war to end the scourge of slavery. The nation paid dearly.

Because we have the most just system of government ever created by man, many champions of civil rights, both black and white, were able to fight for your rights by standing on a granite foundation—our Constitution. Because America's foundations are just, we were able to dismantle systemic racism once and for all. The past is gone. Today, America is the nation where anyone who wants to succeed can do so. There are no laws that stand in your way. In fact, for all Americans, the only thing that stands in our way is ourselves.

There will always be people who may hate you because of your skin color. That is their problem, not yours. Racism will only be completely eradicated from the face of the earth when someone discovers a cure for stupidity.

Today, millions of our black countrymen thrive in this great land. You are doctors, lawyers, scholars. You are physicists, athletes, entertainers. You are electricians, plumbers, and truckers. You are senators and CEOs and have even risen to the presidency.

Despite the successes, the statistics show that a significant portion of our black population still lags behind all other racial groups in economic success and education. Together all Americans, hand-in-hand, arm-in-arm, must ask why? We must engage in honest discourse, fearless self-questioning, and search for answers. There are baiters out there who would have you remain forever in the role of victim. To do so surrenders all of your personal power. Stop listening to them.

While systemic racism is a bygone thing, black oppression can readily be found in the inner-city neighborhoods of our major urban centers where high crime rates and failed school systems are the norm. What do all these cities have in common? They are controlled with an iron fist by Democrats who claim to be helping, but very little ever changes for the better.

In 1960, 78% of black children were raised by two-parent households. Just 30 years after the Democrats started "helping," 66% of black children were raised in single-parent households. This is a statistic cited by the great Thomas Sowell, a successful and proud black man who was raised in Harlem. Democrat policies have failed you, and the black leaders who are in league with Democrats have long since sold you out. Do you think it's time to do something different?

As a white man, I make no claim to fully understand the situation of a black person from the inner city. But I ask you, "Is common sense determined by skin color?" Surely not. Therefore, it is possible to imagine what one should do if living in an inner-city, crime-ridden neighborhood. So, I offer suggestions based on common sense and common human brotherhood. These suggestions do not require me or anyone else to be black. Simply engaging the mind and thinking things through with honesty and clarity would lead anyone to the same conclusions.

1. ***Know who your friends are.*** *Realize that Democrats are not your saviors. They do not love you. They only demonstrate contempt for you. Stop voting for them.*
2. ***Fight like hell for school choice and charter schools.*** *The fact that no Democrat supports this idea proves #1.*
3. ***Teach respect and virtue.*** *Teach young boys to respect girls and teach both boys and girls to refrain from sexual activity until such time as they are ready to accept responsibility for a family. I offer this same advice to any white kid in the suburbs.*
4. ***Strive for self-sufficiency.*** *Turn away from government hand-outs to the greatest extent possible. Hand-outs create dependency and are as damaging as crack cocaine.*
5. ***Demand safety.*** *You need more police presence, not less, but it must be combined with community interaction and mutual trust.*
6. ***Clean out public housing.*** *Public housing projects are for decent people who need a hand up. Demand that drug users and criminals be removed from public housing.*
7. ***Identify the liars.*** *Any community organizer who doesn't stand for numbers one through six is a liar. Don't trust him.*
8. ***Whites are not racist simply because they are white.*** *Any community organizer who tells you that white people are the enemy is again a liar.*
9. ***Read the works of Thomas Sowell. Make him your guide for life.***

Respectfully, with peace and love,

Dan Shyti

DEFINITIONS AND USAGE

America. An alternative name for the United States and used interchangeably.

Black and White. For practical reasons I opted to consistently use "black" throughout the text when referring to people of African descent. The word appears over 250 times in the main body. Using "African American" would have needlessly complicated the text.

African-American is the preferred politically correct term that the left likes to use. It is particularly popular with white liberals who enjoy virtue signaling. I grew up when the civil rights slogan "black is beautiful" was popular.

Also, black people commonly refer to themselves as such unless they intend to stick with their white liberal allies for political effect. I have never encountered a single black person who told me they were offended by being called black.

The left has no problem calling Caucasians white. So, I also considered the value of setting the discussion on equal footing. If you want to delve more deeply into the origin of races, you will quickly find that black and white are artificial terms and neither is racially accurate. Black and white simply reflect today's vernacular.

Conservative. A supporter of conservative political policies such as limited government, traditional American values, and most importantly that the Constitution is not a living document that can be reinterpreted to fit the times or the whims of activist judges. Conservatism hinges on consistency derived from the Constitution as a deliberate static framework specifically designed to protect people against the concentration of government power in the hands of the few.

Critical Race Theory (CRT). This is a repackaging of Marxism that replaces economic class conflict with racial conflict to create social division by casting white people as oppressors and black people as oppressed. The left often expands the "oppressed class" by adding people of color (often abbreviated as POCs) to include anyone they don't consider white.

Democrat. When I refer to Democrats within this text, I speak primarily about the leaders of the Democratic Party. Obviously, in common language, people use the term for anyone who is a party member or voter. I've tried to add additional clarifying words when referring to average voters.

Left (Leftist). I've often used the terms "the left" and "leftist" throughout the text to refer to people who oppose conservative thought and values. Leftists favor Marxist and Socialist approaches as solutions to America's challenges.

Marxism. The economic and social philosophy created by Karl Marx and Friedrich Engels as defined in their Communist Manifesto. Marxism advances the doctrine of oppressed vs. oppressor. In essence that capitalism is the tool of the elite ruling class used to exploit the masses. Under Marxism, the state controls all means of production with the stated goal of creating a classless society.

Marxist. Anyone who professes ideas consistent with the philosophy of Marxism.

Marxist Democrat. I've used this term when I specifically wanted to highlight the Marxist nature of the modern Democratic Party leadership.

Republican. When I refer to Republicans, I'm also mostly referring to party leadership. Just like Democrat, common usage in everyday language also refers to a member of the Republican Party. Where appropriate I draw a distinction for clear interpretation.

Socialism. Effectively the half-step to full blown communism as described by Marxism. Socialism is the system where the government exercises direct control over major aspects of the economy.

Woke (Wokester). A philosophy that opposes nearly all traditional American social and political structures. It advocates that our structures must be torn down and reconstructed usually into a system resembling Marxism. Wokesters believe that America is systemically racist and generally subscribe to the tenets of CRT. Woke beliefs are advanced overwhelmingly by white leftists who think they are helping minorities. A woke person readily advocates censoring any speech that disagrees with woke views. Woke philosophy is Marxism in disguise.

References

1) Cretella, Michelle, MD et al, *Gender Dysphoria in Children*, American College of Pediatricians, November 2018

2) Douglass, Frederick, *Narrative of the Life of Frederick Douglass*, Anti-Slavery Office, 1845, Boston, Massachusetts

3) Du Bois, W.E.B., *The Crisis: My Impressions of Woodrow Wilson*, *The Journal of Negro History 58, no. 4*, The Association for the Study of African American Life and History, 1973, Chicago, Illinois

4) Fransworth, Ward, *The Socratic Method: A Practitioner's Handbook*, Godine, 2021, Boston, Massachusetts

5) Gill, Indermit, *Deep-sixing Poverty in China*, Brookings Institute, 2021, Internet publication

6) Kahneman, Daniel , *Thinking, Fast and Slow*, eBook, MacMillan, 2011, New York, New York.

7) Kessler, Ronald, *Inside the White House: The Hidden Lives of the Modern Presidents and the Secrets of the World's Most Powerful Institution*, Pocket Books, 1995, New York, New York

8) Kreeft, Peter, *Socratic Logic*, Third Edition, St. Augustine's Press, 2008, South Bend, Indiana

9) Marx, Karl and Engels, Frederick, *Communist Manifesto*, Socialist Labor Part of America, 2006, Internet publication

10) Ming Francis, Megan, *Civil Rights and the Making of the Modern American State*, Cambridge University Press, 2014, New York, New York

11) Riley, Jason L., *Please Stop Helping Us*, Encounter Books, 2014, New York, New York

12) Sarkis, Stephanie , Ph.D., *Gaslighting: Recognize Manipulative and Emotionally Abusive People—and Break Free*, First Edition, Da Capo Press, 2018, New York, New York

13) Shyti, Daniel A., *Ten Timeless Rules for Life – Things Every Young Person Should Know for a Perfect Launch,* First Edition, 4 Power Enterprises, 2018, Potomac Falls, Virginia

14) Shyti, Daniel A., *4 Power Leadership: Your Pathway to Leadership Success,* First Edition, 4 Power Enterprises, 2013, , Potomac Falls, Virginia

15) Sparks, Randy J., *Where the Negroes Are Masters,* Harvard University Press, 2014, Cambridge Massachusetts

16) Thomas, Hugh, *The Slave Trade: The Story of the Atlantic Slave Trade: 1440-1870,* Simon & Schuster, eBook, New York, New York

17) US Census Bureau, *Income and Poverty in the United States: 2020,* September 2021

18) Various Authors, *The Not-So-Great Society,* The Heritage Foundation, 2019, Washington D.C.

19) Wilson, Woodrow, *The New Freedom,* Doubleday, Page, & Company, 1913, New York, New York and Garden City, New Jersey

Index

1

1619 Project, *52, 53, 61, 62, 64, 117*

A

Abdul-Jabbar, Kareem, *176*
abortion, *197, 198, 199, 200, 203, 204, 205, 206, 229*
Abrams, Stacey, *168*
African, *46, 48, 49, 51, 246*
Age of Enlightenment, *10*
Age of Propaganda, *174*
Age of Reason, *10, 32*
Alinsky, Saul, *22, 33*
Annamaboe, *48*
Antifa, *192*
Asante, *48*

B

Bader-Ginsberg, Ruth, *25*
Barrett, Amy Coney, *206*
Bell, Derrick, *101*
Biberaj, Buta, *237*
Biden, Joe, *36, 124, 164, 165, 166, 167, 183, 191, 195, 210, 211*
Bill of Rights, *12, 28, 60, 67*
Black Lives Matter, *56, 116, 118, 175*
Blackrock, *179*
BLM, *56, 119, 120, 122, 123, 124, 192, 228, 229*
Bowser, Muriel, *118*
Brees, Drew, *225, 226, 228, 233*
British, *57, 60, 64, 65*
Brown v. Board of Education, *144*
Brown v. Mississippi, *143*
Brown, Michael, *118, 119*

Buchanan v. Warley, *143*
Build Back Better, *169, 170, 171, 210*

C

Capitalism, *4, 26, 93, 178, 180, 231, 247*
Carson, Johnny, 78
Centers for Disease Control (CDC), *175, 182, 183*
Cher, *176*
China, *22, 23, 33, 91, 180, 181, 230, 249*
Chinese Communist Party, *180, 181*
Churchill, Winston, *26*
Civic Nation, *164*
Civil Rights Act, *148*
Civil Rights Era, *141, 146*
Civil War, *5, 146*
Coca-Cola, *103, 167, 168*
cognitive dissonance, *158, 216, 217, 223*
Columbus, Christopher, *43*
Communist Manifesto, *26, 86, 247, 249*
Confederacy, *30, 144, 146, 147*
Confederates, *144*
Constitution, *4, 5, 13, 15, 25, 28, 32, 45, 58, 60, 82, 83, 141, 145, 157, 158, 164, 192, 198, 243, 247*
COVID-19, *20, 33, 34, 151, 168, 169, 180, 182, 183, 192, 218, 230*
Critical Race Theory, *28, 31, 98, 247*
CRT, *28, 31, 98, 99, 101, 116, 158, 179, 180, 181, 192, 222, 228, 231, 233, 247, 248*
Curtin, Philip, *46*

D

Davis, Jefferson, *147*
de Blasio, Bill, *118*, 122
DeAngelo, Robin, *101, 102, 103, 104,*
    105, 106, 107, 109
Declaration of Independence, *5, 58,*
    60, 62, 64, 70, 81, 82, 116
Delta Airlines, *168*
Democrat, *24, 128, 135, 137, 140,*
    144, 146, 147, 149, 156, 158, 187,
    210, 211, 238, 244, 245, 247
Disney, *211, 232*
District of Columbia, *33*
Don't Say Gay Bill, *232*
Douglass, Fredrick, *54, 56, 96, 155,*
    176
Dred Scott v. Sandford, *141*
Du Bois, W.E.B., *138*

E

Election Integrity Act, Georgia, *167*
Environmental Sustainability and
    Governance, *179*
equity, *21, 27, 124, 179*
eugenics, *199, 200, 202*
Executive Order 14019, *165, 166*

F

Facebook, *39*
Fante, *48, 51*
Fascism, *23, 24*
Fauci, Dr. Anthony, 184
Fifteenth Amendment, *142*
Foreign Intelligence Surveillance
    Court, *190*
Founding Fathers, *10, 11, 15,* 66, *83,*
    137
Fransworth, Ward, *214*

G

Gamble, Clarence, *200, 201, 202*
Garland, Merrick, *191*

Gender dysphoria, *37*
global warming, *19, 20*
God, *4, 13, 18, 32, 59, 80, 83, 116,*
    149, 161, 162, 233
Gold Coast, *48, 49*
Goldwater, Barry, *149*
Great Reset, The, *180, 211*
Guinn v. United States, *142*
Gutenberg, Johannes, *10*

H

H.R. 5376. *See* Build Back Better
Hamilton, Patrick, *1*
Hannah-Jones, Nikole, *58, 59, 62, 64*
Hitler, *24, 111*
House Resolution 1, *168, 169*

J

James, Lebron, *125, 176*
Jarrett, Valerie, *164*
Jefferson, Thomas, *15, 31, 49, 58, 60,*
    61, 62, 65, 70, 81, 83, 119, 128,
    137
Jenner, Caitlyn, *230*
Jim Crow, *106, 137, 138, 142, 167*
Johnson, Lyndon B., 145, 146, 148,
    149, 150, 156, 157

K

Kaepernick, Colin, *176*
Kahneman, Daniel, *20, 21, 39, 249*
Kaine, Tim, *211*
Kendi, Ibram, *101, 109, 110, 112,*
    113, 115, 116, 117, 233
Kennedy, John F., *146, 147, 149,* 209
Kennedy, Robert F., 147
King, Martin Luther, *31, 59, 60, 62,*
    70, 115, 116, 147, 202
Ku Klux Klan, *147*

L

Lee, Robert E., *30*

Lenin, Vladimir, *196*
Lerner, Lois, *169*, *189*
life, liberty and the *pursuit* of
    happiness, *15*
Lightfoot, Lori, *118*
Lincoln, Abraham, *31, 53, 54, 56, 70*
Loudoun County, *237*
lynching, *137*

M

Madison, James, *28, 128*
Major League Baseball, *168, 178, 228*
Manchin, Joe, *169, 210*
Mao Zedong, *197*
Markey, Edward, *24*
Marx, Karl, *30, 86, 119, 120, 247, 249*
Marxism, *23, 24, 26, 60, 85, 88, 97,*
    160, 170, 174, 247, 248
Marxist, *3, 4, 5, 6, 16, 22, 25, 26, 27,*
    32, 39, 40, 44, 45, 51, 52, 56, 60,
    62, 64, 118, 119, 122, 123, 127,
    137, 158, 164, 165, 166, 167, 168,
    169, 170, 171, 174, 175, 176, 192,
    196, 205, 210, 211, 213, 247
Maslow, *12, 13, 15*
mass formation psychosis, *184*
Mayflower Compact, *58*
Mayorkas, Alejandro, *241*
McAuliffe, Terry, *28*
McConnell, Mitch, *25*
Milano, Alyssa, *176, 205*
Mitchell, Arthur Wergs, *135, 137, 138*
Moore v. Dempsey, *143*
Mussolini, *24*

N

NAACP, *139, 147, 202*
National Basketball Association, *178,*
    181
National Colored Democratic League,
    138
National Progressive Party, *80*
Negro Project, The, *200*
Nicks, Stevie, *206*

Norton, Eleanor Holmes, *56*

O

Oath Keepers, *194*
Obama, Barrack, *8, 16, 149, 161, 162,*
    163, 164, 165, 166, 169, 191, 211
Orwell, George, *25*

P

Palihapitiya, Chamath, *181*
pandemic, *20, 33, 182, 218*
Parental Rights in Education Bill, *232*
PATRIOT Act, *189, 191*
Pelosi, Nancy, *169, 195*
Planned Parenthood, *198, 199, 200,*
    204
Plessy v. Ferguson, *142, 144*
Portuguese, *48, 49*
progressives, *78, 105*
progressivism, *76, 85*
Putin, Vladimir, *162, 163*

R

Reagan, Ronald, *150*, 209
Republican, *16, 80, 121, 128, 140,*
    141, 210, 211, 248
Revolutionary War, *62, 64, 65*
Rhodes, Stewart, *194*
Rice, Susan, *164, 166*
Rittenhouse, Kyle, *187*
Robinson, Jackie, *105*
Roosevelt, Franklin, *141*
Roosevelt, Theodore, *77, 80*
Rose, Florence, *200*
Rowling, J.K., *230, 231, 233*
Rufo, Chris, *178*
Russell, Richard B., *137*

S

Sanger, Margaret, *199, 200, 201, 202*
Sarkis, Stephanie, *22, 249*
self-censorship, *218*

Sinema, Kyrsten, *169, 210, 211*
slave trade, *46*
slavery, *5, 21, 30, 31, 48, 50, 54, 56,*
    57, 62, 64, 65, 67, 73, 96, 141,
    142, 154, 155, 176, 181, 205, 212
Smith, Howard, *144*
Smith, Scott, *237*
Smith, Will, *176*
Social Media, *124, 224*
Socialism, *23, 248*
Soros, George, *165*
Southern Democrats, *137, 144, 146,*
    148, 149
Southern Manifesto, *144, 146*
Southern Strategy, *149*
Sowell, Thomas, *154, 244*
Systemic Racism, *126, 157*

T

Taft, William H., *80*
The Great Depression, 134, 135
The Great Migration, 134, 135
The New Deal, 136
Thomas, Lia, *230*
Trudeau, Justin, *192*
Trump, Donald, *25, 120, 121, 122,*
    191, 194, 195

U

Universal Basic Income, *170*
Uyghur Muslims, *180*

V

Virginia Company, *57, 58*

W

Wallace, George, *147, 148, 202*
Walters, Alexander, *138*
war on women, *229*
Warner, Mark, *211*
Washington, George, *71, 128*
Waters, Maxine, *23, 122*
Wilson, Woodrow, *80, 81, 82, 83,*
    119, 138, 249
woke, *225, 231, 232, 233, 235*
wokesters, *30*
World Economic Forum, *165, 179,*
    180, 181, 211

Z

Zimmerman, George, *118*

ABOUT THE AUTHOR

Identity politics is destroying America. Pandering politicians use every demographic identity they can think of to divide Americans. Abraham Lincoln once said, "A house divided against itself cannot stand." Today politicians use a variety of tools rolled into woke ideology that seeks to systematically dismantle our constitutional republic. Once again, our house is divided.

If like me, you see our country swirling down the drain, you must become active in opposing woke ideology. This corrosive ideology is a perverse combination of brainwashing and anesthesia designed to create a compliant and passive populace that can easily be led into the tyranny of totalitarian government.

There really is only one identity that matters—the American Identity. That's where each American commits to self-restraint, the rule of law, and equal justice under the law. This requires a commitment to the Constitution as our unifying framework.

Despite our challenges, I'm optimistic that the American spirit will undergo a resurgence. Share that optimism with everyone you know, and let's make it happen together.

Dan

- Professional Speaker
- Author
- Speech Coach
- Political Commentator
- Leadership Expert
- Engineer
- Patriot

Book Dan for Speaking Engagements
Admin@mindunion.com

Other Titles by Daniel A. Shyti

Available on Amazon

https://www.amazon.com/Daniel-A.-Shyti/e/B00H0FS6NQ